# POLICING THE SOUTHERN CITY

# POLICING THE SOUTHERN CITY
## New Orleans, 1805–1889

DENNIS C. ROUSEY

LOUISIANA STATE UNIVERSITY PRESS

*Baton Rouge and London*

Designer: Amanda McDonald Key
Typeface: Janson Text
Typesetter: Impressions Book and Journal Services, Inc.
Printer and binder: Thomson-Shore, Inc.

Portions of Chapters 1, 2, 3, 5, and 6 were first published in the articles "Cops and Guns: Police Use of Deadly Force in Nineteenth-Century New Orleans," *American Journal of Legal History*, XXVIII (January, 1984), 41–66, and "'Hibernian Leatherheads': Irish Cops in New Orleans, 1830–1880," *Journal of Urban History*, X (November, 1983), 61–84, copyright © 1983 by Sage Publications, Inc., and are reprinted by permission. Portions of Chapters 1, 4, 5, and 6 were also published in the article "Black Policemen in New Orleans During Reconstruction," *Historian*, XLIX (February, 1987), 223–43, and are reprinted by permission.

Library of Congress Cataloging-in-Publication Data:

Rousey, Dennis Charles, 1951–
    Policing the southern city—New Orleans, 1805–1889 / Dennis C.
Rousey.
      p.  cm.
    Includes bibliographical references and index.
    ISBN 0-8071-2046-4 (cl : alk. paper)
    1. Police—Louisiana—New Orleans—History—19th century.
    2. Police administration—Louisiana—New Orleans—History—19th
century.   I. Title.
    HV8148.N4R68   1996
    363.2'09763'3509034—dc20                                      95-50128
                                                                      CIP

*For Dad, Mom, and Linda*
*and for BJ, Chris, Bryan, and Matthew*

# CONTENTS

Acknowledgments  xiii

Introduction  1

## 1
Into and Out of the Orbit of Mars: The Military
Style of Policing, 1805–1836  11

## 2
From One, Many: Policing the Partitioned
City, 1836–1852  40

## 3
"A Perfect Hell on Earth": A Time of Troubles
in the Reunified City, 1852–1861  66

## 4
The Shock of Change: War, Occupation,
and Early Reconstruction, 1861–1868  102

## 5
Crisis of Legitimacy: The Metropolitan
Police, 1868–1877  126

## 6
"The Wonder Is That Thieves
Don't Pick Up the Town and Carry It Off":
The Crescent City Police, 1877–1889  159

Conclusion  197

Bibliography  201

Index  221

# ILLUSTRATIONS

*following page 101*

Norman's Plan of New Orleans
and Environs

Map of New Orleans in the early
nineteenth century

Leonard Malone

Henry K. Nixon

A black Metropolitan policeman
of the 1870s

The Reconstruction-era Metropolitan
Police badge

Michael P. Creagh

Dexter S. Gaster

David C. Hennessy

The rapid-response patrol wagon of the
late nineteenth century

The policeman as public servant

Members of the dwindling contingent
of black policemen

# LIST OF TABLES

1  Nativities of City Guardsmen in 1814, 1820,
1828, and 1830   27

2  Police Absenteeism as a Percentage of
Man-Days Worked   55

3  Annual Police Turnover as a Percentage of
Authorized Strength of Force   55

4  Annual Number of Delinquencies per Policeman   56

5  Married Policemen Admitted to Charity
Hospital   57

6  Age of Policemen Admitted to Charity Hospital   57

7  Length of Residence in New Orleans of Policemen
Admitted to Charity Hospital   57

8  Nativities of the Aggregate Police Forces of the
Three Municipalities in 1850   59

9  Nativities of the Police by Municipalities in 1850   60

10  Nativities of the Police in 1850 and 1855   73

11  Nativities of the Police in 1860   74

12  Percentage of Irish Natives in Police and Control
Samples in Fifteen Southern Cities, 1850 and 1860   75

13   Police Arrests, November, 1853–January, 1856   93

14   Percentage of Blacks in Police and Total
Population in Twenty Southern Cities, 1870 and 1880   137

15   Nativities of White Police in 1870   145

16   Percentage of Irish Natives in Police and Control
Samples in Seventeen Southern Cities, 1870 and 1880   146

17   Incidence of Arrest by Nativity Group, 1868–1874   148

18   Number of Policemen per 10,000 of Population in Eighteen
Southern Cities, 1870 and 1880   163

19   Nativities of White Police in 1880   168

# Acknowledgments

I am indebted to the Cornell University history department for support and guidance when this project was in an early phase, and especially to Mary Beth Norton and to Stuart Blumin, who introduced me to social and urban history. At the New Orleans Public Library I have been fortunate to enjoy the expert help of the staff of the Louisiana Division, particularly its head, Colin Hamer, and the city archivist, Wayne Everard. The members of the history department at Arkansas State University have for many years provided a network of friendship and support for historical scholarship, and one in particular, Larry Ball, has given me the professional lagniappe of a colleague who is a specialist in criminal justice history and generous in the exchange of ideas and information. I am also grateful to Margarett Daniels and her staff, who have affably and expeditiously handled a vast legion of interlibrary loan requests at the Dean B. Ellis Library of Arkansas State University.

In preparing the manuscript for publication, I was fortunate to have the courteous and efficient help of Joan Caldwell of the Louisiana Collection, Howard-Tilton Memorial Library, Tulane University, and John Magill and Sally Stassi of the Historic New Orleans Collection in obtaining illustrations. The professionalism and experience of the people at LSU Press, especially Margaret Dalrymple and Catherine Landry, and of my copy editor, Trudie Calvert, proved a great boon in transforming the manuscript into a book.

My greatest debt is to my family, who have given me love, nurture, respect for learning, and shelter from the storms of life: my parents, Merle and Nancy Rousey; my sister, Linda vanDoorninck; and my wife, BJ. I hope the new generation, Chris Lawrence, Bryan Harvey, and Matthew Rousey, will be as blessed.

# POLICING THE SOUTHERN CITY

# INTRODUCTION

At the time of this book's inception more than twenty years ago, published studies of American police history by modern scholars were rare. Roger Lane's 1967 case study of policing in nineteenth-century Boston and James Richardson's 1970 history of the New York police were the most valuable published monographs then available. In 1974 no book-length case study of a nineteenth-century southern urban police force had yet been published, although a few unpublished dissertations offered glimpses into southern policing, especially Selden Bacon's "Early Development of American Municipal Police: A Study of the Evolution of Formal Controls in a Changing Society" (1939) and George A. Ketcham's "Municipal Police Reform: A Comparative Study of Law Enforcement in Cincinnati, Chicago, New Orleans, New York and St. Louis, 1844–1877" (1967). These works left many questions unanswered. Bacon devoted no more than 40 percent of his dissertation to Charleston and New Orleans, and Ketcham's analysis of New Orleans constituted only about 20 percent of his; neither spanned the entire nineteenth century. Even more chronologically limited was an article by Eugene Watts published in 1973, "The Police of Atlanta, 1890–1905," which dealt only with the turn-of-the-century police in a late-blooming southern city. Richard Haunton's 1972 article "Law and Order in Savannah, 1850–1860" included less than two pages on the police. Both articles lacked any useful treatment of the time period before the one given in the title.[1] Anyone with a serious interest in the history of policing in the

---

1. Roger Lane, *Policing the City: Boston, 1822–1885* (Cambridge, Mass., 1967); James F. Richardson, *The New York Police: Colonial Times to 1901* (New York, 1970); Selden D. Bacon, "The Early Development of American Municipal Police: A Study of the Evolution of Formal Controls in a Changing Society" (Ph.D. dissertation, Yale University, 1939); George Austin Ketcham, "Municipal Police Reform: A Comparative Study of Law Enforcement in Cincinnati, Chicago, New Orleans, New York and St. Louis, 1844–1877" (Ph.D. dissertation, University of Missouri, 1967); Eugene J. Watts, "The Police of Atlanta, 1890–1905," *Journal of Southern History*, XXXIX (1973), 165–82; Richard H. Haunton, "Law and Order in Savannah, 1850–1860," *Georgia Historical Quarterly*, LVI (1972), 1–24.

nineteenth-century South was bound to be more tantalized than satisfied with the available literature, especially someone intrigued by the prospect of applying some of the methods and questions of the "new" social history to the history of law enforcement. Since 1974 American police history and, more broadly, criminal justice history have developed a great deal, and an impressive number of case studies have been produced in the form of books, articles, dissertations, and several broad-gauge synthetic histories— yet until now there has been no published major monograph about the nineteenth-century police in the cities of the Deep South.[2]

Historians of American criminal justice disagree significantly about many factual and interpretive issues, but they generally concur about certain features of the transition from colonial to mid-nineteenth-century urban policing. In the colonial era, several institutions of local government inherited from English tradition shared responsibility for urban law enforcement. A night watch patrolled the towns during the hours of darkness, manned initially by adult freemen serving in compulsory, uncompensated rotation. Distaste for this service resulted in major absenteeism. At first, town governments hired temporary substitute watchmen with funds derived from fines collected from the absentees and later hired watchmen for more or less permanent service, paying them with money generated by a general tax levy. Constables worked during daylight hours mainly as process servers for magistrates, paid not by salary but by fees for specific services performed. In some places the constables were elected by the freemen and in others appointed, usually by the justices of the peace. Constables in

2. Books published on police in other parts of the South are Kenneth G. Alfers, *Law and Order in the Capital City: A History of the Washington Police, 1800–1886* (Washington, D.C., 1976); Louis J. Marchiafava, *The Houston Police, 1878–1948* (Houston, 1977); very little of Marchiafava's book deals with the nineteenth century, and both books are short (the text and notes together cover ninety-nine pages in Marchiafava and just fifty-five pages in Alfers). Important works of broad scope are James F. Richardson, *Urban Police in the United States* (London, 1974); Samuel Walker, *A Critical History of Police Reform: The Emergence of Professionalism* (Toronto, 1977); Robert M. Fogelson, *Big-City Police* (London, 1977); Samuel Walker, *Popular Justice: A History of American Criminal Justice* (New York, 1980); David R. Johnson, *American Law Enforcement: A History* (St. Louis, 1981); Eric H. Monkkonen, *Police in Urban America, 1860–1920* (Cambridge, Eng., 1981). Two important comparative studies are Wilbur R. Miller, *Cops and Bobbies: Police Authority in New York and London, 1830–1870* (Chicago, 1977); and Michael Stephen Hindus, *Prison and Plantation: Crime, Justice, and Authority in Massachusetts and South Carolina, 1767–1878* (Chapel Hill, 1980). For other valuable secondary works, see the Bibliography.

some jurisdictions exercised authority over the night watch, but ordinarily constables did not patrol, and neither they nor the night watchmen routinely wore uniforms or carried firearms or swords. Their standard weapon and badge of office was a wooden staff. Sheriffs and their deputies usually played only a small role in enforcing the criminal law because collecting taxes, supervising elections, and maintaining a jail occupied most of their energies. Occasionally local militia companies might be called out to patrol in times of crisis, but rarely did such mobilizations last for long.[3]

This system endured in the big cities of the Northeast until about the middle of the nineteenth century, according to the prevailing historiographical view, when, for reasons much debated by historians, a new form of police emerged, characterized by around-the-clock patrols, a unified administration, salaries rather than fees, and eventually uniforms and revolvers as routine, if not always legal, sidearms. Boston and Philadelphia introduced partial reforms in the 1830s and 1840s, but by the mid-1840s New York had become the first city to adopt most of the features of the new or modern police. In the existing histories of police reform, southern cities have been either ignored or regarded as peripheral and eccentric, with only brief references to their "elaborate" patrol system or to a militia-like organization providing police services.[4]

In fact, the first major reform of the traditional system did not occur in any of the big northeastern cities in the mid-1800s but in the cities of the Deep South in a much earlier period. As early as the 1780s Charleston introduced a paramilitary municipal police force primarily to control the city's large concentration of slaves. In later years Savannah, New Orleans, and Mobile did the same. These police forces, usually called city guards,

3. For the English background, see Leon Radzinowicz, *A History of English Criminal Law and Its Administration from 1750* (4 vols.; New York, 1948–68); and T. A. Critchley, *A History of Police in England and Wales, 900–1966* (London, 1967). For the American colonial approach to law enforcement, see Douglas Greenberg, *Crime and Law Enforcement in the Colony of New York, 1691–1776* (Ithaca, 1976), 156–68; Richardson, *Urban Police*, 4–5; Johnson, *American Law Enforcement*, 4–8; Walker, *Popular Justice*, 17–21; Allen Steinberg, *The Transformation of Criminal Justice, Philadelphia, 1800–1880* (Chapel Hill, 1989), 120–21; Michael Feldberg, *The Turbulent Era: Riot and Disorder in Jacksonian America* (New York, 1980), 108–12; Monkkonen, *Police in Urban America*, 33–35.

4. On the emergence of a new police, see Richardson, *Urban Police*, 19–34; Johnson, *American Law Enforcement*, 22–31; Walker, *Popular Justice*, 55–65; Steinberg, *Transformation of Criminal Justice*, 144–45, 148–82; Feldberg, *Turbulent Era*, 112–19; Monkkonen, *Police in Urban America*, 39–49.

wore uniforms and carried formidable weapons, usually muskets or swords; though they resembled the militia in appearance, they were separate and distinct organizations. City guardsmen were municipal employees, typically exempted from militia duty. They ordinarily patrolled at night, though a reserve force was on call for daytime emergencies. Their compensation was principally in the form of salaries rather than fees.[5]

My thesis—that the first major reform of American urban policing was the establishment of military-style police forces in Deep South cities with large slave concentrations—is novel in its sum but not in its parts. Other historians have propounded at least some fragmentary elements of this interpretation. Selden Bacon suggested in his dissertation that Charleston's uniformed and armed police of the late eighteenth and early nineteenth centuries differed in these characteristics from the police of New York, Boston, and Philadelphia. Bacon also noted that during some portion of the first quarter of the nineteenth century New Orleans had an armed and uniformed police force, but at the time he was doing his research the chaotic condition of the municipal records of New Orleans prevented him from developing a clear understanding of policing in the Crescent City throughout the antebellum period. In his 1956 classic *The Militant South, 1800–1861*, John Hope Franklin noted that the Old South's cities needed "special guards" and "patrols" to buttress slavery, but he seems to have concluded that these were militia units rather than municipally employed police forces. Richard Wade recognized something distinctive about the urban police of the antebellum South in his *Slavery in the Cities: The South, 1820–1860* (1964), observing that southern cities "established elaborate patrol systems" noteworthy for "their size and complex structure." But Wade focused on the last four decades of the antebellum period and hence did not compare antebellum policing with colonial law enforcement in southern towns, and he did not fully capture the innovative and distinctively military configuration of the antebellum police in the Deep South's larger cities.[6]

Wade's conclusions were echoed by James Richardson in 1974 in his

5. For colonial and revolutionary-era background on law enforcement in Charleston, see Carl Bridenbaugh, *Cities in the Wilderness: The First Century of Urban Life in America, 1625–1742* (New York, 1955), 112, 298–99.

6. Bacon, "Early Development of American Municipal Police," II, 598–605, 646, 668–70, 685; John Hope Franklin, *The Militant South, 1800–1861* (Cambridge, Mass., 1956), 74–77; Richard C. Wade, *Slavery in the Cities: The South, 1820–1860* (New York, 1964), 98, 100.

*Urban Police in the United States* ("The cities that did have more elaborate police arrangements were those with large slave populations where white masters lived in dread of possible black uprisings") and by Samuel Walker three years later in *A Critical History of Police Reform: The Emergence of Professionalism* ("the first modern-style police systems appeared in southern cities as part of a general approach to the control of slaves"). Walker trenchantly observed, though, that "historians have never given the matter adequate attention."[7]

That lack of attention has inhibited efforts to synthesize case studies of the police of individual cities into a general history of American urban policing. Walker's *Popular Justice: A History of American Criminal Justice* (1980) merely noted that "Southern cities developed more elaborate systems of police patrol in an effort to control the slave population." Another broad survey, David Johnson's *American Law Enforcement: A History* (1981), offered no treatment of the distinctive features of antebellum southern policing. The lack of a forceful description of the Deep South's characteristic regional model of urban policing in the published literature of American police history also distorted the results of Eric Monkkonen's imaginative and intriguing *Police in Urban America, 1860–1920* (1981). Monkkonen attempted to date the emergence of modern police forces in fifty-nine U.S. cities by determining the year that each police force first donned uniforms, but, forced to work around the lacuna of southern police historiography, Monkkonen attributed dates of adopting uniforms to Charleston, New Orleans, and Savannah which were at least half a century later than the actual initiation of a policy regarding uniforms in each of those cities. His thesis about the spread of uniforms would have fit the data more closely if the Deep South cities with large slave concentrations were treated as following a separate and distinct regional pattern. To his credit, he sensed a major purpose of the police in some southern cities, noting that Savannah's "police were clearly used as a means of slave control, their size and organization more akin to a militia or military occupation forces," and that "the Charleston police served as a militia for slave control."[8]

Of the limited published work about southern policing, Laylon W. Jordan's brief 1979 study "Police Power and Public Safety in Antebellum Charleston, 1800–1860" described the military style most clearly and

---

7. Richardson, *Urban Police*, 19; Walker, *Critical History of Police Reform*, 4.
8. Walker, *Popular Justice*, 20; Monkkonen, *Police in Urban America*, 163, 166–68.

forcefully. Jordan observed that the police force in Charleston "was para-military in dress, weapons, discipline, and tactics" and "an integral part of a system of race relations predicated on the notion that all Negroes were 'domestic enemies' who had to be kept constantly under surveillance and 'completely subordinate.'" His exclusive focus on Charleston, however, prevented the development of a thesis broad enough to encompass other Deep South cities as well.[9]

New Orleans initiated its military-style police in 1805 but demilitarized the police force in 1836, dropping the uniforms and weapons. At the same time a daytime police force, organizationally integrated with the night police, was formed to provide twenty-four-hour active patrolling with a unified chain of command—nine years before New York's similar reform. Within a few weeks, however, the Louisiana state legislature partitioned New Orleans into three separate municipalities to defuse ethnic conflict in the city, incidentally preventing the police reform from taking effect. All three of the autonomous municipalities adopted the new system of policing by 1840. This might seem to entitle New Orleans to recognition as the first major U.S. city to install the style of policing for which New York would be credited five years later, but because of the partitioned government the police in the Crescent City lacked the organizational unity that distinguished the reformed New York police of 1845 and after.

New Orleans was thus unique in first adopting the Deep South model of a paramilitary police and then shifting in the years 1836–1840 to the civil style characteristic of northern police reform in the 1840s and 1850s. The primary cause of the organizational change in the New Orleans police in the 1830s was ethnic conflict among the white population of the city, particularly elite Franco-American and Anglo-American distrust of a city guard increasingly staffed by immigrants from other ethnic backgrounds. Indeed, ethnic issues exerted enormous influence on policing in the Crescent City. By 1850 Irish immigrants were the most overrepresented ethnic group on the police force, and during the 1850s they became prime targets of nativist hostility in the bloody political struggle between the Democrats and the American party. The Know-Nothings gained the upper hand during the latter half of the decade and threw many immigrants off the police force, but the Irish recouped their position of influence by 1870 and sus-

9. Laylon Wayne Jordan, "Police Power and Public Safety in Antebellum Charleston, 1800–1860," *South Atlantic Urban Studies*, III (1979), 122–40.

tained it thereafter. In the South, Irish overrepresentation on the police force was not unique to New Orleans—nor was the nativist conflict of the 1850s. The Irish played a strong role in policing many southern cities before the American party was formed and were overrepresented in most after the Know-Nothing movement collapsed.

Racial conflict also had a considerable effect on policing in New Orleans. At least a few free African American men served on the force up until 1830, but apparently none could obtain such appointments during the period 1830–1867. Once slavery had been abolished, black New Orleanians sought access to many opportunities formerly denied to them, including places on the police force. The police were desegregated in 1867, and African Americans won a proportionate share of police appointments and a full-fledged role in policing as long as the Republicans dominated the state government (this finding contrasts with Howard Rabinowitz' observation that black policemen in many southern cities during Reconstruction were subordinated to a second-class status, permitted to arrest only other blacks).[10] Under Republican control the police in New Orleans also considerably increased their social service and public health roles. But once the Republicans lost power in Louisiana in 1877, the number of black policemen fell sharply and black influence on policing shrank accordingly, thus encouraging more abusive treatment of the African American community by the overwhelmingly white police force.

The Democrats' return to power in 1877 brought not only a diminution of African American involvement in policing but also financial retrenchment and drastic reductions in the size of the police force, characteristics of all southern cities in the post-Reconstruction period.[11] During the last two decades of the nineteenth century, the police role narrowed to one primarily of controlling crime and maintaining order, with a reduction in the social service activities that had expanded under the Republican administration of the Reconstruction era. Efforts at police reform in New Orleans during the late nineteenth century followed national trends, in-

10. Howard N. Rabinowitz, *Race Relations in the Urban South, 1865–1890* (New York, 1978), 41–43.

11. Memphis was an exception to this trend. A series of yellow fever epidemics there in the 1870s encouraged the hiring of black policemen because they were less vulnerable to the disease than whites, especially the Irish immigrants who dominated the force. See Dennis C. Rousey, "Yellow Fever and Black Policemen in Memphis: A Post-Reconstruction Anomaly," *Journal of Southern History*, LI (1985), 357–74.

cluding some modest technological advances—such as an emergency-response patrol wagon system cued by patrolmen's signals from telegraph or telephone call boxes—and the adoption in 1889 of a civil service program that was supposed to end partisan political influence on policing. Civil service did have a moderating effect on political influence but fell far short of ending it.

Throughout the nineteenth century, those who made policies for the police or influenced public discourse about police practices—mayors, city councilmen, state legislators, district attorneys, attorneys general, judges, police commanders, journalists—grappled awkwardly and ineffectually with the nettlesome problem of police use and abuse of deadly force. Despite the importance of this issue, the historical record of nineteenth-century New Orleans cannot be readily or fully compared with the experiences of other urban police forces of the period. Although criminal justice history has grown and developed impressively in the last quarter-century, specialists in the field have devoted relatively little attention to police use of force. Probably the best efforts so far to explore nineteenth-century police violence are those of David Johnson and Wilbur Miller for the American police; Clive Emsley has done valuable work on their English counterparts. More cursory treatments have appeared in published works by Roger Lane, James Richardson, Samuel Walker, Robert Fogelson, and John Schneider, although all of these explorations have left several important questions not only unanswered but unasked.[12]

Although historians of criminal justice have expended scant effort on police use of force, serious scholarly study of the subject is needed. Incidents in which police resorted to force have precipitated some of the worst race riots in American history. The 1964 Harlem riot and the 1966 riots in San Francisco and Atlanta started after white policemen shot black teenagers, and rumors of police brutality in connection with routine traffic stops of black motorists triggered riots in Philadelphia, Watts, and Newark

12. David R. Johnson, *Policing the Urban Underworld: The Impact of Crime on the Development of the American Police, 1800–1887* (Philadelphia, 1979), 137–40; Johnson, *American Law Enforcement*, 30–31, 33; Miller, *Cops and Bobbies*, 21–22, 51–54, 145–47; Clive Emsley, "'The Thump of Wood on a Swede Turnip': Police Violence in Nineteenth-Century England," *Criminal Justice History*, VI (1985), 125–49; Richardson, *New York Police*, 113, 157–58, 263; Lane, *Policing the City*, 103–104, 134, 203; Walker, *Popular Justice*, 63–64, 168, 237; Fogelson, *Big-City Police*, 15; John C. Schneider, *Detroit and the Problem of Order, 1830–1880: A Geography of Crime, Riot, and Policing* (Lincoln, 1980), 117–18.

between 1964 and 1967—indeed, such incidents incited more than eighty riots in the 1960s. Riots in Miami in 1980 and 1989 and one in Chattanooga in 1982 began under similar circumstances, and in 1992 news of the acquittal of four white policemen on charges stemming from the beating of an African American motorist, Rodney King, set off the devastating riot in Los Angeles that led to at least fifty deaths.[13]

Identifying the unique characteristic of policing as an occupation in American civil society also suggests the need to study the police use of force. A high occupational death rate does not make policing unique—rates for teamsters and steelworkers are higher than for police—and although police suicide rates are high, so are those for physicians. Police are not the only law enforcers, either; building inspectors, public health officials, and pollution control authorities are responsible for enforcing some laws. What is unique to policing as an occupation in American civil society is the broad authority and concomitant obligation of police to make arrests and—when circumstances require it—to use force that could be deadly.[14]

The democratic ideals of American civic virtue signal the importance of close scrutiny of police use of force, both historical and contemporary. In fundamental American law, particularly the Declaration of Independence and the Fifth and Fourteenth Amendments to the United States Constitution, the first in the trinity of sacred rights that government must not abridge without due process is life. When a police officer, as an agent of government, has the unilateral power to destroy a human life without reference to the courts, every thoughtful citizen should want to know if such an individual act conforms to the highest practicable standards of law. Issues of this importance compel the historian to pose questions about police resort to force. What formal rules—constitutional provisions, legislative statutes, judicial decisions, city ordinances, and administrative regulations—governed police use of force, and how did they evolve? Under what circumstances and with what consequences did police officers resort to force? The answers to these questions are complex, but one important lesson can be succinctly stated here. In nineteenth-century New Orleans a great gulf separated the formal policy prescriptions of lawmakers from

13. Walker, *Popular Justice*, 224; Peter Scharf and Arnold Binder, *The Badge and the Bullet: Police Use of Deadly Force* (New York, 1983), 10.

14. For background on the development of broadening police authority to arrest, see Jerome Hall, "Legal and Social Aspects of Arrest Without a Warrant," *Harvard Law Review*, XLIX (1936), 566–92.

the actual behavior of rank-and-file policemen at work. Despite the efforts of some public officials to impose reasonable constraints on police behavior and despite occasional small increments of progress in that direction, legal theory and practical reality often remained quite apart from and at odds with each other. Indeed, this observation could describe the fate of most efforts at police reform in nineteenth-century New Orleans.

# 1

## INTO AND OUT OF THE ORBIT OF MARS
### The Military Style of Policing, 1805–1836

WHEN the United States acquired Louisiana from France in 1803, the territory had been in the possession of the French for only one month. Although originally a French colony, Louisiana had been held and governed by Spain from the 1760s to 1803. New Orleans, nestled in a bend of the Mississippi River seventy-five miles upstream from the Gulf of Mexico, was a community of people who were mostly of French, African, or Franco-African descent. The relationship between the French and Spanish in New Orleans had been uneasy, leading to an abortive rebellion in 1767–1769, but thereafter the tensions had moderated considerably.[1]

By regional standards, New Orleans was a large urban place, the most populous in the lower Mississippi Valley. In 1805 the city had a population of about 8,500 people. Whites constituted 42 percent of the total, slaves accounted for 37 percent, and free people of color for 19 percent. The census of 1810 showed approximately 17,000 inhabitants, with whites as 37 percent of the total and blacks constituting a majority (35 percent enslaved and 29 percent free). The suburban and rural remainder of the parish of Orleans had a little more than 7,000 residents.[2]

New Orleans was ethnically heterogeneous, a city of immigrants as well as slaves and free people of color. Blacks outnumbered whites, and this imbalance profoundly influenced the laws of the territory and the city ordinances. Among whites, people of French descent were most numerous,

---

1. John Preston Moore, *Revolt in Louisiana: The Spanish Occupation, 1766–1770* (Baton Rouge, 1976); Carl A. Brasseaux, *Denis-Nicolas Foucault and the New Orleans Rebellion of 1768* (Ruston, La., 1987).

2. *New Orleans in 1805: A Directory and a Census* (New Orleans, 1936); *Aggregate Amount of Each Description of Persons Within the United States of America, and Territories Thereof, Agreeably to Actual Enumeration Made According to Law, in the Year 1810* (Washington, D.C., 1811). In 1805, 2 percent of the inhabitants were classified as "other"—probably Indians. The total of 101 percent for the 1810 figures merely reflects natural rounding error.

followed by Anglo-Americans and natives of Great Britain. Despite forty years of Spanish colonial rule, few Spaniards resided in New Orleans. A smattering of people from all over Europe and Latin America completed the white population.[3]

New Orleans served as an important commercial hub through which flowed the agricultural products of most of the Mississippi Valley, brought downriver by flatboats and shipped out by sail to the eastern seaboard of the United States and to Europe. By European standards, or even in comparison to Boston, Philadelphia, New York, and Charleston, New Orleans was scarcely more than a frontier outpost. The streets of the town were unpaved and only partially lighted; swamps lay beyond its crumbled earthwork walls; and its cultural attainments were few and unsophisticated. It boasted a Catholic church, a convent, a monastery, a theater of sorts, and a charity hospital. But the center of activity was the marketplace on the levee and the levee itself, where vessels were loaded and unloaded. Although sugar manufacturing was an important industry in the countryside, the town itself had no major industry or manufacturing. New Orleans was a burgeoning center of commerce, a river port and a seaport with prospects of a great future.

New Orleans grew rapidly between 1805 and 1836 despite the economic hardships of the embargo and nonintercourse policies of the Jefferson and Madison administrations, the years of war with Britain, the depression caused by the Panic of 1819, and the horrific cholera epidemic of 1832–1833. The city spilled out of the old walls into the principal upriver and downriver suburbs, the faubourg St. Marie and faubourg Marigny, and newer suburbs grew up beyond them. The river and swamps shaped the city's physical growth as it began to take on the crescent configuration of its bend in the river, which would provide the nickname the Crescent City.[4]

The arrival of steamboats in force in the 1820s conferred on New Orleans its greatest commercial advantage of the century. Even in the early years of American rule the city had served as the outlet for the agricultural products of the Mississippi and Ohio river valleys, but the difficulties of upstream transportation had severely limited the distribution of goods from New Orleans to its vast hinterland. Before trans-Appalachian canals

---

3. William Darby, *A Geographical Description of the State of Louisiana* (Philadelphia, 1816), 185–86.
4. *Ibid.*

were built, the country west of the mountains was handicapped in the east-west trade by the great cost of hurdling that mountainous barrier. There-fore, westerners turned to New Orleans for manufactured goods, which were brought in by sail from the eastern seaboard and Europe. The steam-boat made the trade between New Orleans and its backcountry a reciprocal relationship, and the economy of the city flourished. The population boomed from 17,000 in 1810 to 27,500 in 1820 and 50,000 by 1830; by 1836, it had reached perhaps 80,000.[5]

The northern traveler Joseph Holt Ingraham visited New Orleans in the mid-1830s and later recorded his excitement at seeing the police of the city in action. As he walked along Chartres Street one evening, Ingraham observed an argument escalate into an armed brawl, and someone called out for the police: "'Gens d'armes, gens d'armes,' 'guards! guards!' re-sounded along the streets, and we arrived at our hotel, just in time to escape being run down, or run through at their option probably, by half a dozen *gens d'armes* in plain blue uniforms, who were rushing with drawn swords in their hands to the scene of the contest." Later Ingraham had an oppor-tunity to peer inside the guardhouse that served as police headquarters, where a "glance *en passant* through an open door, disclosed an apparently well-filled armory." What Ingraham found worthy of note—the uniforms, the swords, the police armory—were distinctive features of southern urban policing, which no northerner was likely to see at home in that era.[6]

Soon after New Orleans became part of the United States, the city government created a municipal police force whose organization closely resembled that of a small army. This martial style of policing stood in stark contrast to the civil style of law enforcement in northern cities, where constables and night watchmen, ununiformed and unarmed, presented a thoroughly unmilitary and scarcely intimidating appearance. Inspired prin-cipally but not exclusively by a desire to control the large local slave popu-lation, the military-style police in the Crescent City was similar to those in Charleston, Savannah, Mobile, and Richmond.

5. *Fifth Census, or Enumeration of the Inhabitants of the United States. 1830. To Which Is Prefixed a Schedule of the Whole Number of Persons Within the Several Districts of the United States, Taken According to the Acts of 1790, 1800, 1810, 1820* (Washington, D.C., 1832); Richard C. Wade, *The Urban Frontier: Pioneer Life in Early Pittsburgh, Cincinnati, Lexington, Louisville, and St. Louis* (Chicago, 1959), *passim*.

6. Joseph Holt Ingraham, *The South-West: By a Yankee* (2 vols.; New York, 1835), I, 95, 111–12.

This distinctive southern model of policing developed much earlier than police reform in northern cities and for differing reasons. The fear of slave crime and rebellion led these southern cities (and in Richmond's case, the state government) to adopt the martial style of policing when their populations were no larger than about 10,000 people. In contrast, significant police reform did not come to New York City until the mid-1840s, when the population was about 400,000; in Boston the first step toward reform took place in 1838, when the population was probably 80,000, and the process was largely completed in the mid-1850s, when the population was near 150,000; Philadelphia experimented briefly with reform in the 1830s and then again more consequentially in the late 1840s and 1850s—its population numbered 220,000 in 1840 and 340,000 in 1850. The most distinctive features of early southern police forces were uniforms, formidable weapons, and wages (rather than fees or compulsory unpaid service); around-the-clock patrolling and unification of day and night forces came later. In the 1840s and 1850s northern cities adopted the twenty-four-hour patrol, organizational unity, and wages for policemen; uniforms and firearms followed later (often northern policemen armed themselves with guns without official authorization or even against the law). New Orleans participated in both types of reform, adopting the southern model in the period 1805–1836 and shifting to the northern model in the years 1836–1854.[7]

The city government of New Orleans, dissatisfied with the colonial arrangements for enforcing the law and maintaining order, first created a strong municipal police force in 1805 and, after a few years of trial and error, settled upon an organization known as the city guard, which served for nearly a generation. Before 1805, a weak and ununified collection of public officers performed the chores of maintaining order and catching criminals. A handful of officers known as the commissaries of police (in the all-embracing eighteenth-century sense of *police*) were general-purpose health officers, traffic controllers, building inspectors, and occasionally crime fighters. In the suburbs and rural periphery of the city, syndics performed duties similar to those of commissaries. During the 1790s the city

---

7. Richardson, *Urban Police*, 19–34, esp. 22–27; Johnson, *American Law Enforcement*, 17–33; Walker, *Popular Justice*, 59–65; Steinberg, *Transformation of Criminal Justice*, 119–82; Lane, *Policing the City*, 37–105; *Sixth Census or Enumeration of the Inhabitants of the United States as Corrected at the Department of State in 1840* (Washington, D.C., 1841); *Seventh Census of the United States: 1850* (Washington, D.C., 1853).

added a small corps of lamplighters, not only to light the newly acquired street lamps imported from Philadelphia but also to patrol the streets when not tending to the lamps.[8] Serious disorders or threats to the peace forced the city to fall back on the services of the militia and the Spanish army. Never conspicuously effective, this system of law enforcement was badly strained by the population growth of the late eighteenth and early nineteenth centuries. Though the problem of law and order had many nettlesome features in a bustling frontier port city with a polyglot population, such as the seasonal influx of rugged and often rowdy flatboatmen and the year-round presence of sailors, the control of slaves most concerned the city's governors.[9]

In the last third of the eighteenth century, runaway slaves from the city joined other runaways as rural maroons and plagued the law enforcers of New Orleans. Militia expeditions attempted to suppress the marauding African bands in the 1770s and 1780s, with uneven but eventually successful results. Even though the activities of the maroons subsided after the militia scored some successes, the Spanish colonial government in New Orleans— the Cabildo—remained worried enough to petition the Spanish Crown in 1796 to forbid further slave importation. The Cabildo also sought to end the immigration of free blacks, many of whom sought refuge in New Orleans after fleeing the rebellion in St. Domingue. The influx of free and enslaved blacks was interrupted temporarily, but the city's population still contained a large proportion of blacks.[10]

When the Americans acceded to power, the city council complained about the poor quality of policing, pointing to the performance of the lamplighter-watchmen, and voted to contract for street lighting. It also created the office of commissary general of police for the city and faubourgs and appointed Pierre Achille Rivery to the post. Two other officers with the title of constable were assigned to Rivery, and, through sheer accident, the council stumbled upon a former U.S. Army officer who was supporting himself by giving fencing lessons and hired him as Rivery's assistant. The

8. Alphabetical and Chronological Digest of the Acts and Deliberations of the Cabildo, 152–55, 157–60, 191–96, in New Orleans Public Library, hereafter NOPL.

9. Michael Allen, *Western Rivermen, 1763–1861: Ohio and Mississippi Boatmen and the Myth of the Alligator Horse* (Baton Rouge, 1990), 112, 127–29, 167, 196, 198.

10. Alphabetical and Chronological Digest of the Acts and Deliberations of the Cabildo, 191–96, 232–40; Gwendolyn Midlo Hall, *Africans in Colonial Louisiana: The Development of Afro-Creole Culture in the Eighteenth Century* (Baton Rouge, 1992), 212–36, 317–74.

council relied on the militia as a stopgap and undertook to reorganize and revitalize that body. The federal government provided some help, too, as the U.S. troops stationed in New Orleans deployed patrols to keep the peace in the newly acquired territory.[11]

But these measures did not prove adequate. As early as 1804, Mayor Etienne Boré recommended the formation of a mounted patrol to capture runaway slaves. Mayor Boré's proposal presaged the creation of the first strong police force, the Gendarmerie, established by the city council in 1805 to perform all the functions of a police force but with special emphasis on slave control. Indicative of its special purpose was the method of financing adopted for the new organization: slaveholders were taxed one dollar for every slave. Moreover, the formative ordinance spelled out in extraordinary detail the system by which the men of the Gendarmerie were to share in the capture fees for runaway slaves. Although it was a salaried force, ranging from the captain's sixty dollars per month to the ordinary gendarme's twenty to twenty-five dollars, the men accrued shares in a pool of capture fees and money from slaves who were caught gambling. To control the slave population, the Gendarmerie would make night patrols to take up any slave without a pass and disperse nocturnal dances "to the beat of the drum." They also inspected slave huts on plantations in the vicinity and confiscated any arms that were found.[12]

To make the police more responsive to the public's needs, the Gendarmerie not only made night patrols but also held a force in reserve during the day for any public official or citizen to call upon when needed. Half of the force was mounted on horses. This was the only time during the century that such a large portion of the police was mounted, and it was very costly. Mayor Boré had recommended that fewer men be mounted to save money, but the city council stipulated that twenty of its thirty-nine men constitute a horse patrol, receiving an extra five dollars per month.

11. Proceedings of Council Meetings, December 28, 1803, January 25, February 22, March 17, May 16, July 9, August 18, November 28, December 1, 1804, NOPL; W. C. C. Claiborne to James Madison, July 27, 1805, in Dunbar Rowland, ed., *Official Letter Books of W. C. C. Claiborne* (6 vols.; Madison, Wisc., 1917), III, 136–38; Documents and Letters of Laussat, Colonial Prefect and Commissioner of the French Government, and of the Commissioners of His Catholic Majesty, November 30, December 6, 1803, NOPL.

12. Ordinances and Resolutions of the City Council of New Orleans, May 18, 1805, NOPL.

Mounted men were considered essential to ensure the capture of runaway slaves in the countryside.[13]

The new organization strongly resembled a military unit. A hierarchical chain of command with military ranks stretched from Captain Edouard Forstal through a lieutenant, a sublieutenant, a sergeant, and three corporals, down to the rank and file of thirty-two gendarmes. The entire force wore blue broadcloth uniforms (the cost of which was borne by the men), with distinctive insignia of rank. Sergeants, corporals, and gendarmes were required to enlist for at least three years. Any man who quit without permission was subject to a penalty of an additional three months in service and forfeiture of one year's pay. Delinquencies were penalized not only by loss of salary but also by corporal punishment. Like army units, the men were compulsorily quartered in barracks. Their arms were not the clubs or staffs carried by night watchmen in northeastern cities. The mounted gendarmes routinely carried single-shot flintlock pistols, and the whole force carried swords slung from shoulder belts. In addition, the Gendarmerie had an armory of muskets for the unmounted men to carry on patrol.[14]

The tenure of this organization was exceptionally brief. After criticisms of the exorbitant cost of maintaining horses and, to a lesser extent, the quality of personnel and their lack of discipline, the city council abolished the Gendarmerie in February, 1806. During the next three years, the city government tried several alternatives. First was a city guard, a slightly less militaristic version of the Gendarmerie but without the expensive horses, that lasted from 1806 to 1808. A financial crunch caused the city to scrap the city guard in favor of a reinforced corps of constables, who worked at the direction of the city's magistrates primarily as process servers rather than as a patrol force, and lamplighter-watchmen in 1808 and 1809, but when this arrangement proved manifestly ineffective, the constables were reduced in number, the lamplighters lost their night watching duties, and the city guard was revived in December, 1809.[15]

13. Proceedings of Council Meetings, April 4, 1805; Ordinances and Resolutions of the City Council, May 18, June 15, 1805; Messages of the Mayors to the City Council, May 6, 1805, all NOPL.

14. Proceedings of Council Meetings, April 4, 1805; Ordinances and Resolutions of the City Council, May 18, June 5, 1805; Messages of the Mayors to the City Council, May 6, 1805.

15. Cavalry had traditionally been regarded as the most aristocratic branch of the army in Western culture, though whether this perception had any role in abolishing the Gendar-

This second version of the city guard served as the police force for New Orleans (augmented by a few constables, commissaries, and syndics and with occasional crisis patrolling by the militia and the U.S. infantry) until a major reorganization in 1836.[16] Its organizational style was distinctly mili-

merie is unknown. See Ordinances and Resolutions of the City Council, December 14, 1805, March 12, 1807; Proceedings of Council Meetings, September 7, 28, November 16, 23, 1805, February 15, 25, 1806, February 7, March 12, December 30, 1807; Messages of the Mayors to the City Council, September 29, December 5, 1805, March 1, 1806, October 6, December 23, 1807; *Louisiana Gazette*, March 18, 1808, March 24, July 25, August 4, 1809; Christian Schultz, *Travels on an Inland Voyage Through the States of New-York, Pennsylvania, Virginia, Ohio, Kentucky and Tennessee, and Through the Territories of Indiana, Louisiana, Mississippi and New-Orleans; Performed in the Years 1807 and 1808; Including a Trip of Nearly Six Thousand Miles* (2 vols.; New York, 1810), II, 200; *Acts of the Orleans Territory*, 1807, pp. 98–102, and 1808, pp. 82–86; *Police Code, or Collection of the Ordinances of Police Made by the City Council of New Orleans. To Which Is Prefixed the Act for Incorporating Said City with the Acts Supplementary Thereto* (New Orleans, 1808), 282, 290–96; *Ordinances Issued by the City Council of New-Orleans, from the Promulgation of the Police Code Until the First of January 1812, with Two Acts of the Territorial Legislature Relative to Said City, to Serve as a Supplement to the Police Code* (New Orleans, 1812), 38–64.

16. The New Orleans city guard, established first in 1806 and revived in 1809, survived two early crises. In January, 1811, a slave rebellion in the parishes of St. Charles and St. John the Baptist electrified New Orleans. The municipal government clamped down on the local slave population, forbidding the common practice of "living out" from masters. Guns and swords were distributed among sailors aboard ships in port, and the mayor put all twenty-five supernumerary (substitute) guardsmen on duty, plus an additional thirty-seven men as temporary police. Refugees from the countryside fled into town, and for several weeks New Orleans was an armed camp awaiting an invasion or uprising of its own. No such cataclysm came to pass. The state militia and federal troops put down the rebellion, and the city guard apparently managed to retain the confidence of the city government. See Proceedings of Council Meetings, January 12, 16, February 6, 11, March 9, 23, 1811; Messages of the Mayors to the City Council, January 12, 16, 1811. See also James H. Dormon, "The Persistent Specter: Slave Rebellion in Territorial Louisiana," *Louisiana History*, XVIII (1977), 389–404; Thomas Marshall Thompson, "National Newspaper and Legislative Reaction to Louisiana's Deslondes Slave Revolt," *Louisiana History*, XXXIII (1992), 5–29; Junius P. Rodriguez, "Always 'En Garde': The Effects of Slave Insurrection upon the Louisiana Mentality, 1811–1815," *Louisiana History*, XXXIII (1992), 399–416.

Soon thereafter New Orleans steeled itself for war with Britain. In the first year of the war, the city council called out nightly militia patrols, laid in a store of ammunition at city hall, had the muskets of the city guard inspected, and put the city's fire engines in first-class condition. Saloons were ordered to close by nightfall, and an ordinance was adopted banning slave gatherings for any purpose other than a funeral. The city guard was specifically directed to make rounds at dusk to disperse slaves who congregated around cabarets. Declining public revenues as a result of the war led the city government to reduce the guardsmen's pay and

tary, though a bit less so than the Gendarmerie. Unlike the gendarmes, city guardsmen did not routinely carry firearms, relying on sabers and half-pikes instead, although the use of muskets was authorized in times of emergency. Corporal punishment was abolished, and terms of enlistment ran for only six months. This city guard was dramatically closer to a military model of organization than were the northern night watches and constabulary of the same period, and slave control remained a very significant goal of the New Orleans police.[17]

When the city's governors decided in 1805 to adopt a military model for a municipal police, they were guided by experience. Military organizations—the militia and the Spanish army—were the only ones capable of wielding force in the colonial era. Even when the French-speaking world acquired a new police organization (the republican Gendarmerie created in France in 1790), it was a wholly military institution—a unit of the French army. Nowhere in the French-, Spanish-, or English-speaking worlds of 1805 was there a strong, successful, purely civil police force. Not until the English Parliament established the Metropolitan Police for London in 1829 did any noteworthy nonmilitary innovation in policing occur for Americans to consider as a possible model. It is not surprising, then, that New Orleans adopted a military style for its police force even though the organization's source of authority was wholly civil.[18]

New Orleans was not alone among southern cities in establishing a strong police force with a martial configuration. Charleston created a city guard in 1783. This police force wore uniforms, carried muskets and swords, mounted a considerable portion of its men as a horse patrol, and marched forth in strong squads to sweep the streets at night—the same tactic used by the New Orleans force—rather than deploying individual

---

then to cut the size of the force in half. The appearance of British troops in the vicinity at the end of the war revitalized the flagging militia patrols but had little effect on the city guard, for its strength was not increased until 1816. See Messages of the Mayors to the City Council, December 28, 1811, October 31, 1812, February 6, March 4, 13, 1813, August 24, 1814; Proceedings of Council Meetings, September 2, 26, October 31, November 2, 3, 4, 1812, March 4, 6, 13, June 26, 1813, August 20, 24, 1814, May 27, 1815, July 20, August 3, 1816.

17. Although city guardsmen were ordinarily uniformed while on duty, some did plain-clothes police work. In 1820, the city council assigned ten guardsmen to police the Orleans Theatre, stipulating that the men "shall be disguised, that is to say wear any other clothes than their uniform" (Ordinances and Resolutions of the City Council, January 22, 1820).

18. Eric A. Arnold, *Fouche, Napoleon, and the General Police* (Washington, D.C., 1979), 24, 26.

beat patrolmen as northern night watches did. Charlestonians were influenced by the same considerations that led New Orleanians to build a new bulwark for their racial and social order, for Charleston also had large black and slave populations. If anything, the Charleston force may have been even more militant than its counterpart in New Orleans.[19]

The Charleston police attracted the attention of numerous travelers. James Stuart, a British visitor to the United States in 1830, observed that "in the appearance of an armed police, Charleston and New Orleans do not resemble the free cities of America; but the great number of the black population, and the way in which they are treated by the whites, render this precaution, I have no doubt, indispensably necessary." Stuart stressed the military appearance of the Charleston police when he described them as a "guard of soldiers, who patrole the city during the night." Another sojourner, Bernhard, Duke of Saxe-Weimar Eisenach, called the Charleston police "a company of police soldiers" and asserted that "this corps owes its support to the fear of the negroes." A traveling actor, Louis Tasistro, observed in the early 1840s that "Charleston possesses one of the best organized systems of police that ever was devised." When the city guard set forth at night, Tasistro noted, "the city suddenly assumes the appearance of a great military garrison, and all the principal streets become forthwith alive with patrolling parties of twenties and thirties, headed by fife and drum, conveying the idea of a general siege."[20]

Travelers' accounts of the early 1850s emphasized the martial character

19. Edward P. Cantwell, *A History of the Charleston Police Force from the Incorporation of the City, 1783 to 1908* (Charleston, 1908); *A Digest of the Ordinances of the City Council of Charleston, from the Year 1783 to Oct. 1844. To Which Are Annexed the Acts of the Legislature Which Relate Exclusively to the City of Charleston*, comp. George B. Eckhard (Charleston, 1844), 88–102; Walter J. Fraser, Jr., *Charleston! Charleston! The History of a Southern City* (Columbia, S.C., 1989), 171; Bacon, "Early Development of American Municipal Police," II, 598–606; Jordan, "Police Power and Public Safety," 122–40. Jordan suggests that the squad sweep system in Charleston was abandoned for the beat system in the 1820s; so, too, does Jack Kenny Williams, in *Vogues in Villainy: Crime and Retribution in Ante-Bellum South Carolina* (Columbia, 1959), 73. The traveler Louis Fitzgerald Tasistro, however, clearly described the deployment of large squads in the 1840s, in *Random Shots and Southern Breezes, Containing Critical Remarks on the Southern States and Southern Institutions, with Semi-Serious Observations on Men and Manners* (2 vols.; New York, 1842), II, 135.

20. James Stuart, *Three Years in North America* (2 vols.; Edinburgh, 1833), II, 139, 236; Bernhard, Duke of Saxe-Weimar Eisenach, *Travels Through North America, During the Years 1825 and 1826* (2 vols.; Philadelphia, 1828) II, 7; Tasistro, *Random Shots and Southern Breezes*, II, 135.

of the Charleston police. An Englishman, J. Benwell, saw the nightly mounting of the Charleston city guard "as if in preparation for, or in expectation of a foe." The American traveler Frederick Law Olmsted found many institutions in Charleston extraordinarily military in appearance, "especially, the numerous armed police, which is under military discipline," and which "might lead one to imagine that the town was in a state of siege or revolution." William Kingsford, writing for a Toronto newspaper in the late 1850s, left an especially perceptive and detailed impression of the Charleston police:

What struck me particularly in Charleston was the police organization. It is a perfect *gens d'armerie*. On passing the barrack, I was attracted by the sentry who was marching his regular distance accoutered with side belts and musket. I could see at once he was not a militia man, for there was nothing of a holiday look about him. Equally could I see that he was not a soldier, for you did not find that smartness and neatness which become inseparable from continuous discipline. I was subsequently enlightened and learned that there was a strong force constantly in readiness to act. Patrols pass through the city at all hours. . . . It struck me that the principal cause of anxiety might be, after all, the slave population. More than once there has been talk of a general rising, and not very many years ago it is averred that only by great skill and courage such a result was averted.

Charleston's dedication to its traditional approach to policing was reflected in the retention of the name *city guard* into the 1850s. For two years during the 1840s the guard was renamed the *police*, but the old organizational title was restored in 1848.[21]

The military style of policing was also adopted in Savannah, where the police routinely carried muskets on patrol duty and wore uniforms as early as 1796. Later a mounted contingent was established, and the police were furnished with pistols. During the late 1850s Charleston municipal au-

---

21. J. Benwell, *An Englishman's Travels in America: His Observations of Life and Manners in the Free and Slave States* (London, 1853), 178, 184–85. Benwell described the preparations of the Charleston city guard as it began its nightly patrols: "It was a stirring scene, when the drums beat at the guard-house in the public square I have before described, preparatory to the rounds of the soldiers, to witness the negroes scouring the streets in all directions, to get to their places of abode, many of them in great trepidation, uttering ejaculations of terror as they ran." See also Frederick Law Olmsted, *A Journey in the Seaboard Slave States in the Years 1853–1854* (2 vols.; New York, 1904), II, 31; William Kingsford, *Impressions of the West and South During a Six Weeks' Holiday* (Toronto, 1858), 77–78. Kingsford also noted that "special care is also taken in the organization of the militia, who I believe assemble more often for drill than in any other State, perhaps owing to the same cause."

thorities visited Savannah and New Orleans to observe their police forces. They found that Savannah had in "successful operation a system of police which seemed to commend it to all." When they reported their findings, the Charleston city council emulated Savannah's example by substantially increasing the number of city guardsmen who patrolled by horse.[22]

Of the four Deep South cities, Mobile was the slowest to develop and consequently the last to establish a military style of policing. As late as 1830 its population had only reached 3,200, and the city watch was based on the traditional system of compulsory rotative service by the white adult males in the community. During the next decade the population grew rapidly, reaching 12,700 in 1840. In 1835 the municipal government decided to reform the policing system. Hired policemen wore a uniform of blue jacket and white pants; the officers carried swords and pistols, and the privates bore muskets and bayonets. As the city grew, the municipal authorities increased the strength of the police and in 1853 established a mounted patrol employing a portion of the force.[23]

Richmond also had a form of martial policing, though in a way significantly different from those of the other four southern cities. Beginning in 1801 (the year after the abortive slave rebellion of Gabriel Prosser), the state government maintained within the city a unique quasi-police institution known as the Public Guard, which was a standing company of the state militia. Although not a substitute for the city police, for the municipal government maintained its own force, the Public Guard performed a police function by guarding the state capitol building, the penitentiary, and the armory and by being a reserve force against the possibility of slave rebellion. Guardsmen were quartered in the armory; they enlisted for three years, worked under the same regulations that applied to U.S. troops (though they were exempt from the death penalty for delinquencies), wore

22. Thomas Gamble, Jr., *A History of the City Government of Savannah, Ga., from 1790 to 1901. Compiled from Official Records by Thomas Gamble, Jr., Secretary to the Mayor, Under Direction of the City Council, 1900* (Savannah, 1901), 58–59, 66–69, 75, 119, 154–55, 197–98, 239–42; Adelaide Wilson, *Historic and Picturesque Savannah* (Boston, 1889), 81, 97; William Harden, *Recollections of a Long and Satisfactory Life* (New York, 1934), 17–18; *A Digest of All the Ordinances of the City of Savannah, and Various Laws of the State of Georgia, Relative to Said City, Which Were of Force on the 1st January, 1858, Together with an Appendix and Index*, comp. Edward G. Wilson (Savannah, 1858), 321–33; Wade, *Slavery in the Cities*, 101. See also Haunton, "Law and Order in Savannah," 1–24.

23. Paul Wayne Taylor, "Mobile, 1818–1859, as Her Newspapers Pictured Her" (Master's thesis, University of Alabama, 1951), 91–94.

uniforms, were armed with muskets, and received a portion of their compensation in rations (privates received a mere eight dollars per month in cash in 1849). With a complement of nearly ninety men, the guard outnumbered the city police by three to one in 1850. The small municipal force was apparently not armed or uniformed; very likely the city authorities thought it superfluous and wasteful to pay for a formidable force when the Public Guard was available at state expense as a check against slave rebellion.[24]

The Public Guard caught the attention of travelers who visited Richmond. When the English tourist Captain Basil Hall visited in 1828, he was advised by his companion that the guard was "necessary, or at all events it is customary in these States to have a small guard always under arms. . . . It is in consequence of our colored population." The captain's wife, Margaret Hunter Hall, wrote: "They parade a sentry round the Capitol merely as a pretence for having soldiers, but the reason for having them is in case of an insurrection amongst slaves of which the Southern people live in constant dread." While in Richmond, Frederick Law Olmsted saw "an armed sentinel" at the capitol, which he likened to "a prison or fortress." The Public Guard, he discovered, had been established "in 1801, after a rebellion of the colored people, who, under one 'General Gabriel,' attempted to take the town, in hopes to gain the means of securing their freedom. . . . Since then, a disciplined guard, bearing the warning motto, 'Sic semper tyrannis!' has been kept constantly under arms in the capital." William Chambers was deeply struck by the appearance of the guard during a trip through Richmond in 1853, commenting that "it was the first time I had seen a bayonet in the United States, and suggested the unpleasant reflection, that the large infusion of slaves in the composition of society was not unattended with danger."[25]

24. *The Code of Virginia; with the Declaration of Independence and Constitution of the United States; and the Declaration of Rights and Constitution of Virginia* (Richmond, 1849), 170–73; William L. Montague, *Montague's Richmond Directory and Business Advisor, for 1850–1851* (Richmond, [1850?]), 12; *The Charters and Ordinances of the City of Richmond, with the Declaration of Rights, and Constitution of Virginia* (Richmond, 1859), 149–55; *Ordinances of the Corporation of the City of Richmond, and the Acts of Assembly Relating Thereto* (Richmond, 1831), 113–20; Censuses of 1850 and 1860, Record Group 29, Records of the Bureau of the Census, National Archives.

25. Captain Basil Hall, *Travels in North America in the Years 1827 and 1828* (3 vols.; Edinburgh, 1829), I, 74–75; Margaret Hunter Hall, *The Aristocratic Journey: Being the Outspoken Letters of Mrs. Basil Hall Written During a Fourteen Months' Sojourn in America, 1827–*

To confront this domestic danger, the four Deep South cities hired large numbers of policemen in comparison with northern cities, and the combination of state and municipal forces in Richmond was also formidable. During the late antebellum period, the ratio of policemen to ten thousand of urban population tended to be quite high: forty-eight in Charleston (in 1850 and 1856), forty-three in Savannah (in 1854), forty-one in Richmond (city police plus Public Guard in 1850), thirty-three in Mobile (in 1842), and even New Orleans, which had already shifted to a civil style, had rather high ratios of thirty-three (in 1854), eighteen in a period of retrenchment (1855), and twenty-seven (in 1860). In New York City the ratio of police to ten thousand of population was just seventeen (in 1855), in Boston fifteen (in 1856), and in Philadelphia seventeen (in 1856).[26]

White fear of slaves thus led not only to a military style of policing in these southern cities but also to an extraordinary commitment of manpower compared to their northern counterparts. Yet New Orleans did not retain the military style of police throughout the antebellum period but changed to a civil alternative much like that which prevailed north of the Mason-Dixon line and the Ohio River. After years of debate, the Crescent City demilitarized its force in 1836 in response to changes in the ethnic composition of the force and, to a lesser degree, the increasing popularization of political life and the decreasing percentage of slaves in the city's population.

Even in the early nineteenth century some influential New Orleanians were dissatisfied with a police force that closely resembled a standing army. Such dissatisfaction was partially responsible for the abolition of the Gendarmerie in 1806 and its replacement by the city guard, which the city council described as "purely civil."[27] This description was certainly an ex-

---

*1828*, ed. Una Pope-Hennessy (New York, 1931), 197; Olmsted, *Journey in the Seaboard Slave States*, I, 22–23; William Chambers, *Things as They Are in America* (London, 1854), 272.

26. The estimates of police manpower are derived from several sources: Cantwell, *History of the Charleston Police Force* (Charleston); *Digest of All the Ordinances of the City of Savannah*, 321–22 (Savannah); Taylor, "Mobile," 91–93 (Mobile); Census of 1850 (Richmond); Lane, *Policing the City*, 238 (Boston); *A Digest of the Acts of Assembly Relating to the City of Philadelphia, and the (Late) Incorporated Districts of the County of Philadelphia, and of the Ordinances of the Said City and Districts, in Force on the First Day of January, A.D. 1856*, comp. William Duane, William B. Hood, and Leonard Myers (Philadelphia, 1856), 462 (Philadelphia); Ketcham, "Municipal Police Reform," 229 (New York).

27. Proceedings of Council Meetings, February 15, 1806.

aggeration, for the city guard was far more military in style than northern police forces, but it suggested that the police had become too military for the city council's taste, even in the pursuit of the much-desired goal of a secure and stable social order.

Disagreement about how martial the New Orleans police should be persisted as a staple of public debate about law and order. In 1825, for example, a writer for the *Louisiana Gazette* argued that the force "should be modeled after the city guard of Charleston, S.C.," and should routinely carry loaded muskets, drill frequently in the "manual of parade and field evolutions," deploy its men in mounted as well as foot patrols, and quarter the guardsmen more strictly in barracks, denying the men daytime employment (only a portion of the New Orleans force actually was available in barracks during the day at that time). Even police remuneration ought to become more like that of soldiers in the army, the *Gazette* suggested— the cash salary should be reduced considerably and the difference paid in rations. Though these recommendations were not implemented, a similar plan for police reform was touted by the *Louisiana Courier* in 1829, with even more emphasis on mounting the police for horse patrols.[28]

Advocates of the military style began to give way within a few years to proponents of a civil model of organization. The most telling commentary, foreshadowing and partially explaining the demilitarization, appeared in the newspapers in the early 1830s. The editorial bills of indictment charged that not only was the martial character of the force objectionable but so also was the increasing number of its men who were neither French nor Anglo-American. Describing the police as "AN ARMED BAND OF FOREIGN MERCENARIES" and "an unfeeling and almost IRRESPONSIBLE SOLDIERY," the *Louisiana Advertiser* in 1834 condemned the force as "a blot on the face of a free country." These "mercenary soldiers" were "ignorant foreigners" who spoke neither French nor English and were accustomed to "the wars of enslaved Europe." A committee of the city council asserted that "most of them are foreigners, ignorant of the English, and many of them of the French language." The *Mercantile Advertiser* claimed that the police "seldom understand an answer given in English or French" and seemed to enjoy mistreating "the natives of that country which affords them relief from the oppression of their own." Another newspaper, the *True American*, also claimed that a majority of the city guardsmen could speak neither

28. *Louisiana Gazette*, October 5, 1825; *Louisiana Courier*, April 7, 1829.

French nor English, despite the requirement that each member of the force should be proficient in both languages. The city council eventually resolved to test every guardsman to ensure his bilingual capacity. Mayor Denis Prieur opposed this initiative, saying that if he had to dismiss every guardsman who was not bilingual, the entire force would have to be disbanded. Other evidence also indicates that some guardsmen spoke only French and some only English.[29]

In fact, the ethnic composition of the force was changing. In 1814 all the city guardsmen were ancestrally French, mostly (90 percent) "foreign French," a term referring to men of French descent born elsewhere than Louisiana (see Table 1). By 1820 about one-tenth of the force was not of French ancestry but was composed of Germans. Ten years later the French proportion had shrunk, and the police were considerably more heterogeneous; 37.5 percent of the men were not of French ancestry. The largest non-French group was the Germans, which provoked notice and exaggeration. One traveler in the late 1820s commented that the "watchmen and lamp lighters are Germans" and that there "are a great many Germans in New Orleans." In 1834 the *Mercantile Advertiser* asserted that it was not true, "as has been stated, that the majority of the guards are Spaniards. We say that the majority of them are Germans." Though not, in fact, a majority, Germans constituted about one-fifth of the force in 1830, and the chief lamplighter, Henry Hoffman, was a German.[30]

29. *Louisiana Advertiser*, February 14, 17, 18, 1834; *Mercantile Advertiser*, June 25, 1831; *True American*, quoted in Albert A. Fossier, *New Orleans: The Glamour Period, 1800–1840* (New Orleans, 1957), 165; Messages of the Mayors to the City Council, December 3, 1835; *Bee*, July 21, 1835. In 1832, the Reverend Theodore Clapp encountered two city guardsmen who evidently spoke only French (Clapp, *Autobiographical Sketches and Recollections, During a Thirty-Five Years' Residence in New Orleans* [Boston, 1857], 117–18).

30. C. Sealsfield, *The Americans as They Are: Described in a Tour Through the Valley of the Mississippi* (London, 1828), 175; *Mercantile Advertiser*, February 17, 1834.

Determining the nativity of New Orleans policemen before 1836 (or before 1850, for that matter) was extremely difficult. Even simple rosters of policemen's names for the period are scarce. For most years, the city directories listed only a small fraction of city guardsmen's names, with the noteworthy exception of a directory for 1830, which contained a virtually exhaustive list. Payrolls are extant only for 1814, 1820, and 1828. Because these yielded no information other than the policemen's names and salaries, I searched through the municipal death certificates and the newspaper obituary file in the NOPL and obtained records of death (which indicated nativity) for as many of the guardsmen as could be found—in each of the four roster years this was only a fraction of the force. Birthplaces for some policemen appear in the Charity Hospital admission books for the 1820s and 1830s. The results were the

TABLE 1
NATIVITIES OF CITY GUARDSMEN
IN 1814, 1820, 1828, AND 1830

| | 1814 | | 1820 | | 1828 | | 1830 | |
|---|---|---|---|---|---|---|---|---|
| | No. | % | No. | % | No. | % | No. | % |
| French | 10 | 100.0 | 15 | 88.2 | 14 | 70.0 | 20 | 62.5 |
| Louisiana | 1 | 10.0 | 2 | 11.8 | 2 | 10.0 | 3 | 9.4 |
| St. Domingue | 7 | 70.0 | 6 | 35.3 | 6 | 30.0 | 4 | 12.5 |
| France | 2 | 20.0 | 6 | 35.3 | 5 | 25.0 | 12 | 37.5 |
| Canada | 0 | 0 | 1 | 5.9 | 1 | 5.0 | 1 | 3.1 |
| Non-French | 0 | 0 | 2 | 11.8 | 6 | 30.0 | 12 | 37.5 |
| Germany | 0 | 0 | 2 | 11.8 | 3 | 15.0 | 6 | 18.8 |
| Switzerland | 0 | 0 | 0 | 0 | 2 | 10.0 | 1 | 3.1 |
| Italy | 0 | 0 | 0 | 0 | 1 | 5.0 | 2 | 6.3 |
| Canary Islands | 0 | 0 | 0 | 0 | 0 | 0 | 1 | 3.1 |
| Ireland | 0 | 0 | 0 | 0 | 0 | 0 | 2 | 6.3 |
| Totals | 10 | 100.0 | 17 | 100.0 | 20 | 100.0 | 32 | 100.0 |

*Sources:* Charity Hospital Admission Books, microfilm, NOPL, March 29, 1825, November 1, 15, 1827, August 4, 1829, April 24, July 8, 30, December 13, 1830, September 8, 1831, November 30, 1833; New Orleans Death Certificates, microfilm, NOPL, I, 296, III, 276, V, 83, VII, 44, 88, 152, 165, 411, VIII, 286, 420, 697, IX, 371, 471, 812, 839, XI, 166, 188, 301, 690, 1560, XVII, 360, XVIII, 200, 534, XIX, 3, XX, 155, XXI, 88, 376, XXIII, 245, 319, XXXII, 525, XXXV, 566, XXXVIII, 737, XLIII, 421; newspaper obituaries, New Orleans *Bee*, January 8, September 25, 29, 1846; *Louisiana Courier*, September 4, 1822, July 14, 1824, October 12, 1842, November 15, 22, 1853, February 26, 1860; *Daily Picayune*, November 21, 1840; *Deutsche Zeitung*, October 27, 1858; *Daily Crescent*, February 19, 1862.

In the late 1820s and early 1830s, the non-French portion of the guard included natives not only of Germany but also of Switzerland, Italy, the Canary Islands, Holland, Finland, Sweden, and Ireland. Irish policemen

---

samples shown in Table 1: all of the nativity data available for the city guardsmen of 1814, 1820, 1828, and 1830, ranging from about one-fifth of the force in 1814 to one-third in 1830. An alternative scheme based on assigning birthplaces according to the apparent ethnicity of surnames produced similar results, except for a slightly larger proportion of Germans in 1830 (about 28 percent versus 18.8 percent). See Payrolls of the City Guard, January, March, April, June, July, August, 1814, July, 1828, Historic New Orleans Collection; Payrolls of the City Guard, May, 1814, December, 1820, Howard-Tilton Memorial Library, Tulane University, New Orleans; John Adams Paxton, *The New-Orleans Directory and Register* (New Orleans, 1830); Charity Hospital Admission Books, microfilm, NOPL; Obituary Index, Card file, NOPL.

made their first appearance on the force in 1830 and evidently became more numerous rather quickly thereafter, though they were probably still a smaller proportion of the force than Germans in 1836. Though precise numbers for all policemen are not available for the 1830s and 1840s, the Irish apparently accounted for 33 percent of the Third Municipality police force in 1841 and constituted 32 percent of all policemen in the city in 1850, making them the largest single nativity group at midcentury.[31]

Thus the Creole (Louisiana-born) French held a nearly constant one-tenth of police jobs throughout the period 1814–1836, while the foreign French were dwindling in number. Evidently there were no Anglo-Americans on the force before 1836.[32]

The city guard also included at least a few free men of color. In the ten-man sample (all those whose nativity could be identified) of the city guardsmen of 1814, two were black; of the seventeen men in the sample for 1820, one was black; and one guardsman in the samples for 1828 and 1830 was a free man of color. It is unlikely that all four of these black guardsmen were passing for white inasmuch as two of them served in a battalion of free men of color in the War of 1812, one was identified as black in the 1820 census, and the other was listed as black on his municipal death certificate. The city government struggled with its own ambivalence in formulating policies that affected the bearing of arms by free blacks. Black militia units were tolerated—barely—in the early years, and black militiamen carried arms when they participated in the emergency patrols with which the militia occasionally supplemented the efforts of the city guard; yet the municipal government barred free men of color from giving or receiving instruction in fencing. When Mayor Etienne Boré recommended the formation of a mounted patrol service in 1804, he called for a company of white men, "or in lieu thereof, of free mulattoes whose officers will be white men." Racial antipathy eventually led the state government to deactivate black militia units in 1834. Perhaps the city government adopted a similar policy—though tacitly—in the 1830s; no formal record of such

31. Pay List of the Day Police, Night Watchmen, and Lamplighters of the 3rd Municipality for the Month of May, 1841, Hill Memorial Library, Louisiana State University, Baton Rouge; Census of 1850, RG 29, NA.
32. None of the names on the rosters for the period 1813–30 was British. One local journalist explained the absence of Anglo-Americans on the police force before 1836 by suggesting that they had no interest in police work (*Mercantile Advertiser*, February 17, 1834).

a policy has survived, but there is no reliable evidence that black men served on the police force between 1830 and 1867.[33]

Clearly, though, the ethnic composition of the force became controversial. The infusion of Germans and other new immigrants distressed some influential New Orleanians. The alien newcomers seemed even more threatening because they looked like soldiers in their police uniforms and carried deadly weapons (always swords and sometimes muskets). Any objections from the public and the city's governors to the military style of policing were thus likely to be intensified by hostility toward the increasing ethnic heterogeneity of the force. Two other developments probably helped spur support for demilitarizing the police: the popularization of the political culture and the relative decline of slave control as a police priority.

Anxiety about slavery had certainly encouraged the creation of the Gendarmerie and the city guard in the first decade of the century. But the proportion of slaves in the city's population, which had been 37 percent in 1805 and 33 percent in 1830, fell during the next decade to 23 percent in 1840 and continued to fall thereafter. Dramatic increases in white immigration and a declining growth rate in the black population thus altered the demographic profile of the city. During the decade 1830–1840, the slave population grew by 41 percent, but the white population grew by 180 percent. Consequently, police interaction with whites occupied a larger share of the city guard's attention by the mid-1830s than had been true a generation before.

33. The identifiable African American guardsmen were Charles Allegre and Constant Michel in 1814, Pierre Aubry in 1820, and Augustus Bolen in 1828 and 1830. Allegre, Aubry, and Bolen were identified as black by municipal death records; Allegre and Aubry served in Fortier's battalion of free men of color; Allegre, Aubry, and Michel appeared in the 1820 census as men of color (only one head of family in that census was named Constant Michel, the only Allegre family was composed just of free people of color, and the household headed by Pierre Aubry included only one adult male, a free man of color between twenty-six and forty-five years of age (Marion John Bennett Pierson, comp., *Louisiana Soldiers in the War of 1812* [Baton Rouge, 1963]; New Orleans Death Certificates, X, 141, XXXII, 525; Census of 1820, RG 29, NA). For Mayor Boré's recommendation, see Proceedings of Council Meetings, March 17, 1804. For militia, see Ordinances and Resolutions of the City Council, May 21, 1816, December 18, 1817; Ira Berlin, *Slaves Without Masters: The Free Negro in the Antebellum South* (New York, 1974), 118–28. For fencing policy, see Proceedings of Council Meetings, July 9, 1804, April 30, 1808. See also Thomas N. Ingersoll, "Free Blacks in a Slave Society: New Orleans, 1718–1812," *William and Mary Quarterly*, XLVIII (1991), 198; and Donald E. Everett, "Emigrés and Militiamen: Free Persons of Color in New Orleans, 1803–1815," *Journal of Negro History*, XXXVIII (1953), 377–402.

Although slave control did not disappear as a police concern, it did apparently subside in the rank order of priorities. The martial style of policing had originated as a response to slavery, but by the 1830s its *raison d'être* was being eclipsed by the whitening of the city's population. Whites certainly did not cease to worry about slave crimes or slave rebellion, but by 1836 a quarter of a century had passed since the Crescent City had witnessed an insurrection. A military-style police to protect against the danger of rebellion no longer compensated for the day-to-day irritation of respectable citizens who found their increasingly alien policemen too menacing and too lacking in deference. Even the Nat Turner insurrection in Virginia in 1831 did not arrest criticism of the military style of policing in New Orleans for long.[34] Thus a committee of the city council argued in 1834 for demilitarizing the police, claiming that "at present they only serve to create disturbances (rather than to prevent them) by their own improper conduct, without rendering any really beneficial services, *beyond dragging disorderly slaves to prison.*"[35] The last phrase in this comment acknowledged some utility in a soldierly police who dealt with slave discipline, while at the same time suggesting that such benefits were outweighed by liabilities.

The increasing proportion of whites in the city coincided with an expansion of republicanism to include poor white men as political participants. Abolition of property requirements for voting and officeholding in most states and aggressive recruiting by the political parties to bring voters to the polls combined to popularize and democratize—to a degree—the national political culture. Andrew Jackson became the first symbolic political celebrity in this new age. Voter turnout did not peak until the hard cider–log cabin–"Tippecanoe and Tyler, too" campaign of 1840 led to the election of William Henry Harrison and John Tyler as president and vice-

---

34. *Fifth Census; Sixth Census.* The Turner rebellion of August, 1831, had remarkably little impact on the police force. The city council proceedings and messages of the mayors show no effort to reinforce or reorganize the police. The strength of the city guard had last been increased on March 1, 1830, from 60 to 80 men; it was not increased again until April 10, 1833, when the number was raised to 133 men; see *A General Digest of the Ordinances and Resolutions of the Corporation of New-Orleans,* comp. D. Augustin (New Orleans, 1831), 173–87; *A Digest of Ordinances, Resolutions, By-Laws and Regulations of the Corporation of New Orleans and a Collection of the Laws of the Legislature Relative to the Said City* (New Orleans, 1836), 99–105. See also Judith Kelleher Schafer, "The Immediate Impact of Nat Turner's Insurrection on New Orleans," *Louisiana History,* XXII (1980), 361–76.

35. *Louisiana Advertiser,* February 18, 1834 (italics added).

president, but even by the early 1830s a surge of political participation was evident.

Until 1845 Louisiana's constitution limited voting to adult males who paid a state tax; it was one of the last states to adopt universal white manhood suffrage. The police reform ordinance and the editorial campaign that led up to it, along with an increase in the rhetoric of popular politics and aggressive electioneering tactics in the late 1820s and early 1830s, demonstrated that the expansive politics of the "common man" were already influencing New Orleans well before the adoption of white manhood suffrage. The old military style of policing seems to have run afoul of the new politics. A standing army had long been anathema to many Americans, a legacy of the colonial and revolutionary experience, which had intensified the lessons of seventeenth-century English politics. The traditional argument against a too-militant police gained support with the increasing need of respectable elites to recruit the support of humbler men of more modest means.[36]

---

36. *Constitutions of 1812, '45, & '52. Also the Constitution of the United States, with Amendments. Articles of Confederation and the Declaration of Independence* (New Orleans, 1861), 38. For a discussion of the popularizing rhetoric and electioneering tactics in New Orleans of the late 1820s and 1830s, see Joseph G. Tregle, Jr., "Louisiana in the Age of Jackson: A Study in Ego-Politics" (Ph.D. dissertation, University of Pennsylvania, 1954), 256, 347–49, 370, 442, 447–58. For the parties' efforts to appeal specifically to Irish voters, see Earl F. Niehaus, *The Irish in New Orleans, 1800–1860* (Baton Rouge, 1965), 71–78. For national attitudes toward the military, see Marcus Cunliffe, *Soldiers and Civilians: The Martial Spirit in America, 1775–1865* (Boston, 1968), 99–144, 177–212; Richard L. Watson, Jr., "Congressional Attitudes Toward Military Preparedness, 1829–1835," *Journal of American History*, XXXIV (1948), 611–36. For Whiggish perceptions of the potential for military dictatorship, see Edwin A. Miles, "The Whig Party and the Menace of Caesar," *Tennessee Historical Quarterly*, XXVII (1968), 361–79.

During the first twenty years after the Louisiana Purchase, the militia and the U.S. infantry were sometimes called out at the request of the city government to patrol the streets of the city. (City guardsmen ordinarily were exempted from militia duty because they were already involved in patrolling.) After the early 1820s, this practice became much rarer. Declining use of the militia as a police force was a reflection of a growing popular disenchantment with the institution of the militia. Militia service required the free men of the community either to miss a day's work or to hire a substitute. It was thus expensive for the militiamen and worked a greater hardship on men too poor to hire a substitute. The poor quality of militia substitutes also provoked public criticism. Within a few days or a few weeks after each militia call-up, public officials would begin to bemoan the slackening zeal and efficiency of the militia patrols. Also, Joseph Tregle has identified internal dissension along ethnic lines within the militia during the 1820s in "The Rise of Nativism in New Orleans," in *St. Patrick's*

Public discourse about the police in the years before the reform was enacted stressed that the military style was antirepublican. In 1834 the *Louisiana Advertiser* described the city guard as "founded on the customs, and continued by the prejudices of ancient despotic governments," as a "blot on the face of a free country, an ancient barbarism in a great commercial and REPUBLICAN city," and as "a glaring remnant of despotism in a land of LIBERTY." "Shall the reproach continue to attach to us," asked the editor, "that in our local institutions our customs and our improvements we are still a century behind the age?" The solution, he argued, was to reform the police, "to dispense with the sword and pistol, the musket and bayonet, in our civil administration of *republican* laws, and adopt or create a system more congenial to our feelings, to the opinions and *interests* of a free and prosperous people, and more in accordance with the spirit of the age we live in." [37]

Newspaper editors and city councilmen alike condemned police mistreatment of even such lowly and minor malefactors as drunken and disorderly sailors and boatmen. The *Mercantile Advertiser* in 1831 criticized the police for alleged abuses: when "an unfortunate sailor, should be found drunk on the Levee, by two of the guard ... he being thus a victim to spirits is shamelessly beaten." Three years later the *Louisiana Advertiser* asked if when "a drunken sailor—not a bad man in reality when sober—a boatman, or a wretched exile from home and friends, becomes riotous and quarrelsome, is that an excuse for beating, brutally beating, aye, sabering this individual, however poor, ragged, vile, or blameworthy he may be?" One journalist commented that city guardsmen were "often insulted by a citizen rubbing against them as he passes by: this is taken as an assault, forth come the swords of the valiant upon one man," and then the citizen would be "dragged to [the] dungeon." A report by a committee of the city

---

of *New Orleans, 1833–1958*, ed. Charles Dufour (New Orleans, 1958), 25. Perhaps antimilitary sentiment also helped minimize calls for patrolling by the army.

For militia mobilizations and demobilizations, see Proceedings of Council Meetings, September 7, November 23, 1805, December 12, 1807, November 29, 1809, March 23, 1811, August 29, September 2, 26, 1812, November 27, 1819, April 8, 1820; Ordinances and Resolutions of the City Council, April 28, 1831; Messages of the Mayors to the City Council, February 14, 1806; Rowland, ed., *Official Letter Books of W. C. C. Claiborne*, V, 95–96, 100. For criticism of the militia, see Messages of the Mayors to the City Council, May 18, 1805; *Louisiana Gazette*, March 18, 1808, August 4, 1809, March 3, 1818.

37. *Louisiana Advertiser*, February 14, 1834.

council in 1834 asserted that policemen frequently provoked arrestees into resisting by excessive use of force and that bystanders often joined in against the police out of "just indignation." "Hundreds of respectable citizens have seen repeated occurrences of this kind, brought on entirely by the improper conduct of the guard." This committee refused to accept the police rationale that "the guard has to deal with sailors, thieves, drunkards, &c. &c., and that they cannot get on peaceably." The remedy, the committee suggested, was to disarm the police and compel them to treat arrestees with courtesy.[38]

The city's political leaders had long shown concern for the possibility of the police misusing force. As early as 1806 one city councilman had tried unsuccessfully to have the city guard stripped of their swords because allegedly several guardsmen had mistakenly assaulted an innocent bystander while trying to arrest some brawling sailors. In 1809 Mayor James Mather asked the council to reestablish an armory with muskets available to the police in emergencies but was careful to note that "I perfectly understand that the usual weapon of the watchmen must be purely defensive." That same year the council laid down the basic rule to govern the guard's use of force. "Should any person or persons resist the patrol, the lieutenant shall summon him or them in the name of the law to surrender; and in case of refusal, after this summons has been thrice made, he shall employ force." Patrolling was done in squads under the command of a supervisory officer, so the decision to use force fell to a leader rather than to an ordinary guardsman.[39]

Police weaponry and use of force were clearly major sources of concern in this public discourse. The *Louisiana Advertiser* addressed the issue in 1834, asking, "In what free country? In what enlightened city? Save New Orleans, do we see a 'watch,' a *civil* police forsooth, parading the streets at noon day in all the panoply of war, 'armed to the teeth,' like the body guard of an eastern despot? The badge of military rule, the sword belt, and the pistol, and . . . the musket and bayonet? and for what? To frighten freemen! To 'dragoon' our peaceful citizens into good behavior!" A committee of the city council contended that "when [the police are] called upon to arrest a delinquent, a great parade is made, they buckle on their swords and

38. *Mercantile Advertiser*, June 25, 1831; *Louisiana Advertiser*, February 17, 18, 1834.

39. Proceedings of Council Meetings, May 7, 14, 21, June 4, 1806; Messages of the Mayors to the City Council, December 5, 1809; *Ordinances Issued by the City Council of New-Orleans*, 38–64.

prepare for meeting resistance, before the object of their pursuit is seen, and of course before they know whether he will or will not prove refractory; the moment they lay hands on a prisoner they at once commence a system of violence towards him." Police use of force was especially controversial in the early 1830s because, apparently for the first time, a citizen was killed by a police officer in 1830. The city guardsman responsible for the slaying was tried on a charge of manslaughter, and despite being found not guilty by the jury, he was reprimanded and admonished by the judge.[40]

The city guard was remote from the people in another sense. Citizens had limited access to the force because there was no "cop on the beat." Instead of having a man assigned to each several blocks, to be walked repeatedly during a single duty shift, the city guard patrolled in squads, setting out from the guardhouse to sweep the streets usually three times per night. During the daytime, a portion of the force remained in the guardhouse to be available for emergency calls, but these men did not conduct routine patrols. Thus the tactical deployment of the police, along with their uniforms and lethal weapons, made them antithetical to the values of the new political culture.

The political system in New Orleans responded to several changes when the city council adopted the police reform ordinance of 1836. In that year, the city council broke with the military tradition of policing and created a system that was entirely new for the Crescent City, based on around-the-clock patrolling by territorial "beat" men. The force was demilitarized and brought closer to the people by eliminating the uniforms and substituting numbered leather caps as the only standard item of apparel. The men were no longer required to enlist for minimum terms of service. To secure an appointment on the force, a candidate had to be recommended by a citizen of his ward or by six citizens who could reside in any ward. A Committee of Vigilance with fourteen members was to be elected by the voters to fill vacancies in the force and be responsible for its administration. Giving this function to a new body that was more representative of the people and presumably more responsive to their will undercut the traditional authority of the mayor to appoint the men with the consent of the council. The Committee of Vigilance was supposed to oversee the behavior of the police, ensure that they complied with the regulations, and keep one of its members at the guardhouse as an inspector.[41]

40. *Louisiana Advertiser*, May 10, 1830, February 17, 18, 1834.
41. *Digest of Ordinances*, 105–15.

The new police system was intended to be more responsive to the popular will and more effective at catching lawbreakers. The squad sweep procedure was replaced by the beat man or watchman. The territory in each district was marked off in beats composed of four squares each, and every night a policeman was to be assigned to patrol each beat. Thus the force would be more widely dispersed and available to prevent crimes and respond to calls by the public. To prevent routinization and corruption, no man was to patrol the same beat two nights in succession. The beat system removed the patrolmen from the direct supervision of officers and placed a greater importance on the intermediate ranks, particularly corporals and sergeants, who were to bear the principal responsibility for making the rounds.[42]

The beat system also placed the patrolman more on his own and made him more vulnerable to assailants, for he would no longer be in company with two or more of his fellows. To call for assistance, the patrolman was to sound his rattle (a wooden noisemaker) to summon men on adjacent beats to come to his aid.[43]

The reform ordinance also sought to improve police efficacy by instituting regular daytime patrols by one-third of the force; only half as many men were on duty during the day as at night, so the day patrolman would have to cover twice as much territory. To provide the manpower necessary for this dispersed deployment, the council authorized an increase in the city guard from 129 to 220 men.[44]

Although the individual man on the beat was to be granted greater discretion, his potential abuse of authority was to be curtailed by reducing his armament. For the first time, the police were deprived of their swords and allowed only spontoons (half-pikes) for weapons. They were supposed to tap the spontoon at each corner so that they could hear one another's progress along their beats, both to supervise one another and to provide a silent alarm if a patrolman was incapacitated and unable to tap. Limiting the police to spontoons was supposed to reduce the possibility of improper use of deadly force against the citizenry. This was in keeping with the limitation on police use of force embodied in an act of the state legislature two years before. That statute had reaffirmed the power of city guardsmen

42. *Ibid.*
43. *Ibid.*
44. *Ibid.*

in New Orleans to make arrests but had warned that "this act shall not be so construed as to justify or authorise the city guard to use either side or fire arms in making arrests, except it be in self defence."[45]

Of course, legal principles did not necessarily operate in practice and were respected in a discriminatory fashion. Slaves did not enjoy the full protection of such principles, nor did others whom the respectable citizenry deemed dangerously deviant. A city ordinance of 1817 allowed more latitude in the use of force against slaves suspected of criminal acts than against other people, and another ordinance in 1828 empowered the policemen guarding the chain gang to use force to compel prisoners to work. The police were expected to treat slaves and convicts differently from respectable citizens, and the laws and ordinances mandated this discriminatory behavior.[46]

The reorganization of the police included another approach to bringing the force more into line with the expectations of the politically powerful. Every member of the guard was required to be an American citizen or to "have made his declaration of his intention to become a citizen." This requirement joined with the reduction in armament to offer an alternative to an "armed band of foreign mercenaries." To attract better candidates, the salary of the ordinary policeman was radically improved, rising from thirty dollars to fifty dollars per month.[47]

Not everyone favored demilitarizing the police. When it was still just a proposal in 1834, the *Mercantile Advertiser* argued against a disarmed police, "although it may suit an eastern or northern public. Are we the only city having an armed police such as our city guard? No—look at Charleston, we there find an armed police of tenfold extent to our own, yet there we hear no murmurs—there we do not see the people on every little occasion arrayed against the police, and yet it is armed in every respect as ours." Speaking for the traditionalists on this issue, Mayor Denis Prieur also objected to the council's proposal for demilitarization, stressing the historic similarity between the police forces of New Orleans and Charleston. (Indeed, the municipal governments of the two cities had customarily exchanged digests of city ordinances to keep each other informed.)

45. *Acts of Louisiana*, 1834, pp. 139–41.
46. Ordinances and Resolutions of the City Council, December 18, 1817, September 1, 1828.
47. *Digest of Ordinances*, 105–15.

In the northern cities, where the organization now proposed has ever been adopted, and watchmen always armed as you would arm yours, experience has no doubt shown the efficacy of the means. But the same argument will also apply to the city of Charleston, for example, where the organization of the police has ever been more military than in New Orleans. If that organization has been found to answer every purpose, is it not to be accounted for by the similarity between the said systems of both cities. Why then change, when experience and habit unite to demonstrate the efficacy of our present organization. Let it be improved, but not altered.

Prieur was correct in suggesting that the proposed changes would transform the New Orleans police into an organization much like those in northern cities. But his advice to the council to hew hard to tradition proved futile. New Orleans would soon part ways with Charleston and tradition.[48]

This change came, however, in a strange way. While the mayor and council were disputing the proposed changes in the police, the state legislature was responding to the importuning of Anglo-American interests by preparing a bill to separate New Orleans into three municipalities. The legislature enacted the bill in March, 1836, creating a partitioned urban government without parallel in nineteenth-century America, in which authority for managing the police was decentralized so that each municipality would determine the organization, discipline, and selection of personnel for its own force. Although the three municipalities would have a common mayor and a General Council that would consist of the separate councils of the municipalities sitting together, all but the most nominal aspects of city administration would be controlled by each municipality. This bizarre system, growing out of ethnic and economic rivalry, was eventually abandoned and the city reunified in 1852. The partition of 1836 only briefly slowed the demilitarization of the police, however, for soon after the city underwent this administrative subdivision, each municipality individually implemented the new model of civil policing.[49]

The shift to a new system apparently resulted in internal organizational

48. *Mercantile Advertiser*, February 17, 1834; Proceedings of Council Meetings, April 10, 1819; Messages of the Mayors to the City Council, August 10, 1831, January 21, 1836.

49. *Acts of Louisiana*, 1836, pp. 28–37; Ordinances and Resolutions of the First Municipality Council, NOPL, February 24, 1837, July 2, 1840; *Digest of the Ordinances and Resolutions of the Second Municipality of New-Orleans, in Force May 1, 1840*, comp. John Calhoun (New Orleans, 1840), 239–42.

problems for the police of the three municipalities. The rate of personnel turnover increased. Delinquencies also seem to have increased after 1836, when patrolmen were removed from immediate, continual supervision and instead merely subjected to periodic checkups by roundsmen. City council records revealed few specific complaints of police delinquencies before demilitarization, but after 1836 police reports showed a considerable disciplinary problem.[50]

Although new problems accompanied the reform of 1836, the governors of the Crescent City seemed willing to abandon a generation-old institutional arrangement. New Orleans was thus set apart from Charleston, Savannah, Mobile, and—somewhat less so—Richmond. During the quarter-century before the Civil War, the New Orleans police would more closely resemble those of New York, Boston, and Philadelphia.[51] Why did the other southern police forces remain so distinctively military?

The primary explanation very likely lies in the differing ethnic compositions of these cities' populations and police forces. Precise evidence about the ethnic origins of these populations before the 1850 census may be unobtainable, but it is clear that in 1850 New Orleans had a much larger concentration of foreigners in its white population than the other southern cities. The foreign share of white population in 1850 was 54.3 percent in New Orleans, 31.4 percent in Mobile, 29.0 percent in Savannah, 23.2 percent in Charleston, and 13.8 percent in Richmond. These proportions would have been lower in earlier years, but it is likely that New Orleans would have had by far the highest concentration of immigrants. Hence the police forces in the other cities probably had considerably fewer foreigners, and native U.S. elites were less likely to view them with the alarm the large foreign contingent in New Orleans engendered. Also, in none of the other

50. Records suitable for computing turnover before 1836 are scant, but in 1814 the annual rate was somewhere between 27 and 39 percent (Payrolls of the City Guard, 1814, Historic New Orleans Collection and Howard-Tilton Memorial Library, Tulane University). Turnover rates after 1836 were much higher: in the Second Municipality 92 percent in 1840–41 and 40 percent in 1850 and in the Third Municipality 133 percent in 1840–41 and 78 percent in 1850 (author's calculations based on Reports of the Day and Night Police, Second and Third Municipalities, NOPL).

51. During the 1850s, New Orleans paralleled New York, Boston, and Philadelphia even in the sense that what was controversial in those northern cities was also controversial in the Crescent City, especially proposals to uniform the police and the adoption of revolvers as police sidearms (Richardson, *New York Police*, 64–66, 113, 120; Lane, *Policing the City*, 103–105; Monkkonen, *Police in Urban America*, 44–46).

cities did the percentage of slaves in the population decline as much as it did in New Orleans, so controlling slaves remained a high priority in those cities.[52]

The significance of the shift from a military to a civil style of policing may have had little to do with the quality of police performance in preserving order, thwarting crime, and catching criminals. Assessing the efficacy of a police force is difficult even when tangible activities such as arrests, civil liberties violations, and internal disciplinary problems can be measured, but the police records for the period before 1836 offer very little such evidence. The most that can be said with reasonable assurance is that the new police were more accessible and less dangerous to the public but more vulnerable and harder to supervise. But the military style of policing was important as an expression of southern urban culture and as evidence that in this respect the South was more militant than the rest of the country. For white urban residents the military style was a symbol and a kind of amulet. Policemen who looked like soldiers probably helped ameliorate the deep anxieties many whites harbored about the dangers of slave crime and revolt, especially in the early years when slaves constituted such a large percentage of the population in New Orleans. Martial policemen served as psychic soldiers, defending the bastion of a people besieged by fear, quite as much as they were quotidian enforcers of the law. But when their ranks were filled with untrusted aliens, native whites found formidably armed policemen unnerving rather than reassuring.[53]

52. *Seventh Census*. While the slave share of population fell in New Orleans from 33.4 percent in 1830 to 22.9 percent in 1840 (a 10.5 percent drop in relation to total city population), the decline in that decade was from 50.7 to 50.1 percent in Charleston (a 0.6 percent fall), from 39.5 to 37.3 in Richmond (a 2.2 percent decline), and from 36.8 to 30.5 percent in Mobile (a drop of 6.3 percent); the 1830 census reported no distinct data for Savannah, but the slave share there was 40.9 percent in 1820 and 41.8 percent in 1840, suggesting little or no change for 1830–40 (*Fifth Census; Sixth Census*).

53. For a discussion of southern militancy, see Franklin, *Militant South*; Rollin G. Osterweis, *Romanticism and Nationalism in the Old South* (New Haven, 1949); James C. Bonner, "The Historical Basis of Southern Military Tradition," *Georgia Review*, IX (1955), 74–85; Cunliffe, *Soldiers and Civilians*; Robert E. May, "Dixie's Martial Image: A Continuing Historiographical Enigma," *Historian*, XL (1978), 213–34.

# 2

# From One, Many
## Policing the Partitioned City, 1836–1852

WHEN Bernhard, duke of Saxe-Weimar Eisenach, visited New Orleans in the mid-1820s, he attended a ball in honor of George Washington's birthday. Somewhat surprised by the sparse crowd, Bernhard discovered that the "creoles appear rather to wish their country should be a French colony, than annexed to the Union. From their conversations, one would conclude that they do not regard the Americans as their countrymen."[1]

By the time the city was partitioned in 1836, its Franco-American and Anglo-American inhabitants had chafed under their uneasy relationship for more than three decades. The French had never been consulted about becoming Americans, and they were neither graceful nor diplomatic about living under the American flag. Spiting the law, they refused to adopt English for official business. Interpreters were required to translate proceedings in the city council, in the state legislature, and in courtrooms. Even as late as the early 1840s, some municipal records were still kept exclusively in French.[2]

In turn, the Anglo-Americans asserted their cultural identity, developing their own theater with English-language productions and building houses of a style that clashed with the Spanish-French colonial architecture of New Orleans. Moreover, they insisted on closing their businesses on the

1. Bernhard, *Travels Through North America*, II, 72.

2. Proceedings of Council Meetings, January 20, 1821, June 15, 1822; John Adams Paxton, *The New-Orleans Directory and Register* (New Orleans, 1823), (unpaginated); Captain Thomas Hamilton, *Men and Manners in America* (2 vols.; Edinburgh, 1833), II, 207–208; Henry Bradshaw Fearon, *Sketches of America* (2nd ed., 1818; rpr. New York, 1969), 275. French leaders wrote voter qualifications and legislative apportionment provisions into the state's first constitution in 1812 which made it harder for Anglo-Americans to qualify as voters and left them underrepresented in the legislature (Joseph G. Tregle, Jr., "Political Reinforcement of Ethnic Dominance in Louisiana, 1812–1845," in *The Americanization of the Gulf Coast, 1803–1850*, ed. Lucius F. Ellsworth [Pensacola, 1972], 78–87).

Sabbath to attend their Protestant churches, while the Catholic French went about their business and recreation as usual. The Anglo-Americans wanted the city divided into separate municipalities because they believed the city government had been favoring French interests.[3]

As a result of the successful Anglo-American lobbying in the legislature to partition the city, New Orleans had three police forces between 1836 and 1852, one for each of its independent municipalities. The municipalities did not cooperate effectively, and sometimes they worked against one another. Efficiency was sacrificed for the sake of ethnic separatism. The partition would prove to be most favorable—or least unfavorable—to the Americans of the Second Municipality, while the First and Third municipalities fared worse.

The three police forces shared a common tradition and faced similar problems. All three municipalities shifted from military to civil styles of policing within four years. At the same time they adopted beat patrolling on an around-the-clock basis, a tactical change that complicated the managerial task of supervising the patrolmen. The policeman on the beat gained a measure of discretion but was rendered more vulnerable and less powerful.

In these years the Irish share of police jobs and influence in the department rose considerably, in part because so many Irishmen came to New Orleans with so little capital and so few skills that police work seemed desirable, and in part because the Irish worked together effectively in politics and achieved a great deal of leverage over the distribution of patronage. The increasing volume of immigration and the growing diversity of the city's population helped intensify ethnic conflict and led to greater violence in the 1850s.

---

3. Theater: Hamilton, *Men and Manners in America*, 208–209; Sealsfield, *The Americans as They Are*, 184. Architecture: Timothy Flint, *Recollections of the Last Ten Years, Passed in Occasional Residences and Journeyings in the Valley of the Mississippi, from Pittsburgh and the Missouri to the Gulf of Mexico, and from Florida to the Spanish Frontier; in a Series of Letters to The Rev. James Flint, of Salem, Massachusetts* (Boston, 1826), 302–303. Sabbath: Benjamin Henry Latrobe, *The Journal of Latrobe, Being the Notes and Sketches of an Architect, Naturalist and Traveler in the United States from 1796 to 1820* (New York, 1905), 175, 220; Sealsfield, *The Americans as They Are*, 184; Hall, *Travels in North America*, III, 330; Rev. William Bingley, *Travels in North America, from Modern Writers* (London, 1821), 166–67; Bernhard, *Travels Through North America*, II, 57. Some members of the city council sought partition as early as 1826 (Proceedings of Council Meetings, December 2, 1826).

✳

The decision to adopt a decentralized and less efficient form of city government proved unwise, particularly at this time. New Orleans had experienced rapid growth ever since it became part of the United States and had enjoyed almost continuous prosperity since the War of 1812. Depressions had had comparatively mild effects. Trade with the western states boomed after steamboats arrived in force in the 1820s. The vitality and value of this commercial position was seriously challenged, however, by the development of cheap east-west transportation after completion of the Erie Canal in 1825. As more canals and then railroads bridged the Appalachians, the trade New Orleans had enjoyed with its hinterland was increasingly opened to northeastern rivals. The merchants of the city signaled their awareness of this threat by supporting the state legislature in adopting a resolution in 1820 that called for collective action by the western states and territories to build hospitals to care for the many boatmen who fell ill while returning home from New Orleans. Not just an expression of humanitarian concern, the resolution acknowledged that the great incidence of illness among the boatmen was inimical to commerce, and stated that "every effort will be made [by the eastern states] to draw the commerce from its old channels, through the valley of the Mississippi, and give it a direction towards the east, by opening different avenues of communication between the Mississippi and Ohio, and the Atlantic States."[4]

The eastern challenge did not significantly damage New Orleans' western trade until the late 1820s and early 1830s. But as canals and railroads proliferated, the city was unable to restore its river trade with the West. Nor were the city's merchants able to develop new trade ties or new economic activities such as manufacturing. Although New Orleans remained the principal outlet for the cotton exports of the Southwest, its share of the agricultural staples of the upper valley shrank. The city's prospects were further dimmed by the disunity that led to its partition.[5]

4. *Acts of Louisiana*, 1820, pp. 120–26.
5. New Orleans had very little manufacturing. In 1840, investments ran five to one, trade over manufacturing (Merl E. Reed, *New Orleans and the Railroads: The Struggle for Commercial Empire* [Baton Rouge, 1966], 7–9). New Orleans controlled no shipping lines, for most commercial trading firms in the city had ties to similar firms on the Atlantic seaboard, especially New York. Furthermore, a bar in the Mississippi River at New Orleans became such an obstacle to navigation by the larger, faster ships that a new type of craft, the "New Orleans packet," had to be constructed to allow oceangoing vessels to reach the city (Harold Sinclair, *The Port of New Orleans* [Garden City, N.Y., 1942], 173–76).

The partition of the city did not affect all New Orleans interest groups equally. The American faction gained some benefit from the division. Americans no longer suffered from discriminatory use of public funds in behalf of French interests, and they proved themselves better managers than the French. The American Second Municipality more than doubled in population during the 1840s, while the First Municipality lost some 20 percent and the Third Municipality almost 25 percent of their respective populations.[6]

Yet even though the Second Municipality fared better than the other two, the Americans eventually favored a reunion of the city. Throughout the period of partition the three governments were constantly strapped for cash. When revenues from taxes on real estate and slaves and from trade exactions such as wharfage dues and market stall licenses did not meet expenses, the municipalities turned increasingly to borrowing. Management of the bonded debt was one of the most important tasks of the three councils, yet none succeeded in servicing the debt and paying off current administrative expenses, let alone retiring the debt. The Third Municipality was not only unable to meet its current obligations, but as late as 1849 it was still in arrears on its quota of the old city debt from the days of unitary government. The financing of city government in New Orleans became so problematic that the state legislature interceded in 1850 with an act designed to enable the municipalities to liquidate their debts. The scheme did not work, however, and ultimately success was achieved by consolidating the city under one government. Resistance to proposals for reunion surfaced through the late 1840s, especially from the Second Municipality, but after the failure of the state legislation of 1850 all three municipalities supported the act of 1852 which restored unitary government.[7]

The losing battle against insolvency was hard on the police forces of the municipalities. The manpower cost of the police constituted a major portion of the budget so the councils resorted to salary reductions and lengthy salary freezes to save money. The reform ordinance of 1836, which

6. Henry Benjamin Whipple, *Bishop Whipple's Southern Diary, 1843–1844*, ed. Lester B. Shippee (Minneapolis, 1937), 104–105; *Sixth Census; Seventh Census.*

7. Ordinances and Resolutions of the First Municipality Council, June 6, 1842, August 5, 1850, December 22, 1851, February 9, 1852; Ordinances and Resolutions of the Second Municipality Council, November 12, 1850; Messages of the Mayors to the Third Municipality Council, May 24, 1842, April 12, 1847, April 9, August 13, 1849, April 14, 1851.

was not implemented because of the partition, had provided for a raise to fifty dollars per month for ordinary patrolmen. Under tripartite government no rank-and-file policeman ever received so much. Police salaries rose and fell according to the municipalities' ability to pay, hovering between thirty and forty dollars per month most of the time in the First and Third municipalities and eventually reaching fifty dollars per month in the Second Municipality for day officers only. Even worse than reductions and freezes for the ordinary policemen was the occasional inability of the councils to meet the payroll on time, which had not occurred since the War of 1812. It became particularly serious in the Third Municipality, where the policemen petitioned the mayor in 1849 because they had not been paid for six months. The council of the Third Municipality resolved to pay the police ahead of other city employees but in the first two months thereafter managed only to issue due bills in lieu of hard money and reduced the men's salary and fired several of them.[8]

The number of men on the forces fluctuated considerably, and the ratio of police to population at its best reached only approximately the level that had been authorized in 1821, 1830, 1833, and 1836. The First Municipality increased the size of its force in February, 1837, almost doubling the number of men mandated in its inaugural police ordinance of the previous year. In the aftermath of the Panic of 1837, the council gradually reduced the size of the force over the next three years. After bottoming out in 1840 and increasing only slightly in succeeding years, in 1850 the police-to-population ratio in the First Municipality was still below that of 1837. The Third Municipality came closer to maintaining its force at a constant proportionate size but temporarily reduced the number of policemen at times when the public purse was empty or nearly so. Only in the Second Municipality did the absolute number of policemen increase, and it merely kept the police in proportion to the burgeoning population.[9]

8. Ordinances and Resolutions of the First Municipality Council, June 12, 1837, July 16, 1838, December 8, 1845; *Digest of the Ordinances and Resolutions of the Second Municipality; and of the General Council of the City of New-Orleans, Applicable Thereto*, comp. F. R. Southmayd (New Orleans, 1848), 320–22; Ordinances and Resolutions of the Third Municipality Council, February 5, March 12, 1849.

9. In the First Municipality, the total number of policemen was first established at 44 (May 13, 1836), quickly raised to 59 (June 24, 1836), and peaked at 126 (February 24, 1837). It fell to 58 (July 27, 1840) and then 55 (May 8, 1843); by May 11, 1850, it had climbed to 105, but this included the day force. The Third Municipality kept its police at about 36 men for most of the 1840s, though it temporarily rose to 56 (May 13, 1850) and fell back to 34

Although the legislative act of division of 1836 had given the General Council nominal authority to regulate the police, in practice this authority was exercised almost exclusively by the individual councils with an occasional veto by the mayor. The General Council consisted merely of an annual meeting of the three councils in common session, and it performed few significant functions. Its efforts to coordinate police operations proved so minimal as to be little more than symbolic. In an ordinance of 1838 the General Council directed the captains of the three police forces to report in detail to the mayor every day and to assign one officer each to the mayor's office between 9:00 A.M. and 3:00 P.M. It took this step only after the mayor's commands to the captains proved fruitless. Mayor Prieur had tried in 1837 to order them to report to him, but the captains of the forces in the Second and Third municipalities had not complied. When the council of the Third Municipality ordered its captain to report to the mayor, Prieur asserted that the order was superfluous because his authority was grounded in the statute that had partitioned the city, but he seemed to accept the council's initiative with some relief. He was still unable to get an officer from each force assigned to his office and was obliged to employ the First Municipality police alone for this duty. The portion of the General Council ordinance requiring the daily assignments was repealed in 1848.[10]

The inadequacy of the system for intermunicipal cooperation stemmed from the delegation of authority for controlling disbursements and appointing policemen to the separate councils. On a few occasions the crankiness of the system drew fire from municipal officials who advocated greater unity in managing the police. Mayor Prieur observed that the divided basis of police organization had inherent flaws because "it often happens that robbers and other instigators of public disorders, retreat in a different section of the City, after being guilty in another; from that follows embarrassment for a recorder [the police court justice of the individual munici-

---

(May 12, 1851). The Second Municipality started with 65 men (July 1, 1836, including the day police) and fell back only once, to 47 (March 28, 1843).

10. *Digest of the Ordinances and Resolutions of the Second Municipality*, comp. Southmayd, 1, 47; *A Digest of the Ordinances and Resolutions of the General Council of the City of New-Orleans*, comp. T. Thiard and J. Reynes (New Orleans, 1845), 22–24; Messages of the Mayors to the Third Municipality Council, March 30, 1837; Messages of the Mayors to the First Municipality Council, March 30, 1837. For examples of the mayors' use of the veto, see Messages of the Mayors to the First Municipality Council, December 20, 1843; Messages of the Mayors to the Third Municipality Council, August 26, 1843.

pality] to have them watched outside his jurisdiction. The law by reserving the superintendence of the police to the Mayor, remedies this inconvenience to a certain extent, since it can send of his own accord, agents to all points of the City." Prieur was actually asking only for control of the secret police funds (basically executive discretionary funds) of the three municipalities, but the problems of partition afflicted the entire system of policing.[11]

Efforts to coordinate the policing system were few and fruitless. The problem also affected other portions of the criminal justice system. Both the mayor and the council of the Third Municipality expressed a desire to establish a house of refuge for juvenile offenders. Each municipality could not afford to have its own house of refuge, yet they were unwilling to cooperate in building a facility for common use.[12]

Beneath this uncooperative approach to common problems lay a jealousy rooted in ethnic and economic competition that was vividly demonstrated in the conflicting attitudes and policies toward gambling in the three municipalities. New Orleans had a well-earned reputation as a gambler's hell and paradise, where fortunes could be made or lost virtually around the clock in any of a multitude of gambling houses. The legislature had tried to ban gambling throughout the state in 1811 but soon conceded that New Orleans would have to be treated as an exception. Gambling by license was permitted until 1835, when the legislature once again banned gambling everywhere in Louisiana.[13]

The law could not be made to work in New Orleans. The councils of the First and Third municipalities repeatedly authorized and licensed new games of chance in an effort to circumvent the law. When the councils enacted ordinances to permit lotto, keno, ronda, or other games of chance, the mayors were obliged to veto the illegal ordinances. This process was repeated so often that it became formulaic. Whenever the pro-gambling forces licensed some form of gambling, the mayor would refer the matter to the state attorney general, who would in turn report unfavorably on the

11. Messages of the Mayors to the First Municipality Council, February 27, 1837, May 7, 1838; Ordinances and Resolutions of the Third Municipality Council, August 3, 1837.

12. Messages of the Mayors to the First Municipality Council, December 1, 1850; Messages of the Mayors to the Third Municipality Council, December 16, 1850; Messages of the Mayors to Third Municipality Council, December 16, 1850; Ordinances and Resolutions of the Third Municipality Council, January 10, 1851.

13. *Acts of Louisiana*, 1835, pp. 134–36.

ordinance. The mayor would then veto the ordinance, and the councils would renew their effort a few months later with yet another game or sometimes with a game that had already been ruled illegal. The First and Third municipalities issued licenses for gambling and permitted establishments to operate in violation of the law until the mayor and General Council (led by representatives of the Second Municipality) moved to suppress the practice in 1846–1847.[14]

As a result of this crackdown the First Municipality was brought to heel for a while, but the Third Municipality refused to surrender. Its intransigence led to a bizarre conflict between the police forces of the First and Third municipalities. On the night of March 13, 1847, a detachment of policemen of the First Municipality under the command of Captain John Youenes raided several gambling houses, one of them run by free persons of color in the First Municipality. At the request of the district attorney, Youenes also raided an establishment in the Third Municipality. In the course of the raids, the police arrested several people and confiscated a quantity of gambling paraphernalia and cash.[15]

The leaders of the Third Municipality reacted with outrage. The Third Municipality Council ordered its police to arrest any policeman from another jurisdiction who set foot inside the municipality with the intention of violating any of its ordinances. The council members declared that they regarded the people of their municipality as "being constituted by law independent in the exercise of their corporate rights from the other Municipalities, as much so as the states in their federal compact." By unanimous resolution the council promised to defend its citizens who had been arrested in the raid from "the aggression of arbitrary measures of the first Municipal police department." The mayor vetoed this resolution (though he was overridden by the council), arguing that the district attorney had the authority to employ the police of any municipality to suppress open violations of state law anywhere in the city. The state attorney general

14. Ordinances and Resolutions of the First Municipality Council, June 27, 1842, April 29, 1844, February 24, June 2, 1845, November 2, 1846, January 18, May 10, 1847; Messages of the Mayors to the First Municipality Council, November 9, 1846, May 4, 1847; Messages of the Mayors to the Third Municipality Council, October 28, 1843, January 25, October 22, 24, 1847.

15. *Bee*, March 15, 1847; *Daily Delta*, March 16, 1847; *Commercial Bulletin*, March 15, 1847.

threatened to prosecute the recorder and council of the Third Municipality, but apparently nothing came of the promise of state intervention.[16]

Overt warfare between the two municipalities over enforcement of the antigambling statute was averted because the First Municipality backed away from further confrontation. The council of the First Municipality complained that keno, lotto, bagatelle, faro, and roulette were sanctioned in the Third Municipality but later in the year ordered its own police force to forbear from making any more arrests for these offenses without orders from the "proper authorities." The location of proper authority was not clear, but the First Municipality maintained a hands-off policy while the gamblers of the Third Municipality conducted business as usual for the next several years.[17]

This intermunicipal conflict over gambling revealed the weakness of partitioned government. The Third Municipality was able to flout the law of the state and the ordinances of the General Council because there was no effective police apparatus to enforce the decisions of these greater entities of government. Most of the policemen in New Orleans were paid by the individual municipality and took their orders from its council. Even the sheriff and the court constables were limited in their authority and tied to local forces, and had the state or the General Council resorted to them as an enforcement arm, their use in putting an end to public gambling would have been as controversial as the use of the First Municipality police. The real power lay with the municipalities, for they controlled the purse and commanded the police.[18]

The reform ordinance of 1836 adopted in the last days of unitary government served as the model for the police of the municipalities. The three councils enacted the principles of that aborted reform act soon after they were separated from one another, though around-the-clock patrolling was not adopted in all three municipalities at the same time.

16. Ordinances and Resolutions of the Third Municipality Council, March 15, 1847; *Bee*, March 18, 1847; *Commercial Bulletin*, March 18, 1847.

17. Ordinances and Resolutions of the First Municipality Council, December 13, 1847. Apparently the Third Municipality agreed to suppress gambling in 1851 (Ordinances and Resolutions of the Third Municipality Council, October 6, November 17, 1851).

18. The sheriff of Orleans Parish did make at least one arrest of gamblers in the Third Municipality, but there is no indication of the continued involvement of his office in gambling enforcement thereafter (*Daily Delta*, March 19, 1847).

The Americans of the Second Municipality were the first to establish regular daytime police patrols. The responsibility for day policing had previously been shared by the commissaries, the constables of the courts, and the reserve force of the city guard kept on call at the guardhouse, but none of these made routine day patrols. The Second Municipality instituted an organization of day policemen under a high constable in June, 1836, and regularized their function as patrolmen and process servers. Soon thereafter the day and night police were coordinated under a common commander. After October, 1837, the captain of the night watch and the high constable of the Second Municipality were one and the same. The First Municipality delayed in implementing the day police envisioned in the reform of 1836, but when its council added a regular day police temporarily in 1839 and permanently in 1840, the new force was immediately placed under the authority of the captain of the night watch. By 1840 the Third Municipality also had a day police under the command of the same officer who headed the night watch.[19]

The numerical strength of the day police never reached the level called for in the 1836 reform ordinance, which had mandated that the day force should have half the number of men as the night watch. The ratio was usually nearer one to four or one to five in the First and Second municipalities. The First Municipality improved the ratio toward the end of the period to about one to three, which was also the relative strength maintained by the Third Municipality during most of its tenure. In the late 1840s the First and Third municipalities improved the ratio of day-to-night police somewhat.[20]

Though few in number, the day policemen usually enjoyed higher pay than their night counterparts. The idea of a salary differential was one of the selling points of the day force when Mayor William Freret proposed one for the First Municipality in 1840: "The prospect of promotion also from the night watch to the day police, and of a consequent increase of pay, would be an incentive to the members of the former, faithfully to discharge their duties with zeal, energy and discretion; and for this purpose,

19. Ordinances and Resolutions of the First Municipality Council, April 22, 1839, July 27, 1840; *Digest of the Ordinances and Resolutions of the Second Municipality of New-Orleans, in Force May 1, 1840*, 205–207, 239–42; Reports of the Day and Night Police of the Third Municipality, July 14–15, 1840.

20. Ordinances and Resolutions of the First Municipality Council, May 11, 1850; Ordinances and Resolutions of the Third Municipality Council, February 26, 1849.

the rule might be adopted of supplying vacancies in the day police by the promotion of the most deserving among the night watch." The day police ordinarily received between five and ten dollars more per month than the night watch, a sum large enough to motivate many night watchmen to seek promotion to day duty.[21]

The municipalities did not all immediately adopt day policing, but they did immediately demilitarize their police forces. The only weapon the men were permitted to carry was the spontoon. As they lost their swords, so also did their uniforms give way to simple leather caps, each painted with a unique roll number to identify the wearer. With the exception of the Second Municipality, the minimum terms of enlistment were abolished. The six-month term initially required of the Second Municipality police was evidently not enforced for long, for by 1838 the municipality was rewarding men who had served six months with a pay increase rather than penalizing men who served less than that term with the stipulated fine of fifty dollars.[22]

The reform of 1836 had placed the power of appointment and discharge in the hands of an elected Committee of Vigilance, but the municipalities distributed these powers among the Committee of Vigilance, the captain of the guard, the recorder, and the council (or a committee thereof). The distribution varied somewhat, but in no case did the mayor retain his old prerogatives. Control of the police was thus shared among a greater number of elected officials, and because of the ethnic lines of demarcation among the municipalities, those officials were often from the same ethnic groups as many of their constituents. The result was that the police were nominally more subject to the will of the people than they had been before 1836.[23]

The old system of squad sweeps was replaced by the assignment of individual patrolmen to territorial beats. This dispersion proved to be one of the most fundamental revisions of police tactics of the entire nineteenth century. Its purpose was to make the police more accessible to the citizenry who might need them and to increase the chance that they might prevent

21. Messages of the Mayors to the First Municipality Council, May 18, 1840.

22. *Digest of the Ordinances and Resolutions of the Second Municipality of New-Orleans, in Force May 1, 1840*, 243, 247.

23. The distribution of control over the police underwent almost continual revision; see, for example, Ordinances and Resolutions of the First Municipality Council, May 22, 1843, April 25, 1844.

crime. The new method had some advantages but also some liabilities.[24]

One of the thorniest of the new problems was how to supervise the men on their beats. Under the old system an officer or sergeant usually led the men in their sweep, but the new tactic depended heavily on the lone policeman's discretion. Officers, sergeants, or corporals supervised the patrolmen by walking around from beat to beat (hence the term *roundsmen* for those supervising in this fashion), and the patrolmen were supposed to supervise each other through mutual surveillance. The men were now on their own much of the time, and the result seems to have been an increase in delinquency in the first few years after 1836.

The fundamental problem with this method of supervision was that the roundsmen could not be everywhere at once. The addition of day police patrols also made supervision by the captain more difficult, for he could hardly walk the streets all day and all night. Individual beat patrolling necessitated more detailed rules of conduct for patrolmen: they were supposed to keep moving, tap their spontoons at the corners and listen for the answers of the adjacent men, and refrain from engaging in conversation except in the line of duty. The old rules against drinking or sleeping while on watch remained in force, but under the new system the most frequent delinquencies were sleeping or resting on the beat, talking unnecessarily with other policemen, and drinking alcohol on the job. Mutual supervision by the patrolmen often became collusion, as evidenced in this 1841 report of the Third Municipality's night watch: "Sergt Bonzon reported no 16 Sass and no 22 Leaf for neglect of duty standing still on their beats Spain street at 3oClock he supposed that they watched for each other by Turns in order to rest."[25]

Supervisory officers were not exempt from the temptations to neglect their duty or abuse their authority, and their improper example and ineffective leadership encouraged deviant behavior by the men under their command. Roundsmen were included among the policemen who were discharged for cause, though less frequently than patrolmen. The authority of their rank and their experience and connections rendered them less assailable than patrolmen, particularly since a patrolman would have to be

24. Ordinances and Resolutions of the First Municipality Council, February 24, 1837; *Digest of the Ordinances and Resolutions of the Second Municipality of New-Orleans in Force May 1, 1840*, 239–42.

25. Reports of the Day and Night Police of the Third Municipality (Night Watch), July 8–9, 1841.

courageous or audacious to challenge a superior officer with an accusation of misconduct—the challenge could easily boomerang and cost the man his job.

One of the most striking examples of failure in police leadership occurred in the Second Municipality in August, 1850, when Lieutenant Charles Petrie was accused of raping a young woman in the guardhouse while she was in custody on a warrant for theft. The acting recorder of the municipality heard the case and the newspapers followed it closely, reporting much of the testimony. The fifteen-year-old complainant testified that she had been incarcerated in the lieutenant's sleeping room instead of a cell, and there he had held her against her will and raped her during the night. She had not cried out, she testified, because she feared even more serious injury, and Petrie's size and strength had made it impossible to resist him successfully. The defense made an issue of the girl's reputation, calling witnesses to establish that she was not chaste and proper and alleging that for this reason her stepfather had banished her from her home. The stepfather, however, testified that he had turned her out only because she had been disobedient. When the defense attorney asked her if she had ever cohabited with a man before, her counsel strenuously objected to the question; when the judge required her to answer, she replied, "Whether I did or not has nothing to do with the case." Petrie's commanding officer, Captain Henry Forno, offered testimony potentially damaging to the lieutenant when he reported that the girl's name had not been entered in the arrest book for the night in question but had turned up corrupted into a masculine name on the following day's record.[26]

The lieutenant's conduct—or misconduct—went unpenalized by the court. The recorder dismissed the case for lack of evidence, amid the triumphant celebration of Petrie's partisans. The case had become a *cause célèbre*, for Petrie's adherents had charged that the accusation of rape stemmed from personal malice and political conspiracy within police ranks. One policeman testified that he and several fellow officers had encouraged the young woman to make the affidavit against Petrie because they thought

26. The newspaper reports of this case offered a variety of versions of the young woman's name: Barbara Dintinger, Barbary Tintinger, and Corvette Dendinger. Captain Forno testified that the name entered in the arrest book was Robert Dentinger. The best newspaper account is that in the *Daily True Delta*, August 21–25, 1850. The young woman's mother did not know if her daughter had reached puberty and gave her age as seventeen or eighteen, then revised her estimate to fourteen.

he had assaulted her. The trial was full of color and emotion. Charges and countercharges flew back and forth among the police who testified, the lawyers railed against one another with personal invective and against the recorder for partiality and incompetence, and two newspapermen in the audience engaged in a brawl during the proceedings. The Petrie case also revealed a double standard when the police acknowledged that "respectable gentlemen" were never locked in cells but were permitted the comfort of the lieutenant's quarters. A double standard also appeared in the magistrate's admission of questions pertaining to the young woman's sexual experience despite her objections and those of the prosecutor.[27]

The new system of policing had other problems besides leadership. Attracting good men to police service was not easy. Not only was the salary less than munificent, but the job was short on prestige and long on tedium, loneliness, political intrigue, and physical danger. The work discipline could be severe because policemen were required to work every day of the year, twelve hours per shift, usually with either one hour of relief or no relief. The night policemen endured a work schedule at odds with the daytime activities of their families and spent many hours on duty guarding several blocks of quiet, sometimes empty buildings. Even the mundane problem of sleeping during the day in the semitropical climate of New Orleans challenged the night policemen's health. Handling a solitary, incapacitated drunk was about the most demanding task the beat patrolman could have confidence in performing without help so the availability and willingness of patrolmen on adjacent beats to come to his aid was vital. Belligerent drunks and career criminals made the lone patrolman a highly vulnerable target, subject to a painful drubbing or worse.

The temptation to default from duty was powerful. At least four policemen were killed in the discharge of their duty during this sixteen-year period, and many others were wounded. A wounded policeman could not rely on being paid for time lost to injuries, nor could he be sure there would be any aid to his dependents if he were killed in the course of his work. Because sick pay could not be counted on, men who were ill often reported for duty anyway, and when these men drank or rested on the job they were likely to turn up as delinquents in a roundsman's report.

27. Lieutenant Petrie encountered other legal troubles, as well; a free black man sued him for false imprisonment several years after the Dintinger case (Ordinances and Resolutions of the Second Municipality Council, January 22, 1851).

Promotion to the day police became an important opportunity for men who endured the night watch long enough to be considered for advancement. There were few opportunities, though, for the day force was small and had considerably less turnover of personnel than the night police. Until the late 1840s it was common practice to employ night watchmen as supernumeraries for the day police, and consequently some night officers were expected to perform twenty-four or even thirty-six consecutive hours of duty to have a chance to serve temporarily on the day force. The impossibility of meeting such demands without hurting the men or their work eventually led to a ban on the practice.[28]

The advantages of day work resulted in lower absenteeism on the day shift than the night (see Table 2). A comparison of the Second and Third municipalities in 1845 and 1849–1852 shows that the rate of absenteeism was substantially less for the day police than the night watchmen. Day work had significant advantages, among them that the day police usually worked in pairs rather than alone. In a system that provided few symbols of a common bond among policemen, no training or occupational indoctrination, and little chance for sociability or even work-oriented interaction, the companionship and protection of working with a partner proved to be an important benefit of the day police.[29]

Another contrast between the day and night forces was the greater rate of personnel turnover among the night men (see Table 3), which owed much to the fact that the day police were usually veterans of night duty and thus were more experienced and competent. The more select personnel and the greater desirability of day police work kept their turnover rate relatively low.[30]

28. Ordinances and Resolutions of the First Municipality Council, August 5, 1850; Ordinances and Resolutions of the Third Municipality Council, June 10, 1850.

29. Ordinances and Resolutions of the First Municipality Council, July 27, 1840; Reports of the Day and Night Police of the Second Municipality, May 1840. The missing data for absenteeism are the result of omissions in the day and night police reports. Absenteeism was not reported during the years for which Table 2 lists no entries. The exact dates for the sample data are as follows: First Municipality, August 2–3, 1840, through November 2, 1840; Second Municipality, May 1, 1840, through April 30, 1841, June 1, 1844, through March 31, 1845, and September 1, 1851, through February 29, 1852; Third Municipality, July 14–15, 1840, through July 13–14, 1841, April 1–2, 1845, through March 31–April 1, 1846, and June 1–2, 1849, through May 31–June 1, 1850. Missing records made it impossible to obtain samples for all three municipalities over precisely the same periods. The very high rates for the Third Municipality in 1849–50 reflect the effects of a cholera epidemic.

30. The data for turnover were calculated from the same sample described in note 29.

## TABLE 2
### Police Absenteeism as a Percentage of Man-Days Worked in Selected Years

|         | Day Police |          |          | Night Police |          |          |
|---------|------------|----------|----------|--------------|----------|----------|
|         | 1st Mun.   | 2nd Mun. | 3rd Mun. | 1st Mun.     | 2nd Mun. | 3rd Mun. |
| 1840–41 | —          | —        | —        | 10.7         | 11.5     | 3.0      |
| 1845    | —          | 1.1      | 4.6      | —            | 14.8     | 16.9     |
| 1849–52 | —          | 4.2      | 19.7     | —            | 14.4     | 30.6     |

*Sources:* Reports of the Day and Night Police, First, Second, and Third Municipalities, NOPL.

## TABLE 3
### Annual Police Turnover as a Percentage of Authorized Strength of Force in Selected Years

|         | Day Police |          |          | Night Police |          |          |
|---------|------------|----------|----------|--------------|----------|----------|
|         | 1st Mun.   | 2nd Mun. | 3rd Mun. | 1st Mun.     | 2nd Mun. | 3rd Mun. |
| 1840–41 | —          | 35.0     | 30.0     | 123.6        | 91.7     | 133.4    |
| 1845    | —          | 0.0      | 28.6     | —            | 64.8     | 66.7     |
| 1849–52 | —          | 4.5      | 9.2      | —            | 40.0     | 77.7     |

*Sources:* Reports of the Day and Night Police, First, Second, and Third Municipalities.

Turnover rates were highest in the early 1840s and dropped about 50 percent during the next decade. A similar trend is visible in the rates of delinquency (see Table 4). The day forces were fairly stable soon after they were formed, but the night forces began with high rates of delinquency followed by dramatic decline. By the end of the decade, delinquency rates for the night police in the Second and Third municipalities stood at only about one-third of the levels in the early 1840s. The percentages of men discharged for cause also appear to have fallen during this decade (though the evidence for this trend is less reliable because in many cases the police reports cited no reason for a man's leaving the force).[31]

---

The figures in Table 3 are averages of accession and separation rates, adjusted so as to factor out changes in the authorized strength of the forces. Turnover in the 1890s averaged about 10 percent annually.

31. Because of differences among the municipalities in the reporting of delinquencies,

## TABLE 4

### Annual Number of Delinquencies per Policeman

|  | Day Police | | | Night Police | | |
| --- | --- | --- | --- | --- | --- | --- |
|  | 1st Mun. | 2nd Mun. | 3rd Mun. | 1st Mun. | 2nd Mun. | 3rd Mun. |
| 1840–41 | 0.6 | 1.0 | 0.9 | 5.1 | 15.7 | 9.5 |
| 1845 | — | 2.3 | 0.7 | — | 10.5 | 4.5 |
| 1849–52 | — | — | 0.6 | — | 5.0 | 3.3 |

*Sources:* Reports of the Day and Night Police, First, Second, and Third Municipalities.

Although the declining rates of turnover and delinquency may have resulted from several causes, the most evident seem to have been an improvement in the quality of recruits and the retention of good men: the police were older, more often married, and longer residents of New Orleans.[32] The municipalities apparently never kept detailed personnel records, and no census records before 1850 would provide such information, but it is possible to construct a tentative social profile of policemen who were treated for injuries and illnesses at Charity Hospital. Hospitalized policemen would not have constituted a perfect cross section of the police because men without families in New Orleans or too poor to afford home care by a physician might have been overrepresented. Most policemen had about the same income, however, and any policeman who was wounded or injured on the job was almost certain to be admitted at Charity Hospital. During this period the median age of hospitalized policemen rose by five years and their median length of residence in the city increased from less than one year to six years (see Tables 5 and 6). Fewer than one-tenth were married in the late 1830s, but by the end of the period married policemen constituted more than one-third of the total (the percentage of married men was almost certainly greater for the force as a whole than for the hospitalized men; see Table 7). The increased maturity and greater life

intermunicipality comparisons are less reliable than observations of change over time within each municipality. Discharges are also calculated from the sample described in note 29.

32. If an insufficient number of roundsmen had accounted for low rates of reported delinquency, then the lowest delinquency rates should have appeared where the ratio of supervisors to patrolmen was least. In fact, the opposite was true. The Second Municipality always had the lowest proportion of supervisory officers, never better than one to six and usually worse, yet reported delinquency was greater there than in the First and Third municipalities, where the ratio varied between one to three and one to six.

## TABLE 5
### Married Policemen Admitted to Charity Hospital

|  | Number Admitted | Number (%) Married |
|---|---|---|
| 1836–39 | 12 | 1 (8.3) |
| 1840–43 | 46 | 11 (23.9) |
| 1844–47 | 29 | 6 (20.7) |
| 1848–52 | 36 | 13 (36.1) |

*Sources:* Charity Hospital Admission Books.

## TABLE 6
### Age of Policemen Admitted to Charity Hospital

|  | Number Admitted | Median Age | Mean Age |
|---|---|---|---|
| 1836–39 | 69 | 30.4 | 32.2 |
| 1840–43 | 47 | 31.9 | 32.5 |
| 1844–47 | 30 | 35.4 | 35.8 |
| 1848–52 | 36 | 35.0 | 35.0 |

*Sources:* Charity Hospital Admission Books.

## TABLE 7
### Length of Residence in New Orleans of Policemen Admitted to Charity Hospital

|  | Number Admitted | Median Length of of Residence | Percentage Less than One Year | Percentage One to Five Years | Percentage Five Years or More |
|---|---|---|---|---|---|
| 1836–39 | 68 | 11 months | 66.2 | 26.5 | 7.4 |
| 1840–43 | 42 | 3 years | 26.2 | 52.4 | 21.4 |
| 1844–47 | 29 | 3 years | 24.1 | 37.9 | 37.9 |
| 1848–52 | 33 | 6 years | 15.2 | 33.3 | 51.5 |

*Sources:* Charity Hospital Admission Books.

experiences of the policemen at the end of the period seem to have made them more responsible and disciplined than those who served at the beginning of the period.

✳

In one of the most famous travel accounts of the Old South, Frederick Law Olmsted recounted his experience asking a New Orleans policeman for directions back to his hotel. With apparent surprise, Olmsted wrote that "a policeman, with the richest Irish brogue, directed me back to the St. Charles." Olmsted's narration of this brief encounter signals one of the most important changes in the police of the Crescent City between 1830 and 1850: a dramatic shift in their ethnic composition. In 1830 very few Irishmen or native Louisianans served on the city guard. By 1850 these had become the largest nativity groups on the police forces of the three municipalities. Most of the Louisianans were men of French descent, but the Irish were new Americans and even newer Orleanians.[33]

Apparently the first Irish policeman in New Orleans was Patrick Donoho, who joined the force about 1830. By 1850, Irishmen constituted the largest nativity group in the police department. At midcentury, 20 percent of the white adult male population of the Crescent City were Irish-born and 32 percent of the police force were natives of Ireland, according to the population schedules of the 1850 census (see Table 8). The Irish were also overrepresented on each of the individual municipalities' police forces (see Table 9). At a time when Irishmen were excluded from police work in some American cities such as Boston and Philadelphia, the Irish in New Orleans expanded a tiny beachhead established by one immigrant in 1830 into an ethnic stronghold two decades later.[34]

The Irish ascendance in policing of the 1830s and 1840s derived in part from the massive influx of immigrants from the Emerald Isle during those decades, although many of the Irishmen who became police officers in this period had come to the United States before the great famine. New Orleans was a major port of immigration in these years, usually ranking second or third behind New York, drawing about 10 percent of America's alien arrivals. Some 58,000 immigrants landed at New Orleans between 1831 and 1840, 188,000 from 1841 to 1850, and 254,000 during the decade 1851–1860. New Orleans was very much a city of immigrants; its white adult male population was 74 percent foreign-born in 1850 and 72 percent

---

33. Olmsted, *Journey in the Seaboard Slave States*, II, 232.

34. Lane, *Policing the City*, 75–78; Richardson, *Urban Police*, 26; Charity Hospital Admission Books, 1830; John Adams Paxton, *The New-Orleans Directory and Register* (New Orleans, 1830).

TABLE 8

NATIVITIES OF THE AGGREGATE POLICE FORCES
OF THE THREE MUNICIPALITIES IN 1850

| | Police | | White Adult Males (sample) | |
|---|---|---|---|---|
| | % | No. | % | No. |
| Native-born | 37.7 | 101 | 26.1 | 842 |
| Louisiana | 28.7 | 77 | 7.5 | 242 |
| Other slave states | 3.7 | 10 | 5.9 | 189 |
| Pa., N.J., N.Y. | 4.1 | 11 | 6.7 | 215 |
| New England | 1.1 | 3 | 5.4 | 173 |
| Midwest | 0 | 0 | 0.7 | 23 |
| Foreign-born | 62.3 | 167 | 73.9 | 2,383 |
| Ireland | 32.1 | 86 | 20.3 | 656 |
| Germany | 16.0 | 43 | 20.3 | 655 |
| France | 4.1 | 11 | 15.7 | 505 |
| Spain | 3.7 | 10 | 3.4 | 109 |
| Italy | 1.9 | 5 | 2.6 | 83 |
| Britain | 1.1 | 3 | 5.3 | 171 |
| Other | 3.4 | 9 | 6.3 | 204 |
| Totals | 100.0 | 268 | 100.0 | 3,225 |

Source: Census of 1850, RG 29, NA.

in 1860. In those same census years, the Irish constituted 20 and 25 percent, respectively, of white adult males.[35]

Irishmen proved more successful than other foreign-born groups at winning jobs on the police force. Police jobs were patronage plums, available through the party system to the well-connected politically faithful. Most of the Irish shared a sense of historic nationalism and grievance, and many shared a common religion. They entered into partisan politics with great élan and exceptional solidarity and were rewarded with a large share of jobs on the police force. Other foreign-born groups got considerably smaller shares. The Germans, though approximately as numerous as the Irish, remained consistently underrepresented on the police force. Unlike

35. U.S. Bureau of Statistics (Treasury Department), *Immigration into the United States, Showing Number, Nationality, Sex, Age, Occupation, Destination, Etc., from 1820 to 1903* (Washington, D.C., 1903), 4366; William J. Bromwell, *History of Immigration to the United States* (New York, 1856).

## TABLE 9
### NATIVITIES OF THE POLICE BY MUNICIPALITIES IN 1850
### (PERCENTAGES ONLY)

| | Second Municipality | | First Municipality | | Third Municipality | |
|---|---|---|---|---|---|---|
| | Police | White Adult Males (sample) | Police | White Adult Males (sample) | Police | White Adult Males (sample) |
| Native-born | 26.7 | 27.9 | 39.8 | 29.5 | 43.1 | 16.4 |
| Louisiana | 8.0 | 4.7 | 34.1 | 8.7 | 37.5 | 8.3 |
| Other | 18.6 | 23.2 | 5.7 | 20.8 | 5.6 | 8.1 |
| Foreign-born | 73.3 | 72.1 | 60.2 | 70.5 | 56.9 | 83.6 |
| Ireland | 53.3 | 46.6 | 23.6 | 6.5 | 22.2 | 17.3 |
| Germany | 14.7 | 13.4 | 12.2 | 19.9 | 22.2 | 30.5 |
| France | 4.0 | 1.7 | 5.7 | 22.8 | 2.8 | 17.6 |
| Spain | 0 | 1.0 | 4.9 | 4.0 | 5.6 | 5.1 |
| Other | 1.3 | 9.4 | 13.8 | 17.4 | 4.1 | 13.1 |
| Totals | 100.0 | 100.0 | 100.0 | 100.0 | 100.0 | 100.0 |

*Source:* Census of 1850, RG 29, NA.

Ireland, Germany was not politically unified until 1871, so German immigrants were not bound together by a common political heritage. Also, the Germans in America were more religiously heterogeneous than the Irish, including Catholics, Jews, several Protestant denominations, and freethinkers. Furthermore, the differences in dialect among the Germans were much greater than among the Irish. Also underrepresented on the police force were the European French and the British immigrants in New Orleans, despite their cultural ties to the two historically dominant ethnic groups in the city.[36]

Police jobs attracted the Irish more than most other ethnic groups. Policing required no formal education, no legal training, no investment capital, and no elaborate skills. As the most uniformly uneducated, unskilled, impoverished white ethnic group in the city, the Irish were most likely to want positions on the force—especially because police work paid somewhat better than unskilled labor (though less than skilled work).

The rough-and-tumble character of police work may also have appealed

36. Although the earliest Irish immigrants in New Orleans were probably disproportionately Protestant, Earl F. Niehaus has suggested that the number of Catholic Irish may have equaled the number of Protestants as early as 1824; Niehaus, *The Irish in New Orleans*, 16.

to many Irishmen. Economic exploitation and political repression in the old country had helped create a culture that legitimized violence. Evicted tenant farmers struck back at landlords with force, individually and collectively in secret societies. The Young Ireland movement of the 1840s led an armed rebellion against the English imperial regime, and in the 1850s a group of Irishmen established the Fenians, an organization committed to the use of violence to achieve independence for Ireland. Violence was a part of custom because fighting was a traditional means of asserting masculinity and an outlet for repressed sexuality. Most Irishmen were pridefully conscious, too, of the heroic Celtic tradition. It was no accident that Irish boxers dominated prizefighting in nineteenth-century America. Cheap liquor was available, and drunkenness exacerbated the problem of violence. The high arrest rates of Irishmen in New Orleans—highest of all groups—and in other American cities suggest that the label "fighting Irish" was not an undeserved ethnic epithet.[37]

Prosopographic information about the Irish policemen of the 1830s and 1840s is scarce, but valuable fragments of biographical data are preserved in the admission books of Charity Hospital. Although a majority of Irish policemen probably had rural roots, more than four out of five had been urban dwellers before migrating to New Orleans. Some 69 percent of those hospitalized between 1836 and 1852 had lived at least temporarily in other American cities, especially New York, before settling in New Orleans, and an additional 13 percent had lived in urban areas in other countries, most

---

37. The arrest rate for the Irish in the years 1868–74 was the highest for any ethnic group in the city, nearly 60 percent over the average and almost three times the rate for the Germans; *Annual Report of the Board of Metropolitan Police to the Governor of Louisiana*, 1868/69–1874/75. John C. Schneider and Eric H. Monkkonen have found high rates of arrest and conviction for Irish immigrants in Detroit and Columbus in the nineteenth century (Schneider, *Detroit and the Problem of Order*, 113, 115; Eric H. Monkkonen, *The Dangerous Class: Crime and Poverty in Columbus, Ohio, 1860–1885* [London, 1975], 85). As evidence of violence in Ireland, Stanley H. Palmer has demonstrated that Ireland had a considerably higher rate of crime than England, with committal rates for riot and assault in the years 1835–41 twelve and fifteen times higher, respectively, than in England (*Police and Protest in England and Ireland, 1780–1850* [Cambridge, Eng., 1988], 45, 380). For further description and analysis of violence among the Irish, see Andrew M. Greeley, *That Most Distressful Nation: The Taming of the American Irish* (Chicago, 1972), 58–61, 103, 129–43; William Forbes Adams, *Ireland and Irish Emigration, from 1815 to the Famine* (1960; rpr. New York, 1967), 22–31; William V. Shannon, *The American Irish* (New York, 1963), 16–18, 41, 95–102; Oscar Handlin, *Boston's Immigrants: A Study in Acculturation* (rev. and enlarged ed.; New York, 1976), 121–22.

notably Liverpool. Undoubtedly many of the Irishmen who moved to New Orleans from elsewhere in America were looking for economic opportunity; New Orleans radiated an allure in this period that drew many migrants in pursuit of the main chance. Probably some Irishmen found the city attractive because of its Catholic tradition.[38]

The growing number of Irish immigrants and their role in politics increased ethnic tensions in New Orleans during the 1840s and early 1850s. When Judge Benjamin Elliott of the city court of Lafayette (a New Orleans suburb later incorporated into the Crescent City) was impeached for selling fraudulent naturalization certificates in the mid-1840s, the indictment made frequent reference to Irish immigrants as his customers.[39] In the 1844 federal election, Democratic senator John Slidell arranged for two steamboats to carry at least 150 men—mostly Irish and German immigrants—from New Orleans downriver to vote in Plaquemines Parish. Plaquemines was in the same election district as New Orleans, and voters were permitted to cast their ballots anywhere within their district, but the Whigs cried "fraud" and accused Slidell's men of voting more than once at different polling places along the way.[40] When a state constitutional convention assembled the following year, several delegates railed against the foreign population of New Orleans. As one delegate put it, electoral fraud was the fault of "the crowds of persons that come from the other States, and more particularly from Europe. To convince one of the motley character of that population, it was only necessary to go in the morning to the market; there was a confusion of tongues there, equal to that of the Tower of Babel." A member of the New Orleans delegation, outraged at attempts to restrict political participation by naturalized citizens and proposals to underrepresent the city in the legislature, asked, "What great harm has New Orleans ever done to the country, that she is now so roughly and unjustly handled,

---

38. Charity Hospital Admission Books, 1836–52. The Irish policemen in the hospital records numbered 22 for 1836–39, 20 for 1840–43, 10 for 1844–47, and 22 for 1848–52. Few policemen persisted in these records for more than one four-year period, and only one man from the period 1836–39 turned up in the years 1848–52.

39. Ordinances and Resolutions of the First Municipality Council, April 15, 1844; Messages of the Mayors to the First Municipality Council, April 22, 1844; Niehaus, *The Irish in New Orleans*, 79–80.

40. *Journal of the Special Committee Appointed by the House of Representatives of Louisiana, to Investigate the Frauds Perpetrated in the State, During the Late Presidential Election* (New Orleans, 1845), esp. 11, 12, 16, 17, 19, 20, 23, 27, and 29 for identification of immigrants as culprits.

and for which they claim so much from her? They tell you it is the Irishmen they fear. *The Irishmen*, is their everlasting cry. That is the bugbear."[41]

Ethnic conflict increasingly affected the New Orleans police. By 1850 all policemen had to stand for election on an annual basis, and partisan competition—intensified by ethnic hostilities—made this process more and more contentious. The council of the Second Municipality was split largely along party lines in 1850 when faced with the question of electing the police: the Whigs favored retention of the incumbent policemen, while the Democrats pressed for a new election. As candidates for the force stood in the lobby, alternately laughing and groaning at the proceedings, the Whigs withdrew from the meeting and deprived the council of a quorum. Two weeks later, after winning a compromise that would require applicants to "prove their qualifications" (meaning principally their citizenship), the Whigs allowed a new election.[42]

Concern for the nativity of policemen was not restricted to the Second Municipality. All three councils held police elections in 1850, and in each case they stipulated that the men had to be U.S. citizens (though the bar to noncitizens was later dropped in the Third Municipality). Naturalized citizens could become policemen in all of the municipalities. Later that same year, the *Daily Orleanian* complained of the situation, suggesting that immigrant men would be better employed as laborers than as police officers: "The police are despised, contemned, and mocked at; they are looked on as mere cyphers and considered unworthy of their pitiful positions. If they possessed a spark of pride, or were imbued with the slightest particle of manly spirit, they would resign in a body—id est—the 'Foreigners'; for the police is said to be mainly composed of Irish and Germans. They are generally stout, lusty fellows, with whom a hard work will not disagree, and cannot come amiss."[43]

Although the Irish and Germans were the largest immigrant groups in the city and those most frequently castigated by nativists, other ethnic groups faced nativist hostility, too. The city's small Spanish population, which numbered 1,150 in 1850 and accounted for 3.4 percent of white

41. *Proceedings and Debates of the Convention of Louisiana Which Assembled at the City of New Orleans January 14, 1844* (New Orleans, 1845), 128, 322.

42. *Bee*, June 5, 1850.

43. Ordinances and Resolutions of the First Municipality Council, May 21, 1850; Ordinances and Resolutions of the Third Municipality Council, May 12, 1851; *Bee*, May 15, 1850; *Daily Orleanian*, August 26, 1850, quoted in Niehaus, *The Irish in New Orleans*, 56.

adult males, found themselves targeted by rioters in 1851. Some New Orleanians complained of Spanish domination of the local fruit trade and consequent high prices for fruit, Spanish smuggling of cigars from Cuba to avoid import duties, and illicit catering to slaves in Spanish coffee houses, but the principal precipitant of the 1851 riot was the failure of a filibustering expedition against Spanish Cuba in August of that year.[44]

New Orleans had served as the base of operations for the filibusters of the Venezuelan-born former Spanish officer Narciso López, and local opinion strongly favored U.S. annexation of Cuba. The second López expedition ended in defeat, the execution of López and his lieutenant John Crittenden, and the imprisonment in Spain of some 150 of his men. When this news reached the Crescent City in August, 1851, a mob sacked several Spanish-owned coffee shops and tobacco stores—plus some fruit stands—invaded the Spanish consulate and defaced a portrait of the queen of Spain, burned the Spanish flag and an effigy of the captain-general of Cuba, and wrecked the office of the Spanish-language newspaper *La Union*, which had editorialized against filibusters. Spanish properties in the Second Municipality sustained the most damage, but considerable property was destroyed in the First Municipality, where the consulate was located. The police forces of those municipalities evidently made little effort to restrain the rioters and arrested only a few in the aftermath. In the words of the *Daily Crescent*: "No watchmen or military were visible, and the authorities were powerless or would not act."[45] Unfortunately, two of the most salient features of this episode—the ethnic dimension of the violence and the failure of the police—would prove to be reliable harbingers of the remainder of the decade.

With the increasing evidence that the partitioned government of New Orleans was still failing to manage public finances, the state legislature in 1852 mandated the reunification of the three municipalities and the incorporation with them of the suburb of Lafayette. The Americans of the

44. *Statistical View of the United States . . . Being a Compendium of the Seventh Census* (Washington, D.C., 1854), 399; Census of 1850, RG 29, NA; Richard Randall Tansey, "Economic Expansion and Urban Disorder in Antebellum New Orleans" (Ph.D. dissertation, University of Texas at Austin, 1981), 21–22; Chester Stanley Urban, "New Orleans and the Cuban Question During the Lopez Expeditions of 1849–1851: A Local Study in 'Manifest Destiny,'" *Louisiana Historical Quarterly*, XXII (1939), 1095–1159.

45. *Daily Crescent*, August 22, 1851; *Daily Orleanian*, August 23, 1851; *Congressional Globe*, 32nd Cong., 1st Sess., 1851, 25, Appendix 33–38.

Second Municipality were the last to support reunification because they had fared better than their rivals under the divided government. It had grown from the smallest to the largest of the sections and was the only one not to decline in population by 1850. The Second Municipality returned to unitary government with the balance of power tipped in favor of its businessmen and politicians. It was symbolically appropriate that the Second Municipality was renamed the First District of the consolidated city; it was certainly first in influence. But rivalry between the French and Americans was becoming less important as the city was flooded with other ethnic groups such as the Irish and Germans. During the troubled, violent 1850s the French and Americans found progressively more in common— including a common nativity as Louisianans—as many of the members of these groups became politically allied against the new immigrants.

Another of the changes in this period that would have a lasting effect was the redefinition of the policeman's role, in part by politics and in part by the transformation of patrol tactics. The adoption of dispersive beat patrolling created a problem in personnel management, weakening the link between roundsman and patrolman but offering more widespread territorial coverage by the police. The reformed police thus became more available to the public yet less powerful as solitary patrolmen, lacking swords and firearms. The new police officer, dressed in his own choice of clothes, was more an individual man and less the impersonal embodiment of police authority, and this new emphasis on the personal element was intensified by the increasing politicization of the police. Greater police involvement in partisan politics made the new police more vulnerable to the instability stemming from the fluctuating fortunes of their political patrons.

The police were becoming more vulnerable in another sense, too, because the public had access to more efficiently lethal weapons in this period, especially the revolver. This era offered grim portents of a violent future, when the first documented instances of policemen killed by gunfire occurred in 1840 and 1848. During the 1850s increased violence and political conflict would dominate policing in the Crescent City.[46]

46. The only apparent earlier instance of a policeman killed in the line of duty occurred in 1818, when a city guardsman named Trouilleux was fatally stabbed by a man he was attempting to take into custody (Messages of the Mayors to the City Council, February 28, 1818; *Louisiana Courier*, March 2, 1818).

# "A Perfect Hell on Earth"
## A Time of Troubles in the Reunified City,
## 1852–1861

WHEN the English journalist William Howard Russell visited New Orleans in 1861, his itinerary included a tour of the parish prison. The parish criminal sheriff informed Russell that the city was "a perfect hell on earth, and that nothing would put an end to murders, manslaughters, and deadly assaults, till it was made penal to carry arms; but by law every American citizen may walk with an armory round his waist, if he likes. Bar-rooms, cock-tails, mint-juleps, gambling-houses, political discussions, and imperfect civilization do the rest."[1] Russell was one of many travelers to the Crescent City who remarked upon the incidence of violence there and the proclivity of New Orleanians to bear weapons. Certainly New Orleans was one of the most violent cities in the United States in the late antebellum period.

One conspicuous source of violence in this era was political conflict, especially between the nativist American party and the multiethnic coalition of Democrats. During the 1840s and early 1850s control of the police force had become an increasingly important issue in municipal politics because of its value as a source of patronage and its influence on elections. After the restoration of unitary government in the city in 1852, the police played an even larger role in the manipulation of elections and resorted more frequently to intimidation and violence. Although the first mayor of the rechartered city was a Whig, the Democrats achieved domination of the police by electing a majority of the members of the Board of Police, which controlled the force from 1853 to 1856. The American party organized and did battle at the polls in 1854–1855, and when its members failed to win a majority on the board, they arranged the impeachment of

1. William Howard Russell, *My Diary North and South* (Boston, 1863), 244.

two Democrats and the substitution of men partial to their own party. Under the rule of the Know-Nothings, the police force was reduced in size and funding, and most of the policemen who lost their jobs were foreign-born Democrats. The result was a force so woefully inadequate to fight crime and maintain order and so abusive of the electoral process that a vigilance committee seized the city in 1858 in a brief and unsuccessful attempt to end what many people considered a reign of terror.

New Orleans shared turbulent ethnic politics with other American cities of the period. Several municipal governments attempted to reform their law enforcement systems in these years. One of the most widespread reforms was the integration of once-separate organizations, usually the day police and night watch, into a single entity with a unified chain of command. New York City had led the country by doing so in 1845, and Boston, Philadelphia, Chicago, Charleston, St. Louis, and Richmond were among those that followed in the 1850s. New Orleans had integrated the day and night forces by 1840 but did not consolidate the three municipalities' police forces until the legislature reunified the city in 1852. New Orleans also tinkered with other common nationwide reforms of the period, such as installing a police telegraph system and creating a "rogues' gallery" stocked with daguerreotypes of prominent career criminals, and it considered the "northern" reform of adopting a police uniform. In characteristically unique fashion, the New Orleans city government—which had uniformed its police force during the period 1805–1836—decided to reuniform the police in 1855 and then rescinded the order before it was put into effect. New Orleans also shared the national problem of increasingly available lethal weaponry, especially the proliferation of revolvers; a state statute forbade the carrying of concealed weapons and at least one mayor tried to enforce that law, but policemen began to carry deadly weapons and usually kept them concealed.[2]

Under the new city charter of 1852, the authority to set regulations for the police department and to appoint its personnel was vested in the mayor, subject to the advice and consent of the Board of Aldermen. This departed from the system of dispersed authority that had prevailed under the par-

---

2. Richardson, *Urban Police*, 19–34; Johnson, *American Law Enforcement*, 17–33; Walker, *Popular Justice*, 59–65; Steinberg, *Transformation of Criminal Justice*, 119–82; Lane, *Policing the City*, 37–105.

tition government, and it made partisan control of the police almost completely dependent on the party affiliation of the mayor. The new charter also created the office of chief of police, subordinate to the mayor.[3] For this post Mayor Abdil Crossman chose a fellow Whig, John Youenes, who had served nine years as captain of the First Municipality police.[4] Youenes, however, held the job for only one year. The city's Democrats procured a charter amendment from the legislature which removed the police from mayoral control and gave that authority to a Board of Police. The mayor served as presiding officer of the board but cast only one of five votes, the other four coming from the city's recorders, each of whom represented a district. Three of the four recorders were Democrats and so constituted a majority of the board. In April, 1853, they elected as chief an Irish-born policeman, Stephen O'Leary, who had fifteen years of police experience in the old Second Municipality. While applicants for the force thronged the corridors of city hall, the board overrode the mayor's objections and appointed a largely new group of men to serve under O'Leary.[5]

It was during O'Leary's tenure as police chief that the police became involved in the first serious political violence of the 1850s. Complaints of electoral fraud tainted elections in May and November, 1853, but both elections were peaceful, and neither Whigs nor Democrats found fault with the police.[6] When the American party presented a slate of candidates in

3. *Daily Picayune*, February 29, 1852; *Acts of Louisiana*, 1852, pp. 42–57.

4. For opposition to the appointment of Youenes, see *Daily Crescent*, April 27, 1852. Youenes was about thirty-five when appointed as chief. He ran unsuccessfully for coroner as a Whig in November, 1853, held the post of city fire warden in the late 1850s, supported the presidential candidacy of John Bell in 1860, and served as an artillery officer in the Confederate army. The U.S. census listed his birthplace as Louisiana, but his death certificate showed his birthplace as Holland (New Orleans Death Certificates, LXIII, 82; Andrew B. Booth, comp., *Records of Louisiana Confederate Soldiers and Louisiana Confederate Commands* [New Orleans, 1920]; *Daily Picayune*, April 15, 1852, February 21, 1856, February 21, 1875; *Daily Delta*, November 9, 1853; *Daily Crescent*, July 2, 1860; *Bee*, August 9, 1860).

5. *Daily Picayune*, April 28, 1853; *Daily True Delta*, April 28, May 3, 1853; *Daily Orleanian*, April 4, 1854; *Daily Crescent*, November 1, 1853; *Louisiana Courier*, October 21, 1853; *Acts of Louisiana*, 1853, pp. 79–83. O'Leary served as an infantry captain in the Confederate army (Booth, comp., *Records of Louisiana Confederate Soldiers*). Although O'Leary was the first Irish-born chief of police for the entire city, Daniel Kennedy of County Limerick, Ireland, had become captain of the city guard in the Third Municipality in 1848—the first Irishman to hold the highest police rank possible in that period (New Orleans Death Certificates, LVII, 511; *Daily Picayune*, March 26, 1873).

6. *Daily True Delta*, November 3, 1852, May 17, 1853; *Daily Picayune*, March 24, 1852,

the regular municipal election in March, 1854, however, the polling turned violent. In one precinct a band of armed men destroyed a ballot box. The local press reported accusations that policemen led groups of men from one poll to another to vote "early and often" and permitted and abetted the intimidation of Know-Nothing supporters. Two Irish-born policemen were killed in the fray. After the second slaying, the nativist *Daily Crescent* claimed the policeman had been trying to prevent a qualified voter from casting a ballot, whereas the Democratic *Daily True Delta* alleged that he had been courageously preserving the peace from nativist outrages. Police chief Stephen O'Leary was among those wounded in the electoral combat.[7]

When O'Leary's term as chief expired in the spring of 1854, the Board of Police appointed William James to succeed him. James quickly made enemies on the board by vigorously enforcing the laws respecting gambling, taverns, and dance halls, consequently increasing the city's license revenues fivefold in just one year. The Board of Police did more than sack James; it abolished the office of chief of police, thereby giving each recorder more control over the police in his district.[8]

Despite the formal consolidation of the police in 1852, the department had continued to resemble four police forces rather than one. The establishment of the Board of Police had exacerbated this tendency, making the recorders "like despots in their respective districts," according to the *Daily True Delta*. The *Daily Crescent* concurred, asserting that "as at present organized, the police force of this city is divided and local." The editorial suggested a remedy: "The police should be organized on a different footing altogether. It should be the police of a consolidated city, and not a district one; there should be but one head to it, who should be held responsible for its acts." The recorders customarily selected the police for their own districts. When the Board of Police rejected the nominees of Recorder H. M. Summers for partisan reasons in April, 1854, he protested that "I

---

November 10, 1853; *Daily Crescent*, November 5, 1852, November 3, 8, 1853; *Daily Delta*, November 4, 1852; *Louisiana Courier*, October 21, November 7, 1853.

7. *Louisiana Courier*, March 28–31, 1854; *Daily True Delta*, March 29, 1854; *Daily Crescent*, March 28, 1854; *Daily Picayune*, March 28, 1854; *Daily Delta*, March 28, 1854.

8. James, a native of New Orleans, was thirty-two years old when he became chief. He had served as chief deputy sheriff of Orleans Parish during the late 1840s under then sheriff John Lewis (*Daily Picayune*, August 27–28, September 1–3, 1854; *Daily True Delta*, August 26, 1854; *Times Democrat*, May 22, 1908).

desired and expected to exercise the previously-conceded right of selecting the entire police of my district."[9]

After only one month a district court judge ruled the excision of the office of police chief illegal and the board was forced to restore the office. But during that month, in a week-long battle in the streets between the Democrats and the Know-Nothings, the police proved almost totally ineffectual at restoring peace. The riots were triggered by the arrest on September 9 of Henry T. Sherman, who was allegedly brutalized by the police who took him into custody. A group of fifty to sixty Know-Nothings assaulted the police station where Sherman was incarcerated, and two Irish policemen suffered gunshot wounds. A police lieutenant found former chief O'Leary carrying a shotgun and confiscated the weapon. Several days later he was found by police to be armed again and was arrested for carrying a concealed weapon.[10]

When the rioting continued after September 9, the police could not restore order. One detachment marched away from a riot in Tchoupitoulas Street when they received a misdirected order; another detachment stood idly by as a band of armed men passed. Three night policemen in the First District ran away from a pair of pursuers only to be overtaken and embarrassed to find that they had run from two day policemen who were coming on duty. A display of military force by a small militia unit failed to halt the violence, and the mayor eventually felt compelled to swear in a special citizen police force of about 250 men, who succeeded where the regular police had not. A few regular policemen did their duty and acquitted themselves honorably during the Sherman riots, but as a whole the force failed miserably.[11]

Democratic control of the police force ended six months later. The American party had won a majority of the Board of Assistant Aldermen in 1854, and in the municipal election of March, 1855, it secured control of both branches of the Common Council. The Democrats accused the Know-Nothings of excluding naturalized citizens from voting in the election, but to no avail. Even though the Democrats still held a majority on

9. *Daily True Delta*, August 26, October 4, 1854; *Daily Crescent*, October 5, 1854; *Bee*, April 24, 1854; Police Board Records, NOPL, April 15, 18, 1854.

10. *Daily True Delta*, September 12–21, 1854; *Louisiana Courier*, September 12–20, 1854; *Daily Picayune*, September 11, 1854.

11. *Daily True Delta*, September 14, 17, 1854; *Louisiana Courier*, September 13, 1854; *Daily Crescent*, September 11–21, 1854; *Daily Picayune*, September 12, 16, 17, 19, 1854.

the Board of Police, the Know-Nothings maneuvered into control of the board by impeaching the two Democratic recorders, Clement Ramos and Peter Seuzeneau. Chief William James, who had been restored to his post by judicial order shortly after the Sherman riots in September, 1854, charged the two magistrates with malfeasance for permitting their subordinates to receive fees for issuing passes and bonds to blacks and for releasing from jail a policeman who was being held for interfering with the election. The Common Council responded to Chief James's accusations by impeaching Ramos and Seuzeneau before the Board of Police made its annual appointment of the force. Although the two Democrats were eventually vindicated in court and restored to their offices, they were replaced in the interim by American party loyalists.[12]

Democratic protests against the impeachment proved fruitless. One of the Know-Nothing acting recorders expressed his willingness to table the police appointments, but the others pressed ahead and the board appointed a new police force over the objection of the lone Democrat, Mayor John Lewis. Even though Chief James had brought charges against Ramos and Seuzeneau he lost his post because he was a Democrat and was replaced by Alexander F. Moynan.[13]

Moynan commanded a radically altered police department. Even before the American party had won control of the Board of Police, its leaders used their Common Council majorities to enact a new police ordinance, reducing the force from 450 to 265 men. The Americans sought to limit other traditional expenditures throughout the municipal government so as to channel money to railroad construction. In July, 1855, Chief Moynan attempted to requisition a ream of paper and a few pens, but the comptroller denied the request because it first had to be endorsed by the Common Council's finance committee. The *Daily Picayune* commented, "The police are busily engaged in scraping up backs of old letters and stray pieces of

12. James was a Democrat, though his party compatriots subsequently branded him a turncoat for his role in the impeachment of Ramos and Seuzeneau (*Daily Crescent*, September 22, 1854; *Louisiana Courier*, March 26, 27, 1855; *Daily Picayune*, September 21, 1854, March 25–27, April 10, 1855; Police Board Records, September 21, 1854). The Common Council, which was the legislative branch of city government, had two chambers: a Board of Aldermen with eleven members and a Board of Assistant Aldermen with twenty-four members. In 1856, the membership of the boards was reduced to nine and fifteen, respectively (*Acts of Louisiana*, 1852, pp. 42–55, and 1856, pp. 136–37).

13. *Daily Picayune*, April 10, 12, 13, 22, 1855; *Daily True Delta*, April 13, 15, 17, 18, 20, 21, 1855; *Louisiana Courier*, April 10, 13, 1855; *Bee*, April 12, 1855.

blank paper for present purposes, and will have to continue doing so till the next meeting of the Financial Committee." Because of its determination to invest in new transportation projects the new administration could not meet many of the city's other expenses. The public school teachers sued the city for payment of back salary and forced the sale of the police department's two paddy wagons, the Red Maria and Black Maria, at public auction. The buyer of the Marias acquired them at half their original cost to the city and promptly informed the police department that he would be willing to hire out the wagons.[14]

When the Know-Nothings scaled down the police force, most of the men who lost their jobs were immigrants (see Table 10). The Board of Police substantially nativized the department, though some foreign-born men remained. Almost every immigrant group lost part of its 1850 share of policemen in the reorganization of 1855. When the American party recast the ethnic composition of the police department, the Irish probably made up about 20 percent of the white adult male population of the city, but they received only 10 percent of the appointments in 1855. Five years layer, the situation had not changed much; immigrants were underrepresented on the police and the Irish still held close to 10 percent of jobs (see Table 11). The struggle in New Orleans between Democrats and Know-Nothings was roughly paralleled in most other American cities of the period, though in some places the Democrats were more successful in meeting the American party challenge, and the level of violence varied considerably from one place to another. A survey of fifteen other southern cities indicates that in 1860 the Irish were substantially overrepresented in six and underrepresented in eight, with nearly proportionate representation in one (see Table 12).

Immigrant policemen who lost their jobs were bitter. One dismissed policeman, William Gotts, reapplied for police work in the early 1860s describing himself as "at one time a Police Officer appointed by the Democrats but removed by the *Know Nothings* when the[y] got into power." Another longtime policeman, John Gallagher, wrote in condemnation of the Know-Nothings: "I am an Irish man by Birth, I am an American by choice, constitutionally a Jeffersonian, I am a man of Family I hold the Thugs in utter abhorence."[15]

14. Ordinances and Resolutions of the Common Council, NOPL, No. 2100, April 5, 1855; *Daily Picayune*, July 22, September 17, 18, October 23, 1855.

15. Applications for Positions as Police Officers, 1862–65, for William Gotts and John

## TABLE 10
### Nativities of the Police in 1850 and 1855

|  | 1850 | 1855 | |
|---|---|---|---|
|  | % | % | No. |
| Native-born | 37.7 | 76.8 | 129 |
| Louisiana | 28.7 | 53.0 | 89 |
| Other slave states | 3.7 | 9.5 | 16 |
| Pa., N.J., N.Y. | 4.1 | 8.3 | 14 |
| New England | 1.1 | 3.6 | 6 |
| Midwest | 0 | 2.4 | 4 |
| Foreign-born | 62.3 | 23.2 | 39 |
| Ireland | 32.1 | 10.1 | 17 |
| Germany | 16.0 | 3.0 | 5 |
| France | 4.1 | 1.8 | 3 |
| Italy | 1.9 | 0.6 | 1 |
| Britain | 1.1 | 3.6 | 6 |
| Other | 7.1 | 4.1 | 7 |
| Total | 100.0 | 100.0 | 168 |

*Sources:* Census of 1850, RG 29, NA; New Orleans Death Certificates; newspaper obituaries.

The drastic reduction in police personnel caused serious problems. Chief Moynan notified the Board of Police in December, 1855, that "this meagre force is inadequate to the wants of the city, and in consequence, I am compelled to leave a very large portion of the city entirely without any watchmen; and on those streets which have watchmen, the beats are necessarily so long that depredations can be committed before they can walk the extent of their beats and return." Citizens had complained "very justly," Moynan said, of being unable to find a policeman when they needed one. His proposal called for doubling the size of the force and returning to the use of a boat police to protect steamboats and other shipping in the river from thievery. The grand jury issued a report in agreement with the chief, suggesting an additional 250 policemen be hired. The New Orleans *Bee*, which supported the Know-Nothing retrenchment in other departments, editorialized in behalf of an increased police budget, deeming an under-

---

Gallagher, Records of U.S. Army Continental Commands, 1821–1920, Part I, No. 1852, RG 393, NA.

## TABLE 11
### NATIVITIES OF THE POLICE IN 1860

|  | Police | | White Adult Males (sample) | |
|  | % | No. | % | No. |
| --- | --- | --- | --- | --- |
| Native-born | 72.2 | 268 | 28.0 | 1,160 |
| Louisiana | 46.4 | 172 | 11.2 | 463 |
| Other slave states | 8.9 | 33 | 7.0 | 291 |
| Pa., N.J., N.Y. | 12.4 | 46 | 6.1 | 255 |
| New England | 2.7 | 10 | 2.5 | 105 |
| Midwest | 1.9 | 7 | 1.0 | 42 |
| Other | 0 | 0 | 0.1 | 4 |
| Foreign-born | 27.8 | 103 | 72.0 | 2,990 |
| Ireland | 10.8 | 40 | 24.7 | 1,023 |
| Germany | 5.9 | 22 | 22.5 | 935 |
| France | 2.7 | 10 | 12.4 | 514 |
| Spain | 1.9 | 7 | 2.0 | 84 |
| Italy | 0.5 | 2 | 1.5 | 62 |
| Britain | 3.2 | 12 | 4.2 | 174 |
| Other | 2.7 | 10 | 4.8 | 198 |
| Totals | 100.0 | 371 | 100.0 | 4,150 |

*Source:* Census of 1860, RG 29, NA.

sized police force a "sordid and ill-judged economy." Mayor John Lewis concurred that the department was undermanned, but the Common Council allowed only 50 new policemen and did not increase the force again for two years. Additions to the department thereafter brought the total number of policemen back to about 450 men in 1860, still proportionately smaller than the force had been in the early 1850s (the city's population in 1850 was 116,000 but had swelled to 169,000 by 1860, though part of the increase came from the annexation of Lafayette).[16]

The police remained politically partisan and controversial during the latter 1850s, still under American party control. Occasionally policemen faced punishment for abuse of the electoral process. Two members of the force were brought before the Board of Police on charges of interfering in

16. Police Board Records, March 8, December 6, 1855; *Bee*, December 12, 1855; *Daily Picayune*, April 23, 1856; *Daily True Delta*, April 23, 1856; *Seventh Census*, 474; *Population of the United States in 1860* (Washington, D.C., 1864), 195.

## TABLE 12

### PERCENTAGE OF IRISH NATIVES IN POLICE AND CONTROL SAMPLES IN FIFTEEN SOUTHERN CITIES, 1850 AND 1860

| | 1850 Police | 1850 White Adult Males (sample) | 1860 Police | 1860 White Adult Males (sample) |
|---|---|---|---|---|
| Savannah | 39 | 24 | 62 | 33 |
| Charleston | 40 | 21 | 58 | 22 |
| Mobile | —a | 19 | 34 | 20 |
| St. Louis | —b | —b | 41 | 25 |
| Montgomery | 21 | 7 | 21 | 8 |
| San Antonio | —a | 9 | 14 | 8 |
| Atlanta | —c | —c | 10 | 9 |
| New Orleans | 32 | 20 | 11 | 25 |
| Memphis | 14 | 19 | 2 | 32 |
| Louisville | 10 | 15 | 8 | 18 |
| Augusta | —a | 15d | 0 | 20 |
| Nashville | —a | 9 | 0 | 19 |
| Lexington | —b | —b | 0 | 17 |
| Petersburg | —a | 3 | 0 | 7 |
| Richmond | 6e | 12 | 10e | 16 |

Sources: Censuses of 1850 and 1860, RG 29, NA.

a Not possible to identify police.
b Not included in the research.
c No data available.
d Richmond County, Georgia.
e Includes both municipal police and state Public Guard.

an election in June, 1855; one received a ten-day suspension for committing assault at the polls, but the other was reinstated without punishment.
More complaints were forthcoming after the November, 1855, election,
when a Democratic newspaper accused two policemen of participating in
a nativist assault against a preelection parade of Democrats. During the
voting, outbreaks of violence occurred in four precincts, resulting in two
deaths and destruction of two ballot boxes. The Know-Nothings systematically excluded from the polls voters who had been naturalized during
the courts' summer recess as well as any whose naturalizations had been
processed in the First District court. Democrats complained that the police
tolerated the intimidation of some voters and actively participated in violence against others. Mayor John Lewis roundly condemned the police for
failing to execute warrants against men charged with offenses stemming
from the election violence even though their identities were well known.
He urged the chief of police to bring all offenders within the department
to justice or, he warned, he would do so himself.[17]

The mayor's appeal for a housecleaning had little effect. As a Democrat,
he was a political outsider in the Know-Nothing administration, and his
efforts were frustrated by the Board of Police, the Common Council, and
the police department itself. The Democratic state legislature and governor
removed one obstacle by abolishing the Board of Police in February, 1856,
and attempted to restrain American party electoral abuses by enacting a
voter registration law and creating a Democratic-controlled election commission for the city in 1857, but the entrenchment of the Americans in
municipal government prevented any substantial reforms. Abolition of the
board restored control of the police to the mayor, a situation Lewis had
little chance to enjoy, for he surrendered his office to a Know-Nothing,
Charles Waterman, in June, 1856. In the election that put Waterman in
the mayor's office, voter turnout was light because the Know-Nothings
excluded many Democrats from voting. Armed men held the polls in three
precincts throughout the day. One exchange of gunfire resulted in the
deaths of two Sicilian immigrants. At least four policemen were beaten
during the polling, and that night a majority of the policemen in three of

17. *Daily Picayune*, August 31, November 6, 7, 1855; *Louisiana Courier*, November 4, 6,
8, 1855; *Commercial Bulletin*, November 8, 1855; *Daily Crescent*, November 7, 8, 1855; *Daily
True Delta*, November 7, 1855; Police Board Records, August 30, November 20, 1855.

the city's four districts absented themselves from duty and absences ran above normal in the remaining district.[18]

Newly elected Mayor Waterman reappointed Alexander Moynan as chief of police. Moynan had stepped down from the office in March, 1856, after being arrested for assaulting and threatening to kill one of his own policemen. The complainant claimed that the chief had referred to him as a "d——d Irish son of ———," threatened to kill all the Irishmen in the city, and employed a knife and brass knuckles as proof of the sincerity of his words. (Similar bigotry was displayed by one of his lieutenants, who was reported by an Irish policeman to have said that "the Board of Police were appointing a parcel of damned Irish and Dutch, and a set of thieves on the police," and by one of his patrolmen, who killed a German immigrant after calling him a "d——d Dutch son of a b——ch.") Moynan served as chief again until December, 1856, when he resigned and was replaced by Henry Forno. Forno had at one time been captain of the guard in the old Second Municipality and during the 1850s had worked occasionally for the governor in extraditing fugitives.[19]

Mayor Waterman promised to reform the police by appointing sober and industrious men without respect to party membership or place of birth, but he failed to create a nonpartisan police. The police made their typically controversial showing in the November election of 1856. A police lieutenant attempted to quell a disturbance at one location, failed and was wounded for his trouble, and then quit the scene, declaring that the disorder had grown too great to handle. One policeman attempting to arrest a man who had broken a table at a polling station found himself single-handedly engaged because other policemen at the scene refused to help

18. Police Board Records, November 22, 1855; *Daily Picayune*, November 23, 1855, February 24, March 8, June 3, 4, 14, 1856; *Daily True Delta*, June 3, 1856; *Louisiana Courier*, June 3, 4, 1856; *Acts of Louisiana*, 1856, pp. 19–20, 131–36; Leon Cyprian Soulé, *The Know Nothing Party in New Orleans: A Reappraisal* (Baton Rouge, 1961), 86–90. Soulé's is the best overall account of the American party in New Orleans.

19. Moynan may have been influenced to resign by the death of his wife in June, 1856. He later served as a private in the Confederate army and died in 1864 (*Daily Picayune*, March 14, June 16, 1856; *Louisiana Courier*, March 25, June 17, December 14, 17, 1856, April 10, 1859; *Daily True Delta*, March 6, 1856; *Bee*, March 25, 31, December 17, 1856; Police Board Records, June 28, August 23, 1855, *Acts of Louisiana*, 1853, p. 171, and 1854, p. 133; Booth, comp., *Records of Louisiana Confederate Soldiers*).

him. If even a fraction of the complaints against the police were true, most stood by and did nothing in the presence of violence.[20]

Election days remained tumultuous into 1858. The last major episode of political violence of the decade came in June, 1858, before and during a municipal election. Running against the regular American party ticket was an Independent organization, led by propertied merchant Know-Nothings, who resented their loss of power to the labor wing of the party, and supported by many Democrats. They chose as their mayoral candidate P. G. T. Beauregard, a popular figure in the city (and later to become a general in the Confederate army). On June 3, 1858, four days before the election, a group of men calling themselves the Vigilance Committee, apparently for the most part Democrats, seized the state arsenal at Jackson Square as well as the police headquarters. They announced their intention to rid the city of thugs and ensure a fair election.[21]

Mayor Waterman convened the Common Council but declined to disperse the vigilantes by force. Waterman went to Jackson Square to negotiate with the vigilantes and, after refusing their demand that they be appointed as a special police force for the election, called out the militia. Major General John Lewis (the former Democratic mayor) reported that the 150 men who could be mustered were insufficient to retake the arsenal. Neither Waterman nor anyone else seems to have expected the regular police to deal with the crisis, though many of them remained on duty during the early days of the siege. On June 4, Mayor Waterman agreed to appoint the vigilantes as special policemen without pay until the election was over. An armed and angry mob opposed to the Vigilance Committee marched toward Jackson Square but retreated when faced there with an imposing barricade and frightened by a single stray gunshot. A citizens' group disclaiming any connection with the vigilantes endorsed the agreement with Waterman, and several officials and civic leaders spoke to anti-vigilante mobs to restrain them from storming Jackson Square. Mayor Waterman delegated the task of swearing in the special police to Recorder Gerard Stith (the Know-Nothing candidate for mayor) but rescinded his action when two lawyers advised him the delegation of authority was illegal.

20. *Daily Picayune*, June 18, November 4, 5, 1856; *Louisiana Courier*, June 19, November 5–7, 1856; *Bee*, November 4–6, 1856.

21. *Louisiana Courier*, November 3, 1857, June 5, 1858; *Daily Picayune*, November 3, 1857; *Daily True Delta*, November 3, 4, 1857, June 3–5, 8, 1858; *Bee*, June 4, 5, 7, 1858; Niehaus, *The Irish in New Orleans*, 96.

Stith ignored the rescinding order, and the men already sworn in served as specials at the election. The Common Council impeached Waterman, and H. M. Summers became acting mayor. Chief of Police Henry Forno abandoned his post and retired to his home in the country.[22]

Acting Mayor Summers appointed Jonathan A. Jacquess as temporary chief of police, and his force joined the special police on election day. The only casualties during the siege were several members of the Vigilance Committee who were accidentally shot by their own people, leaving four of them dead. After the election had ended in victory for the Know-Nothings, the vigilantes peacefully evacuated Jackson Square and the special police retired from the streets.[23]

The new Know-Nothing mayor, Gerard Stith, appointed as chief of police Thomas E. Adams, a businessman and member of the state legislature, who served for the next two years. Mayor Stith was remarkably candid about the political role of the police, acknowledging that "the force is mainly constituted of men favorable to the principles which are professed by the American Party" and asserting that the "efficiency of the department requires that the men who compose it, so long as they take a part and feel an interest in politics, should sympathize with the chief in political opinion." But Stith sought to limit the influence of political partiality on police appointments, noting that the force did include "many . . . adopted citizens" and that "political brawlers, and those who would make their injudicious activity at the polls a passport to office, have not been preferred." As proof that merit was important, he noted that 269 men had been dismissed from the force during the first fifteen months of his administration. Stith castigated the New Orleans police for their political involvement, describing the "entire police organization of the city" as "radically wrong" and recommending that they be made independent of municipal politics and placed under the authority of the state legislature. Such a change took

22. *Communication of Charles M. Waterman, Mayor of the City of New Orleans, to the Board of Assistant Aldermen, and Their Action Thereon (June 18, 1858)* (New Orleans, 1858); *Daily Picayune*, June 5, 7, 8, 1858; *Louisiana Courier*, June 6, 8, 1858; *Daily Crescent*, June 7, 1858. Forno, a native of Charleston, South Carolina, distinguished himself in the Mexican War and as a colonel in the Confederate army, so lack of courage seems an unlikely explanation for his behavior in this instance. A rumor circulated in the city to the effect that he had accepted a bribe to withdraw. In any event, he died after the Civil War as the result of a locomotive boiler explosion (*Daily Crescent*, February 2, 3, 5, 1866; *Daily Picayune*, February 1–4, 1866; Soulé, *Know Nothing Party in New Orleans*, 94–104).

23. *Daily Crescent*, June 8, 1858; *Bee*, June 8, 9, 1858.

place in New York in 1857, in Baltimore, St. Louis, and Kansas City in the early 1860s, and in other cities later. It did not happen in New Orleans until 1868, and like the other cities in which the state took control of their police forces, the reform changed the party that controlled the police but did not extricate the police from politics.[24]

After June, 1858, election days ceased to be times of bloodletting and terror, at least for a while. The American party held such complete control of municipal government—despite being defunct at the state and national levels—that the Democrats, hobbled as well by a deep split within their party, had difficulty turning out voters. As one Democratic newspaper reported in April, 1861, "It is now becoming a trite remark that in our city the quietest days of the year are those on which elections are held." Thus elections had become peaceful and their outcome predictable.[25]

Policemen in New Orleans lived and worked in a world of chronic and pervasive violence. Few other cities in the United States in the 1850s could have matched the level of violence in New Orleans; indeed, the Crescent City may well have been the darkest stain on the butcher's apron. Virtually the dueling capital of the South, a major headquarters for career criminals, site of some of the most intense ethnic strife in the country, New Orleans earned a reputation as one of the most dangerous places in America.

Widespread carrying of revolvers, duckfoot and pepperbox pistols, knives, and slungshots was routine in New Orleans (a slungshot was a lead ball connected by a wire to a short wooden handle—a pocket-sized, unspiked version of the deadly medieval morningstar). An Englishman traveling in the United States at midcentury, Edward Sullivan, encountered this practice in the Crescent City, where he attended one of the renowned quadroon balls. "These balls take place," Sullivan reported,

in a large saloon: at the entrance, where you pay half a dollar, you are requested to leave your *implements*, by which is meant your bowie-knife and revolvers; and you leave them as you would your overcoat on going to the opera, and get a ticket with their number, and on the way out they are returned to you. You hear the pistol and bowie-knife keeper in the arms-room call out, "No. 46—a six-barrelled repeater." "No. 100—one eight-barrelled revolver, and bowie knife with a deaths'-head and cross-bones cut on the handle." "No. 95—a brace of double-barrels." All this is

24. *Louisiana Courier,* June 22, 1858; *Daily Picayune,* October 12, 1859; Richardson, *Urban Police,* 38–40.

25. *Bee,* April 2, 1861.

done as naturally as possible, and you see fellows fasten on their knives and pistols as coolly as if they were tying on a comforter or putting on a coat.

As I was going up stairs, after getting my ticket, and replying to the quiet request, "whether I would leave my arms," that I had none to leave, I was stopped and searched from head to foot by a policeman, who, I suppose, fancied it impossible that I should be altogether without arms. Notwithstanding all this care murders and duels are of weekly occurrence at these balls, and during my stay at New Orleans there were three. There are more murders here than in any other city in the union.[26]

The invention of the revolver and its circulation into widespread ownership provided Americans from the late 1830s onward with a lethal weapon well adapted to urban use. It was more reliable in wet weather than the flintlock; the percussion system of ignition was united in one mechanism with a rotating cylinder to permit five or six shots in rapid succession. The user was limited only by the speed with which he could cock the hammer and pull the trigger and his accuracy in aiming the piece. The device did have mechanical deficiencies. It was prone to accidental discharge and misfire, the crude sights allowed a large error in aiming, and the black powder that propelled the separate lead bullet corroded the chambers when the gun was left loaded for any length of time. Most models were, however, small enough to be concealed upon the person.[27]

26. Edward Sullivan, *Rambles and Scrambles in North and South America* (London, 1852), 223–25. Comparative generalizations about the level of violent crime in nineteenth-century America are necessarily somewhat tentative and conjectural because reliable statistical evidence from that period is sparse and very difficult to find. The available quantitative and literary evidence does suggests that New Orleans had a very high level of violent crime in the 1850s, however, probably more than any other large city in the United States. Among southern cities, the incidence of political violence was probably also high in Baltimore and Louisville. See Charles E. Deusner, "The Know Nothing Riots in Louisville," *Register of the Kentucky Historical Society*, LXI (1963), 122–47; Wallace S. Hutcheon, Jr., "The Louisville Riots of August, 1855," *Register of the Kentucky Historical Society*, LXIX (1971), 150–72; Jean H. Baker, *Ambivalent Americans: The Know Nothing Party in Maryland* (Baltimore, 1977).

27. For a discussion of revolvers, see Lee Kennett and James LaVerne Anderson, *The Gun in America: The Origins of a National Dilemma* (Westport, Conn., 1975), 89–90; Charles T. Haven and Frank A. Belden, *A History of the Colt Revolver and the Other Arms Made by Colt's Patent Fire Arms Manufacturing Company from 1836 to 1940* (New York, 1940), 17–82; Arcadi Gluckman, *United States Martial Pistols and Revolvers* (Harrisburg, Pa., 1960), 91–93, 153–210; Frederick Wilkinson, *Antique Firearms* (Garden City, N.Y., 1969), 180–88.

Regarding the custom of carrying weapons, see Dr. Thomas L. Nichols, *Forty Years of American Life* (2 vols.; London, 1864), I, 184–86; George Vandenhoff, *Leaves from an Actor's*

New Orleans policemen armed themselves with revolvers in the 1850s, in violation of the law and in response to the arming of the public. During the 1840s policemen armed only with spontoons or clubs had frequently confronted citizens carrying firearms. Officer James Norton of the First Municipality was shot to death in 1840 while attempting to execute a warrant, and in the scuffle his partner, Thomas McGovern, was stabbed several times. Eight years later policeman John Foster was found floating in the Claiborne Canal, dead of a gunshot wound received in the line of duty. Other police officers were shot but, like Thomas Hennessey in 1847, survived. Yet others, including Corporal Petard of the Third Municipality, were fired on without suffering wounds or death. Working under such conditions placed a considerable demand on policemen's courage. The temptation to look or run the other way when faced by armed opponents must have been strong. Some did resist the temptation. A night policeman named Kruse in 1840 interceded in a domestic quarrel to wrestle a gun away from an irate husband and was fortunate enough to avoid injury. In 1844 the captain of the guard in the Second Municipality, J. L. Winter, captured in a swamp outside of the city a murder suspect who was armed with "one of Colts revolving pistols."[28]

The burgeoning political conflict of the 1850s and the proliferation of revolvers in private ownership made it increasingly unrealistic for the public or the city's governors to expect the police to arm themselves less formidably than their opponents. In September, 1854, the *Daily True Delta* observed that "it is all nonsense to expect a police armed with batons only, to disperse mobs of ruffians conscious of impunity for their crimes, and

---

*Note-Book; with Reminiscences and Chit-Chat of the Green-Room and the Stage, in England and America* (New York, 1860), 206–207; Charles Mackay, *Life and Liberty in America; or, Sketches of a Tour in the United States and Canada, in 1857–8* (2 vols.; London, 1859), I, 173; Benwell, *An Englishman's Travels in America,* 113–16; Alex Mackay, *The Western World; or, Travels in the United States in 1846–47* (2 vols.; Philadelphia, 1849), II, 88–89; Whipple, *Bishop Whipple's Southern Diary,* 115; Tasistro, *Random Shots and Southern Breezes,* I, 229–30, II, 36–37; Bernhard, *Travels Through North America,* II, 61, 70–71; Ingraham, *The South-West,* I, 90, 208; Fearon, *Sketches of America,* 275.

28. *Bee,* December 25, 1840; Messages of the Mayors to the First Municipality Council, March 13, 1848; Charity Hospital Admission Books, April 5, 1847; Reports of the Day and Night Police of the Third Municipality, October 22–23, 1840 (Night Watch), November 21, 1849 (Day Police); *Daily Picayune,* May 26, 1851; Ordinances and Resolutions of the Third Municipality Council, August 11, 1851; Reports of the Day and Night Police of the Second Municipality, July 6, 1844 (Day Police).

armed to the teeth with murderous weapons." Mayor John Lewis addressed the Common Council the following month to request limited authority to arm the police: "The propriety, also, under certain exigencies, of arming the force merits due consideration; at present the law forbids their being armed. In cases like those which have recently occurred, it is hardly fair to require unarmed men to march up and quell a mob or riot, and be met by an array of deadly weapons in the hands of their opponents."[29]

But the police had already taken the matter into their own hands. At the trial of a policeman indicted for murder, Chief of Police William James testified that during the September, 1854, riots following the arrest of Henry Sherman, "it was usual for the police to carry arms. Witness [James] had several times given orders to the police to carry arms when sent on some special duty." The new practice took root despite its illegality. A policeman who carried a concealed weapon—and most apparently did conceal their guns, knives, and slungshots—broke the law just as surely as other citizens who did so, for the statute covering the offense exempted no one. The punishment for a first offense was lenient: until March, 1855, a maximum fine of fifty dollars and thereafter one month in jail or a maximum fine of five hundred dollars. In September, 1855, Mayor Lewis wrote to Chief of Police Alexander Moynan that "inasmuch as it is reported that members of the police department in this city are in the habit of carrying concealed weapons, and there being no law permitting them to do so, I direct that you issue peremptory orders, commanding a cessation of the practice in the department."[30]

This order proved ineffectual, and Lewis soon showed at least a partial change of heart. When he swore in special policemen for the municipal election in June, 1856, he advised them to arm themselves before reporting for duty at the polls. Despite its illegality, the revolver became a basic tool of the policeman's trade during the remainder of the decade. Knives and slungshots also found their way into the waistbands and pockets of some policemen. In 1854 a policeman was dismissed from the force for drawing

29. *Daily True Delta*, September 14, 1854; *Daily Picayune*, October 6, 1854.

30. *Daily Picayune*, September 17, 1855, October 13, 1854; *Louisiana Courier*, September 19, 1855; *Acts of Louisiana*, 1813, pp. 172–74, 1855, pp. 131, 146, 1858, pp. 32–33; *The Consolidation and Revision of the Statutes of the State, of a General Nature*, comp. Levi Pierce, Miles Taylor, and William W. King (New Orleans, 1852), 187. According to a Louisiana appellate decision in 1856, even partial concealment was illegal (*State v. J. T. Smith*, 11 Louisiana Annual Reports 633 [1856]).

a knife on his sergeant, and two others were brought up on charges for resorting to knives in 1856. When policeman W. Oscar Somers was murdered on his levee beat in 1860, his partner, Peter McMullen, testified that Somers carried a "Colt's five shooter" and a slungshot, the same armament borne by McMullen. "When the officers go upon the Levee," observed McMullen, "they have to be like arsenals."[31]

Police adoption of firearms led to accidents. Lacking any training in safety or marksmanship, members of the police force had no claim to technical mastery of their guns. In one instance, a police officer accidentally shot his partner in the head, killing him, when the two men broke into a room to make an arrest while carrying cocked revolvers. A former policeman who was sitting in a coffee house in November, 1859, lost his life when accidentally shot by a day police officer. Another policeman drew his revolver to stop a brawl and shot an innocent bystander by mistake. One unfortunate member of the river police patrol attempted to pull a gun from underneath a boat seat and fatally wounded himself when he caught the hammer on a projection and involuntarily discharged the piece.[32]

Deliberate misuse of firearms also became a serious problem. In 1854 policeman Michael Nugent dispatched a man he believed to be trifling with his wife by shooting him in the head. In that same year, one of the chief's special officers (special officers performed detective duties) drew his revolver on a militia captain without identifying himself as a policeman. The special officer lost his job but was subsequently reappointed to the force and came before the Board of Police again the following year for drawing a gun and threatening to shoot a butcher in one of the city's meat markets. He escaped punishment on the charge, but another policeman who drew his gun to settle a dispute was dismissed from the force. One policeman attempted to shoot his sergeant but was clubbed and sent to the hospital

---

31. *Bee*, June 3, 1856, October 12, 1860, January 17, 1861; *Daily True Delta*, June 28, 1860.

32. *Daily Picayune*, August 2, 1856; *Commercial Bulletin*, August 2, 1856; *Louisiana Courier*, June 12, 1856, June 7, 1859; Charity Hospital Admission Books, June 11, 1858.

The police manual issued in 1852 (and apparently never revised during the 1850s) offered only brief and vague guidance about the use of force and made no reference to the possibility that the police might employ firearms. It advised that the policeman "must never use his club, except in the most urgent case of self defence," and that when endeavoring to arrest or disperse rioters "force will not be resorted to until it become absolutely necessary, but when necessary must be exercised to the degree required" (*Rules and Regulations for the General Government of the Police Department of the City of New Orleans* [New Orleans 1852], 30, 48–49).

by the roundsman. Two officers were arrested in 1856 for beating and shooting at a citizen, but their poor marksmanship kept them from being charged with murder, manslaughter, or mayhem. During a gun battle between a policeman and a private citizen in Canal Street, the latter discharged five shots without harming his opponent, while the policeman fired two ineffectual shots before his revolver misfired and jammed.[33]

Mere possession of a revolver did not confer safety on the carrier. It put policemen on the same footing as a large segment of the public, who commonly carried deadly weapons. The custom was not new, but it posed even greater danger to life and health because of the increase in political and ethnic strife and the greater availability of efficient lethal weaponry. The state legislature in 1855 enacted a slightly stricter law against carrying concealed weapons. But in his report for 1856, the state attorney general observed that the number of crimes of violence was growing. In the four years 1857–1860, at least 225 criminal homicides were committed in New Orleans, an annual rate of about 35 per 100,000 of population. (In Philadelphia during the years 1853–1859, the homicide rate was 3.6 per 100,000, and in Boston it was about 7.5 during the years 1855–1859.) In the latter half of the 1850s, the attorney general complained about the crime in New Orleans, stating that the police force was ineffective, witnesses to crimes were frequently afraid to testify, too many people were exempted from jury service, jurors received no per diem compensation and were called for too many days of service, the recorders' courts failed to keep written records of testimony in preliminary hearings, and the district attorney's office was grossly undermanned and overworked. As a consequence, the criminal justice system was not very effective at catching or prosecuting murder suspects; of the murders committed during 1857–1859, only 21.5 percent were resolved by conviction on a charge of either murder or manslaughter.[34]

33. *Daily Picayune*, October 8, 13, 1854, October 18, 26, 1855, February 14, 28, 1856; *Bee*, March 18, 1856; *Daily Delta*, November 14, 1859; *Louisiana Courier*, November 9, 1858; Police Board Records, August 10, 1854, June 14, 1855; Record of Inquests and Views, Coroner's Office, 1844–90, microfilm, NOPL, IX, 664.

34. For the period 1892–1900, the homicide rate for New Orleans averaged 14 per 100,000 population, and for metropolitan New Orleans during the years 1965–72 it averaged about 13 per 100,000; *Annual Report of Board of Police Commissioners and Superintendent of Police*, 1892–1900; *New Orleans Police Department 1973 Annual Report* (Metairie, La., [1974?]); Roger Lane, *Violent Death in the City: Suicide, Accident, and Murder in Nineteenth-Century Philadelphia* (London, 1979), 71; Theodore N. Ferdinand, "The Criminal Patterns of Boston

The police suffered in this violent environment. At least seven police-men were murdered while on duty from 1854 through 1860. John and William Mocler died of wounds received in the election riots of March, 1854. John Dunn was stabbed to death at the polls the following year. In 1856 Alexander Algeo was shot in the head and died, leaving a widow and two children. When police officer Gustave Lafferanderie was stabbed to death in 1860, he also left a family without a breadwinner. W. Oscar Somers was murdered in May of the same year, and James McIntosh was killed in December.[35]

Over a period of four years, at least eight policemen received gunshot wounds which they survived. One of them was the same Gustave Laffer-anderie who would be killed in 1860; he was shot in the thigh in 1856 while wrestling a pistol away from a man he was attempting to arrest. Others encountered pistol-wielding assailants with less dire consequences, and still others were threatened with being shot. Knife-wielding assailants were also a danger. In the same four-year period, at least seven policemen were

---

Since 1849," *American Journal of Sociology,* LXXIII (1967), 89; First District Court, Parish of Orleans, Docket Books, 1857–59, Minute Books, 1857–59, NOPL; *Report of the Attorney General to the Legislature of the State of Louisiana,* 1854, pp. 1–3, 1856, pp. 3–5, 1857, pp. 6–11, 1858, pp. 3–7; *Annual Report of the Attorney General to the Legislature of the State of Louisiana,* 1855, pp. 4–7, 1859, pp. 4–5, 1860, p. 7, 1861, pp. 3–5, 11.

Another suggestive indicator of the incidence of violence in New Orleans can be found in arrest rates for assault and assault and battery. The annual arrest rate for these minor crimes of violence in Boston in 1856 was 84.2 per 10,000 population, whereas the annual rate for New Orleans for the years 1854–56 was more than twice as high at 194.4 per 10,000. Because the Boston police seem to have been more efficient and vigorous than the police in New Orleans, and because both private citizens and policemen in the Crescent City were more likely than Bostonians to treat assaults as affairs of honor to be settled privately without the intervention of the police and the courts, it is likely that the real differential in the rates of minor violence between the two cities was even greater than that indicated by the nominal arrest rates; for arrest data, see *Daily Picayune,* June 15, December 12, 15, 1854, January 7, February 24, March 18, April 22, May 12, 1855; Police Board Reports, May, 1855–January, 1856; and Lane, *Policing the City,* 230–31.

35. *Daily True Delta,* March 28, 1855; *Commercial Bulletin,* March 26, 27, 1856; *Louisiana Courier,* March 20, 1856, *Daily Picayune,* March 29, 1854, June 13, 1855; *Bee,* March 19, 1856, December 24, 1860, January 10, March 4, 25, 1861; Messages of the Mayors to the City Council, December 26, 1860; Record of Inquests, VIII, 171, 173, XII, 58, XVI, 137, 343; State v. Rosana Chilarri, First District Court, Docket Books, Case No. 15095, acquitted May 2, 1861; State v. John Mulholland and Peter McCabe, First District Court, Minute Books, Case No. 14535, sentenced December 24, 1860, to hang.

stabbed while on the job without fatal results. Many others were beaten in the course of their work. One former policeman narrowly escaped being hanged in revenge for an arrest he had made while on the force; a bystander intervened to rescue him from three assailants. An assault could be charged with indignity as well as danger, as one officer discovered when he became the target for "slops, urine and other filthy matter" thrown by five individuals while he stood on the corner of Julia and Levee streets.[36]

Some of the men who joined the police force brought with them a taste for violence that was fed by their work. Several policemen of the 1850s stood trial for murder. Antoine Cambre, a native of Plaquemines Parish and formerly a carpenter, was a Know-Nothing appointee in 1855. Cambre also worked as a ballroom watchman (a notorious occupation because ballrooms were linked to many illegal activities). In 1859 he shot and killed a German lamplighter whom he mistook for another man with whom he had a score to settle. He was subsequently convicted of murder and sentenced to death. Cambre cheated the hangman by dying of a fever in prison. He shared a cell with Eugene Adams, another former policeman, who had been convicted in the stabbing murder of one man not long after having shot another. Adams was rumored to be willing to offer evidence in another murder case but was soon thereafter found in his cell dead of poison.[37]

One of the most gruesome cases of the decade involved police officer Jean Gros. Gros slipped into the room in which his free quadroon mistress lay sleeping beside her six-year-old son and shot her through the head with his pistol. The result was, according to a newspaper account, that "one side of the head was blown off and the bed and wall bespattered with bone, hair and brains, while a stream of gore had run down upon the floor in pools." Gros escaped by cab and was presumed by the police to have left the city. Six months later, the murdered woman's mother noticed him sitting in a house as she walked past one Saturday evening. She turned her head away

36. Ordinances and Resolutions of the Common Council, No. 3338, April 9, 1857; Charity Hospital Admission Books, December 27, 1857, February 20, May 3, 1858, May 27, October 8, 23, 1859, May 29, June 4, 1860; *Daily True Delta*, April 24, 1855; *Daily Crescent*, November 8, 1859; *Daily Picayune*, August 24, October 25, 1855, June 15, 23, August 28, 1856, January 3, 1860; *Bee*, April 8, 9, June 3, 1856, July 27, 1857.

37. *Daily True Delta*, July 3, 1860; *Louisiana Courier*, April 10, 1859; *Bee*, June 21, August 8, 1860; Record of Inquests, XVI, 179; *State* v. *Antoine Cambre*, First District Court, Minute Books, Case No. 14369, sentenced July 2, 1860, to hang; *State* v. *Eugene Pepe alias Eugene Adams*, First District Court, Docket Books, Case No. 14066, sentenced June 14, 1860, to hang.

and walked to the corner, then ran to a police station. Three officers returned with her and made the arrest, but he was eventually released and the district attorney entered a *nolle prosequi* in the case.[38]

One of the most enduring men of violent appetite who served on the police force was Arthur Guerin, a native of New Orleans. He lost his job as a policeman in 1855 after knifing two men, and in the two months thereafter he was arrested once for stabbing a man, once for assaulting a girl, and once for shooting a man in the back. He managed to stay out of prison, however, and in subsequent years was acquitted of murder on three occasions. He died in a courtroom in 1871, shot to death by a deputy sheriff who claimed Guerin had menaced him. Another policeman came to grief in a courtroom in 1856. Nathaniel McCann, known as "Old Hardweather" to his compatriots, was dismissed from the force and sought out a recorder to plead for reinstatement. When the magistrate refused to hear the case any further, McCann shot him in the neck with a pistol, but a policeman seized the gun and clubbed McCann to the floor. Another particularly serious offender on the police force was John Poole. Poole struck a black man in 1853, and his victim fell into the water and drowned, resulting in a murder charge against Poole.[39]

Other policemen were prosecuted or at least arrested for serious crimes. A policeman who committed robbery was nearly charged with murder when his victim died soon after the robbery; the coroner ruled that pneumonia was the cause of death, so the policeman faced only a count of robbery. A former police lieutenant, who had once been shot by Eugene Adams, was himself arrested for shooting two men. In 1857 the chief of police and his special officers, acting on a tip, lay in wait outside the home of a widow in the fourth district, expecting a burglary. When four burglars appeared shortly after midnight, the police fired on the men, wounding one in the thigh. The others escaped, but the wounded man proved to be a member of the police force.[40]

38. *Bee*, April 23, 1860; Record of Inquests, XV, 386; *State v. Jean Gros*, First District Court, Minute Books, Case No. 14514, *nolle prosequi*, December 20, 1861.

39. *Daily Picayune*, December 24, 1849, October 16, 1853, October 12, 1855, February 17, 1856, August 26, 1871; *State v. Arthur Guerin*, First District Court, Docket Books, Case No. 12868, *nolle prosequi*, December 20, 1857. John Poole was acquitted of murder (*Annual Report of the Attorney General to the Legislature of the State of Louisiana*, 1855, p. 17).

40. *Louisiana Courier*, April 12, 1857; *Daily Picayune*, October 7, 1857; *Bee*, January 30, February 1, 1861.

Violent behavior characterized the lives of many policemen in a variety of other ways. In one instance, two policemen were arrested by their commanding officer for attempting to fight a duel. Another time, a police captain was accused of participating in a lynching in Biloxi, Mississippi. Leaving the police department did not end a man's violent behavior. Several former policemen were arrested in 1854 in a plot to drown an active member of the force. Others died in the streets or in coffee houses as participants in brawls and shooting affrays. Less severe episodes of violence were legion. In a sample of cases covering a twenty-one-month period during 1854–1856, the Board of Police adjudicated forty-three cases of assault, assault and battery, or brutality by policemen, dismissing thirteen of the accused from the force and penalizing nine others with fines or loss of rank. Almost certainly many instances of police misuse of force never eventuated in any formal charges, or went unreported.[41]

The problem of violence in New Orleans was multifaceted and complex, deriving from many sources. New Orleans was a large city—the most populous in the Deep South—and perhaps more ethnically diverse than any other in the United States (though certainly New York, St. Louis, and Milwaukee were also diverse). It was a major port with many trade relationships with Latin America and second only to New York as a port of entry for immigrants in the 1850s. It had a large transient population of sailors, boatmen, and commercial travelers, and once the danger of yellow fever in the late summer and early autumn was over, the city experienced a large seasonal influx of population, including many professional criminals. As a southern city, New Orleans had problems distinctive to the region. The institution of slavery helped brutalize the sensibilities of whites. Widely prevailing notions of masculine honor spurred gentlemen and workingmen alike to retributive acts of violence, in formal duels and informal brawls, whenever they perceived any slight or insult. Prickly personalities more readily indulged in bellicose behavior when or after visiting one of the city's thousands of saloons and coffee houses that dispensed alcoholic beverages. The large number of men who went about formidably armed made affrays more likely to result in deaths or serious injuries.[42]

41. Police Board Records, 1854–56; *Daily Crescent*, September 11, 1854, March 5, 1860; *Deutsche Zeitung*, May 5, 6, 1856; *Commercial Bulletin*, June 28, July 8, 1855; *Daily Picayune*, August 9, 10, 13, 15, 1850, February 2, August 2, October 18, 1854, September 13, 1855, July 25, 1856, February 13, 1858.

42. New Orleans had a relatively large concentration of white men in the high-crime-

To ameliorate the problem of violence to any substantial degree would have required state and municipal policies—and perhaps federal policies as well—for which there was not enough political or community support in the 1850s. Similarly, any realistic strategy to restrict or prohibit police use of arms would have necessitated a comparable policy to limit or prohibit ownership and carrying of firearms by all citizens, which was a political impossibility. With the exception of some decline in the level of political conflict, violence remained largely untouched by government policy in New Orleans in the late antebellum period.

The formal law and the public generally expected the police to catch criminals and suppress crime, to maintain order, and to render emergency aid to the victims of crime, accident, and misfortune. The crime-fighting role was perhaps the most dramatic of these—although maintaining order could sometimes become a spectacle—but most police work fell into the latter two categories. For a policeman to catch a criminal in the act was a rare and usually celebrated event. On one occasion, a policeman observed a black man stealing a thousand-dollar bill that had been dropped by a white man who was intoxicated and half asleep. The officer gave chase and after a long run captured the thief and restored the bank note to its owner. Long pursuits sometimes occurred, and New Orleans policemen made several arrests after tracking their prey to remote parts of Louisiana or, in one case, all the way to Illinois. Premeditated crimes were, however, very difficult to stop and their perpetrators very elusive. Policemen who succeeded in making arrests in such cases had to learn the skills of a detective, using informants, promising leniency for confessions, coercing and intimidating

---

age cohort of twenty to forty years who lived without the stabilizing and civilizing influence of wives and families. In the Crescent City in 1850 the number of white males twenty to forty years old per 100 white women in the same age bracket was 167 to 100, while the ratio was 93 men per 100 women in Philadelphia County (Pennsylvania), 92 per 100 in Suffolk County (the Massachusetts county consisting mostly of Boston), and 100 to 100 in New York County (which consisted almost entirely of New York City). By 1860, the disparity had diminished somewhat but still remained substantial: New Orleans had 113 men per 100 women, Philadelphia had 88 per 100, Suffolk County had 88 per 100, and New York had 89 per 100 (*Seventh Census*, 48, 88–90, 154–55, 466–67; *Population of the United States in 1860*, 188, 218, 322, 406).

On honor and violence, see Edward L. Ayers, *Vengeance and Justice: Crime and Punishment in the 19th-Century American South* (New York, 1984), esp. 9–33, 266–76; Bertram Wyatt-Brown, *Southern Honor: Ethics and Behavior in the Old South* (New York, 1982), esp. 350–401.

potential informants, and identifying the likeliest suspects from discernible patterns of criminal behavior.[43]

As maintainers of order, the police enforced a host of laws and ordinances proscribing public intoxication, disturbing the peace, vagrancy, and other minor offenses. They devoted considerably more time to this category of enforcement than to more serious crimes. Strikes, riots, traffic control, and Mardi Gras celebrations all fell within the police purview of keeping order. Riots were the most extreme form of disorder and often exposed the weaknesses in police training, organization, and discipline.[44]

A regionally distinctive example of the police responsibility for preserving order was the problem of slavery. Slaves had more laws to violate than did whites or free people of color, for they were forbidden to congregate in cabarets, buy liquor, gamble, walk the streets after curfew, rent rooms, or even move about without a pass. In addition to the normal police patrolling to curb such offenses, in one instance a police sergeant disguised himself as an African American to capture a cabaret keeper in the act of selling liquor to slaves. The fear of slave insurrection lay behind the plethora of legal restrictions on bondsmen, and the press was quick to congratulate policemen who claimed to have nipped an uprising in the bud.[45]

Maintaining the "moral" order of society (a nebulous notion) was also one of their tasks. The police made arrests for simple intoxication, gambling, prostitution, and circulation of "obscene and improper" publications. They even arrested women for wearing men's clothing. Enforcement of the laws against gambling and prostitution offered immense opportunity for malfeasance. The exact extent of clandestine corruption can only be a matter for conjecture, but the occasional scandals and grand jury reports of extensive networks of graft suggest that the problem was huge and remained largely unremedied.[46]

43. Police Board Records, November 29, 30, 1855; *Daily Picayune*, August 22, 1850, June 4, 13, September 6, 1855; *Louisiana Courier*, November 18, 1858; *Bee*, January 19, February 15, March 6, 1861.

44. *Daily Picayune*, April 13, 1852, August 1, 2, 1854; *Daily Crescent*, August 1, 1854; *Daily True Delta*, August 1, 1854; *Bee*, February 14, 1861.

45. *Daily Picayune*, June 16, 1853, October 30, November 1, 1855.

46. *Daily Picayune*, November 3, 1855, February 22, 24, March 11, July 30, 1856. Richard Tansey, "Prostitution and Politics in Antebellum New Orleans," *Southern Studies*, XVII (1980), 449–79, and Tansey, "Economic Expansion and Urban Disorder in Antebellum New Orleans," 37–79, describe the failure of efforts to curb prostitution in the late 1840s and 1850s, noting that politicians from the Democratic, Whig, and American parties permitted

The police also helped the needy. Policemen transported the sick and injured to Charity Hospital, attempted to prevent suicides, and responded to emergencies. In one instance, a police corporal pulled a drunken man from a rapidly filling gutter during a rainstorm, saving him from drowning. They were also called upon to succor lost children and find their families. The police played a major role as a primitive relief agency, sheltering the homeless in the city's jails, where men and women were lodged and fed (minimally) without charge or penalty and in large numbers during inclement weather.[47]

Although arrest data are notoriously biased and fragmentary indicators of police activity, a compilation of arrest reports from the 1850s suggests some of its dimensions (see Table 13). Most involved minor offenses related to maintaining order. Intoxication, disturbing the peace, vagrancy, suspicion, and minor assaults accounted for about two-thirds of all arrests, and arrests for slavery-related offenses constituted an additional one-eighth of the total. The gravest violations, murder and other serious violent crimes, were less than one-twentieth of all arrests and, when added to professional crimes for profit, barely exceeded one-tenth. In addition, a total of 2,505 persons, mostly overnight lodgers, received help from the police from November, 1853, through January, 1856. Most official police activity involved routine transactions.

If arrests had been equally shared among policemen, each man would have made about forty-seven per year in the mid-1850s. During the summer and early autumn the population of the city fell to its annual nadir, and arrests dropped accordingly. Few women were arrested except for gambling and prostitution. Females accounted for only 17.1 percent of all arrests, but they constituted 71.1 percent of those in the gambling-prostitution category—and almost all prostitution-related arrestees were women. In 1850–1851, 25.3 percent of those arrested in the First and Third municipalities were slaves or free persons of color, with slaves predominating over free blacks by slightly better than two to one. (African

---

brothels to operate largely unhindered. The Know-Nothings did try in 1857 to restrict prostitution to multiple-story bordellos because some of their constituents complained that single-story houses of prostitution were driving down property values, but even this restriction was quickly defeated by brothel managers and landlords.

47. *Daily Picayune*, August 24, September 7, 1850, January 13, August 17, November 29, 1855, March 13, 1856, June 9, 1858, January 1, 1860; *Bee*, January 3, 1861.

TABLE 13

Police Arrests, November, 1853–January, 1856

| Offense | % of Total Arrests | No. of Arrests |
|---|---|---|
| Intoxication and disturbing the peace | 39.3 | 19,363 |
| Vagrancy and suspicion | 17.8 | 8,786 |
| Assault and battery, other minor crimes of violence | 13.3 | 6,542 |
| Slavery-related offenses | 12.4 | 6,090 |
| Professional crimes for profit | 7.5 | 3,669 |
| Serious crimes of violence, excluding murder | 3.2 | 1,567 |
| Gambling and prostitution | 1.4 | 675 |
| Murder-related offenses | 0.3 | 124 |
| Other unclassified | 4.8 | 2,436 |
| Totals | 100.0 | 49,252 |

Sources: Daily Picayune, June 15, December 12, 15, 1854, January 7, February 24, March 18, April 22, May 12, 1855; Police Board Records.

Americans made up 30.8 percent of the 1850 population of these two districts.)[48]

Evidence regarding the nativity of arrestees in this period is very sparse. The federal census for 1850 included the inmates of the First Municipality jail: the Irish were highly overrepresented, natives slightly overrepresented, and immigrants other than Irish very underrepresented.[49]

48. Messages of the Mayors to the First Municipality Council, December 1, 1850, November 17, 1851; Messages of the Mayors to the Third Municipality Council, December 16, 1850. The percentage of arrestees who were black is a weighted average for two years of First Municipality data and one year for the Third Municipality, and the general population comparison percentage is also a weighted average. The arrest report of the Second Municipality police for the year ending June 30, 1851, did not include data about black arrestees (Bee, October 1, 1851).

The average number of arrests per policeman of 47 per year was neither very large nor small; in the years 1868–77, the average varied from as high as 62 to as low as 38; in the 1890s it ranged from a low of 67 to a high of 105; and in 1973, the average was 32 (Annual Report of the Board of Metropolitan Police to the Governor of Louisiana, 1868/69–1873/74; Annual Report of Board of Police Commissioners and Superintendent of Police, 1891–1900; New Orleans Police Department 1973 Annual Report.

49. Census of 1850, RG 29, NA. The jail population included 61.1 percent illiterates. It

Some arrests involved a highly controversial form of police activity—misconduct. When a police officer was accused of wrongdoing, his supervisors suspended him temporarily, and if the charge was serious, his case would be heard before the Board of Police during the years 1853–1856 or by the mayor in the other years of the period. The number of temporary suspensions was staggering, two or three per policeman each year, but between two-thirds and four-fifths of these suspensions did not lead to trial before the board. Yet even the minority of cases that came to trial revealed a glaring incidence of delinquency. During the year before the Know-Nothings came to power, more than one-fourth of the police force was dismissed for cause and one-sixth more received punishment by spending additional time under suspension before being reinstated.[50]

Derelictions of duty constituted the largest category of offenses. These included standing, sitting, lying down, or sleeping on the beat; drinking on the job; and other forms of neglect. This class of offenses also drew the second highest proportion of dismissals. Abuse of authority was the next most numerous category and included brutality, interference in elections, extortion, and other forms of misfeasance and malfeasance. Disruption of the chain of command was a distant third in numerical rank but was the type of offense most likely to result in dismissal from the force. It included disobedience, insubordination, improper treatment of patrolmen by supervisors, and intrapolice assaults. Incidents of misbehavior off duty (or "conduct unbecoming a police officer") were fewer than disruptions of the chain of command.[51]

---

may, however, have somewhat overrepresented the poor, who were less likely to make bail or be released on their own recognizance.

50. Dismissals from the force in the 1940s amounted to a mere 0.2 percent annually and in the years 1965–69 ran between 1.1 and 1.5 percent per annum. In the latter period, total complaints against policemen averaged one-third to one-half of one complaint per man annually, and not all complaints led to even temporary suspension (Police Board Records, 1854–56; Bruce Smith, *The New Orleans Police Survey* [New Orleans, 1946], 35; International Association of Chiefs of Police, Field Operations Division, *A Survey of the Police Department: New Orleans, Louisiana* [Gaithersburg, Md., 1971], 136; *Daily Picayune*, December 12, 1854).

51. Of the 672 cases adjudicated by the Board of Police between April, 1854, and February, 1856, 59.2 percent involved charges of dereliction of duty, 17.4 percent abuses of authority, 7.2 percent violations of the chain of command, and 5.5 percent conduct unbecoming a police officer; 1.2 percent were for other specified offenses and 9.5 percent for unspecified offenses. Charges of violating the chain of command led to dismissal from the force of 33.0 percent of the men charged, followed by dismissal of 30.8 percent of those

The records of police delinquency indicate that Irish policemen were substantially more likely to be brought before the Board of Police than were others. They were, however, slightly less likely to be dismissed from the force than other men on trial, both before and after the American party had consolidated its power over the police department in May, 1855.[52]

One source of problematic behavior was the city's failure to train its policemen. One police chief made a brief effort to offer guidance to his men. When Chief Stephen O'Leary's force went on duty for the first time in May, 1853, he lectured the men on the responsibilities of their job. O'Leary "explained what he conceived to be the best method of carrying" out the "minor details of police duties" and discouraged brutality and religious or national prejudices. Although the first manual for policemen was issued in 1852, no apparent effort was made to ensure that they were familiar with its contents.[53]

Most new appointees to the force first became supernumeraries. This was a probationary status; the supernumerary officers worked as substitutes for absentees among the regulars. These men were required to report for roll call daily but only occasionally got the chance to work. "In my present situation," wrote one supernumerary in the early 1860s, "I work only a few

---

charged with dereliction of duty, 21.6 percent of those accused of conduct unbecoming a police officer, and 18.4 percent of the men charged with abuses of authority (Police Board Records, 1854–56).

52. Irish policemen were overrepresented among those tried by the Board of Police, both before and after the Know-Nothings gained control of the board. During the period April, 1854–April, 1855, Irishmen held about 26 percent of police jobs but constituted approximately 40 percent of the accused; between May, 1855, and February, 1856, the Irish accounted for roughly 10 percent of the police force but about 21 percent of those tried by the board. But Irish policemen brought up on charges were somewhat less likely than other policemen to be dismissed from the force. Between April, 1854, and April, 1855, 35 percent of Irish policemen tried by the board were fired for cause, while 37 percent of other accused policemen were terminated; for the period May, 1855, to February, 1856, the dismissal rate for the accused Irish policemen was 14 percent, and for other policemen before the board on charges it was 22 percent. Thus, although the American party members of the board were evidently less willing to employ Irish or other immigrant officers, they do not appear to have judged accused Irish policemen more harshly than men from other ethnic backgrounds. The dismissal rates after the Know-Nothings gained control of the board were markedly lower than under the Democrats, suggesting that the Know-Nothing board was less likely than its Democratic predecessors to respond to complaints about police misconduct with the most severe administrative punishment of dismissal.

53. *Daily True Delta*, May 3, 1853.

days in the month and barely earn enough to get through life." Another wrote that "as a Supernumary I cannot gain a livelihood." Several men complained of their inability to earn enough to support their families. One man went so far as to assert that the "system of supernumeraries is a humbug, by reducing the men to the level of serfs."[54]

Policemen received no sick pay except by special dispensation of the Common Council, and they could not look forward to pensions. Turnover of personnel was high, ranging from 30 to 60 percent annually among the regulars, though by 1860–1861 the rate had dropped to 17 percent. Absenteeism was also high, running between 13 and 20 percent. Although many men served on the force for a short period, some persisted for years, often discontinuously, and so constituted a core of experienced veterans. They were probably the best policemen in some ways, but they also had the greatest opportunity to partake of graft. For most, policing was a short-term occupation. Untrained, they impressed their individuality on the beat in a highly informal, personalized style.[55]

Their economic status may also have had a significant influence on policemen's behavior. Most fell below the white population median in wealth and income but came from or soon achieved a status materially above the bottom rungs of the socioeconomic ladder. Patrolmen received a salary of $45 per month from 1852 to 1855 and $50 thereafter. The daily wage of $1.50 to $1.70 was more than the $1.00 to $1.50 earned by day laborers. Patrolmen's compensation was below that of carpenters, which was $2.30 and up, and longshoremen, who made between $2.50 and $3.00 per diem. Policemen were subject to less seasonal unemployment than day laborers and many skilled laborers, however, and had opportunities for

54. Applications for Positions as Police Officers, for A. Hoff, John Sass, Henry Hoff, Henry Parr, Joseph Nunnemacher, and George Washington Hopkins, RG 393, NA.

55. The turnover data do not include the change in personnel as a consequence of annual reappointments. These figures describe turnover only among the full-time policemen, not the supernumeraries. If supernumeraries were included, the turnover rates would be much higher. Supernumeraries are not included to allow comparison with the turnover rates of 1840–52, for which no information about supernumerary turnover was available (turnover calculated from Police Board Records, 1854–56, and Personnel Records of the Police Department, 1856–61, NOPL). Absenteeism in the 1940s was 4.5 percent, twice the average for police departments with strict medical discipline (absenteeism estimated from the Reports of the Third District Police, 1855–56 and 1860, NOPL, and for the 1940s see Smith, *New Orleans Police Survey*, 39).

illegal compensation through graft. Barring illness, injury, or a change in administration, their standard of living surpassed that of day laborers.[56]

Policemen were about as likely as any white adult male to own as much as $100 of personal property, but only a few owned real estate. Supervisory officers fared better than patrolmen: sergeants earned $55 to $58 per month, lieutenants $55 to $83, captains $75 to $100, and the chief $167. Several chiefs of police were modestly prosperous. The first chief of the period, John Youenes, was assessed for tax purposes on real estate worth $6,670 and two slaves valued at a total of $1,000. William James appeared in the tax books with $1,500 in real estate and one slave worth $600. Henry Forno, the chief who left the city during the Vigilance Committee crisis of 1858, owned real estate with a taxable value of $4,500 in 1852 and in 1856 held $1,500 plus slaves assessed at $1,000 altogether. He also owned a home outside the city that was not subject to municipal taxation. Other supervisory officers below the rank of chief also owned real estate.[57]

The case histories of a few men suggest that those with education tended to rise more than other men. Formal schooling was not, however, the surest route to upward mobility in the police department. Political favors and personal influence were extremely valuable in furthering a career. During the early 1860s, for example, several applicants for police jobs were endorsed by influential men under whom they had previously served,

56. Ordinances and Resolutions of the Common Council, No. 2100, April 5, 1855; *Daily Picayune*, May 14, 1852; *Daily True Delta*, August 1, 1854; *Statistical View of the United States*, 164.

57. In 1860, 35.3 percent of the police force owned as much as $100 in personal property, while 34.6 percent of a control sample of the white adult male population held at least that much personalty. But the mean value of the personal property of policemen was less than for the control sample—$400 for the former and $2,445 for the latter. Age was not the reason for the disparity, for an age-specific analysis shows lower values for policemen in every ten-year age bracket from twenty-one through seventy.

In 1850, 9.9 percent of policemen owned realty and in 1860, 8.7 percent; the control sample of white adult males revealed 10.0 percent to be owners of real estate in 1850 and 11.6 percent in 1860. But the mean values of realty for the police were lower than for the control sample—$2,149 for the police in 1850 and $11,143 for the control sample, and $1,427 for the police in 1860 compared with $8,792 for the control sample. An age-specific analysis shows that age differences did not cause the disparity between police and the control sample. The 1850 sample consisted of 3,232 white adult males drawn from the Census of 1850, RG 29, NA. The 1860 sample consisted of 4,566 white adult males drawn from the Census of 1860, RG 29, NA. Tax information came from Tax Registers and Ledgers, City of New Orleans, 1852–60, NOPL.

including former mayor Gerard Stith, former chief of police John Youenes, and businessman-politician Benjamin F. Flanders. Membership in a volunteer fire company could also boost a career. One police application included a recommendation from a city assessor, who asserted that the candidate's "appointment would be acceptable he having been a regular fireman of Louisiana Co. No. 10 in which company he became exempt after Seven or Eight years since." Further evidence of the value of belonging to a fire company can be found in a sample of the 1855 Know-Nothing appointees, at least 21 percent and perhaps considerably more of whom were members of fire companies.[58]

Politics clearly influenced the police department, but some people—perhaps many—were displeased by that influence. Civil service was not adopted in New Orleans until 1889, but even in the 1850s there was support for a nonpartisan merit principle. In 1854, Mayor John Lewis and Recorder H. M. Summers advocated hiring on merit. Mayor Charles Waterman offered a brief and ineffectual plea in 1856 for the eradication of the "political features" of the force. His successor, Gerard Stith, advanced a more forceful—though ineffectual—proposal for reform in 1858, arguing for the economic benefit of a nonpartisan police department: "If a law should be enacted by the Legislature making the tenure of office dependent

58. Applications for Positions as Police Officers, for Wendover and Smart, Anthony Vierira, Augustus Miller, and Jacob Lieser, RG 393, NA. Fire company sample information is derived from newspaper obituaries for former members of the Know-Nothing force. For an example of political influence on one policeman's career, see obituary for Patrick Creagh, *Daily Picayune*, November 14, 1903; Creagh left the police department after a short term of service and subsequently held a multitude of political offices. Formal education probably helped Thomas N. Boylan get a rapid start in his career as a policeman, and he eventually rose to become superintendent of police; see his obituary, *Daily Picayune*, May 20, 1902.

Although literacy was a nominal requirement to become a policeman, census records showed four illiterate men on the force in 1860 (about 1 percent of the force), and nine illiterates in 1850 (about 3 percent of the force). In 1841, 7 percent of the city guardsmen in the Third Municipality were unable to sign the payroll (Pay List of the Day Police, Night Watchmen, and Lamplighters). The actual number of functional illiterates was probably higher than any of these figures suggest. For policemen who could speak neither French nor English, see Police Board Records, August 23, 1855.

In 1850, 70.5 percent of the police force was 40 years of age or younger, while the mean and median ages were 34.6 years and 28.9 years, respectively. In 1860, 74.8 percent were 40 or younger, the mean age was 35.3, and the median was 32.9 (Censuses of 1850 and 1860, Orleans Parish). In 1970, 80 percent of the police were 40 or younger (International Association of Chiefs of Police, *Survey of the Police Department*).

on good behavior and peculiar efficiency, thus elevating the present mere temporary appointments into the dignity of a profession, and securing as officers only such as had proved to possess special qualifications for their duties, it might be possible to accomplish more good with a small police force." Making policemen independent of the results of municipal elections would, he advised, remove the incentive to favor members of their own party. Both the *Louisiana Courier*, a Democratic paper, and the moderately Know-Nothing *Daily Picayune* endorsed Stith's recommendation. Stith repeated this recommendation in 1859, but again to no avail.[59]

Reform proponents debated the most effective way to reduce partisan influence on the police. Calling the police department the most abused of municipal institutions, the *Daily True Delta* in 1859 branded both the mayoral and police board systems of control as failures. "Whatever party may possess the power, so long as it is deposited as at present, will prostitute it to its own advancement and perpetuation of its rule in office." Mayor Stith suggested electing a board of police commissioners composed of two persons from each ward. Noting that this inevitably meant two persons of the party then in power, the *Daily Delta* argued for a board of commissioners to be appointed by the governor or the legislature. Support for this proposal came also from the *Daily True Delta*, which stressed the success of the English system of commissioners appointed by the national government. The state legislature eventually produced a police reform bill that would create a board of commissioners, but not until January, 1862, and its effect was undercut by the Union occupation in April of that year.[60]

Their involvement in politics was not the only complaint about the police. The parish grand jury as well as several newspapers objected to their inefficiency and their entanglement in a web of corruption. In 1854 the grand jury found that there was "every reason to believe that there has been a general system of dishonesty and peculation carried on for some time past in the First District at least." Gambling dens and bordellos operated in defiance of the law and on such a large scale as to require police protection. Another common complaint against the police was simple inefficiency: they caught too few criminals. Also, some people found the

59. *Daily Picayune*, June 30, July 16, 1858; *Louisiana Courier*, June 20, 1858; *Message of Gerard Smith, Mayor of the City of New Orleans, to the Common Council* (New Orleans, 1858), 13.

60. *Daily True Delta*, November 1, 1859, February 15, 1860, January 19, 1862; *Daily Delta*, January 17, 19, 1860, January 18, 1862.

police to be uncooperative in working with other departments of city government.[61]

Reform efforts were largely ineffectual in this period. A minor reform, putting the police back into uniforms, seemed about to succeed in the middle of the decade. The ordinance that led to the reorganization of 1855 also authorized the mayor to provide uniforms for the force. After a considerable delay, the mayor ordered the chief of police to have the day force outfitted in a blue frock coat, with standing collar and metal buttons.[62]

The Common Council objected to the expense of the uniforms, said they were too conspicuous, and complained about purchasing city-owned uniforms for a force whose personnel changed frequently. The aldermen considered the crescent badge a sufficient symbol of police authority, but some of the men refused to display it. In other cities, especially New York and Philadelphia, policemen disliked wearing a uniform because, according to the New York correspondent for the New Orleans Bee, it was a "kind of dishonorable livery." Police resisted uniforms and even badges because an obvious and distinctive uniform would make shirking more difficult. Renewed attempts in the Crescent City to adopt a police uniform in 1858 and again in 1860 failed as well.[63]

A few minor reforms did occur in the late antebellum period. Chief Stephen O'Leary had begun a rogues' gallery of daguerreotypes of professional criminals as early as 1853, but the project withered without an appropriation of funds from the Common Council. When the council refused to authorize money for the purpose in 1858, Chief Thomas Adams began daguerreotyping prominent criminals at his own expense. The council finally funded the operation beginning in February, 1860. A few months later, the city completed and put into service a fire alarm and police telegraph system. It was more valuable to firefighting than policing because it merely allowed the several district stations to communicate directly with

61. Police Board Records, August 31, 1854, June 21, July 19, 1855, February 14, 1856; *Louisiana Courier*, May 7, 1857, May 30, 1858, November 2, 1859; *Daily True Delta*, April 4, 1855; *Daily Crescent*, March 24, 1854, October 31, 1859; *Daily Picayune*, February 4, April 30, 1854, March 30, 1855.

62. Journal of the Proceedings of the Board of Assistant Aldermen, NOPL, October 9, 1855; *Bee*, October 10, 1855; *Daily Picayune*, July 16, August 20, 1856.

63. Journal of the Proceedings of the Board of Assistant Aldermen, October 16, 1855; Messages of the Mayors to the City Council, June 26, October 2, 1860; *Bee*, October 20, 1853, October 24, 1855, March 27, June 27, 1856, June 27, 1860; *Commercial Bulletin*, July 8, 1858; *Daily Delta*, June 27, 1860; *Daily True Delta*, July 11, 1860.

one another and made no provision for emergency signals from citizens to police or from beat patrolmen to the stations.[64]

These small reforms did little to improve the quality of policing in New Orleans.[65] Ironically, the most popular reform of this period was achieved by the state legislature: the consolidation of the police forces of the three formerly independent municipalities and the city of Lafayette as part of the formal reunification and expansion of the city of New Orleans. But at the end of this period the police force satisfied only a narrow segment of the public—for the most part white nativists—and them only partially. Recruited from the ranks of the American party; commanded by stridently partisan politicians; subject to only intermittent supervision on the job; lacking training, sick pay, pensions, attractive salaries, compensation for experience, and a uniform to emphasize the official character of their role, the police continued to display an individualistic, partisan, and frequently abusive style of operation.

64. Ordinances of the Common Council, No. 4974, February 18, 1860; *Daily Crescent,* May 19, 1853; *Louisiana Courier,* November 13, 21, 1858; *Bee,* June 6, 1860; *Daily Picayune,* April 6, 1853; *Daily True Delta,* June 7, 1860.

65. Neither the Democrats nor the American party cared much about improving the condition of the city's jails. In 1854, the Orleans Parish Grand Jury complained that the Third District lockup was dilapidated and the prisoners needed blankets, the city surveyor reported that the principal police jail needed extensive repair, and the chief of police called the First District lockup a disgrace to the city. Two years later the mayor and chief of police both asserted that the Third District lockup was in poor condition (the chief said that "it would fall into the river if not repaired"), and the Grand Jury called it the "Black Hole of New Orleans." The Grand Jury also reported that both the boys' and girls' houses of refuge were old and unfit structures, that the main police jail was filthy and the prisoners were underfed, that the city workhouse was a fire hazard, and that the inmates of the parish prison were overcrowded and needed more food. The Second District lockup had cells exposed to the elements, and at least one prisoner died in the winter of 1860–61. When William Howard Russell visited the parish prison in 1861, he reported overcrowding, intermingling of serious and minor offenders, "wretched cells," and a "stench . . . so vile that I could not proceed further," and denounced the whole as "a disgraceful institution" (*Daily Picayune,* February 4, April 30, June 8, November 26, 1854, April 23, August 6, 1856, January 4, 1860; *Daily Crescent,* November 8, 1852; *Bee,* April 5, 1856; Russell, *My Diary North and South,* 245–48).

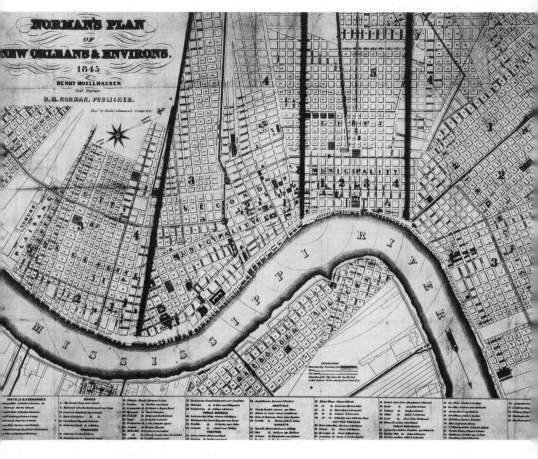

Norman's Plan of New Orleans and Environs, showing the
partitioned city in 1845

*Courtesy Historic New Orleans Collection, Museum/Research Center, Acc. No. 1949.7*

The urban frontier: New Orleans in the early nineteenth century

*Courtesy Louisiana Collection, Howard-Tilton Memorial Library, Tulane University*

Leonard Malone, whose police
career spanned half a century
*Courtesy Louisiana Collection, Howard-Tilton
Memorial Library, Tulane University*

Henry K. Nixon, who first joined
the police force in the 1850s
*Courtesy Louisiana Collection, Howard-Tilton
Memorial Library, Tulane University*

Sketch of a black Metropolitan policeman of the 1870s, published in *Scribner's Monthly* in December, 1873

*Courtesy Historic New Orleans Collection, Museum/Research Center, Acc. No. 1974.25.25.181*

The Reconstruction-era Metropolitan Police badge, which departed from the traditional crescent shape

*Courtesy Historic New Orleans Collection, Museum/Research Center, Acc. No. 1959.38.2*

Michael P. Creagh, whose father, Patrick, started a political career as a policeman in the 1850s

*Courtesy Louisiana Collection, Howard-Tilton Memorial Library, Tulane University*

Dexter S. Gaster, who began his career on the Reconstruction-era Metropolitan Police force

*Courtesy Louisiana Collection, Howard-Tilton Memorial Library, Tulane University*

David C. Hennessy, whose assassination led to a mass lynching of
Italian-Americans

*Courtesy Louisiana Collection, Howard-Tilton
Memorial Library, Tulane University*

The rapid-response patrol wagon of the late nineteenth century

*Courtesy Historic New Orleans Collection, Museum/Research Center, Acc. No. 1974.25.3.238*

The policeman as public servant

Members of the dwindling contingent of black policemen at the end of the
nineteenth century: (from top left) Benjamin J. Blair, George Doyle,
Henry Labeaud, William H. Robinson, George St. Avide, and Louis J. Therence

*Courtesy Louisiana Collection, Howard-Tilton Memorial Library, Tulane University*

# 4

# THE SHOCK OF CHANGE
## War, Occupation, and Early Reconstruction, 1861–1868

H ATH not the morning dawned with added light?" wrote the South Carolina poet Henry Timrod to celebrate the creation of the Confederate government at Montgomery, Alabama, in February, 1861. Many proslavery whites in New Orleans (though not all) shared in the joy of this "Ethnogenesis," as Timrod called it. Louisiana adopted a secession ordinance effective January 27, 1861, and transferred the military force of the state to the Confederate government on March 15, thereby giving the Confederacy its financial capital, its most populous city (the sixth largest in the United States, with a population of 169,000 in 1860), and its premier port (New Orleans exported more of "the snow of southern summers" than any other city in the South).[1]

The Civil War marked the beginning of a decade and a half of national attention to the Crescent City. After a year under Confederate rule, the city was occupied by federal troops and administered by a military government from May, 1862, to April, 1866. During 1866 and early 1867, white conservative Democrats regained control of the city government, and their police force joined in a murderous attack on black and white Republicans who were attempting to reconvene a state constitutional convention at the Mechanics' Institute in 1866. This violent episode helped persuade Congress to adopt military Reconstruction, which in turn led to a mandate from the military government of Louisiana compelling the New Orleans municipal government to replace many former Confederates on the police force with white Union army veterans and some black men. In 1868 the

1. Henry Timrod, "Ethnogenesis," in *The Literature of the South*, ed. Richmond Croom Beatty, Thomas Daniel Young, and Floyd C. Watkins (Glenview, Ill., 1968), 291–94 ("the snow of southern summers" was Timrod's metaphor for cotton); *Acts of Louisiana*, 1861, p. 113; *Population of the United States in 1860*, 195.

Republicans created a metropolitan police system run by a commission of the state government. The Republicans held power at the state level, so the Democratic municipal authorities were effectively excluded from control of the police. For a time, at least, black New Orleanians rather than racist whites had reason to hope that "the morning dawned with added light."

In the patriotic fever of spring, 1861, many New Orleans policemen prepared to march off to war. Policemen were not the most eligible group of volunteers; few were under twenty-five years of age, most had dependents to support, and their salaries were larger than those of most soldiers. Nonetheless, from the early months of 1861 several high-ranking policemen volunteered as commissioned officers and others enlisted in the ranks of the Confederate army. The men who stayed behind were promoted more readily than ever before. Most of the police appear to have supported the Confederacy. In October, 1861, Chief of Police John McClelland returned to New Orleans from a tour of the front in Kentucky and Tennessee, bringing with him letters from the volunteers and affirming the connection between the city and its troops hundreds of miles away.[2]

While the Confederates ruled New Orleans a major police role was to suppress disloyalty to the Confederacy. Shortly after the bombardment of Fort Sumter in April, 1861, Judge Philip H. Morgan of the Second District Court in New Orleans spoke at a mass rally at the Henry Clay statue on Canal Street, opposing the resort to force against the Union, and the crowd burned an effigy of Morgan bearing a placard labeling the straw man "P. H. Morgan—Traitor." This act proved indicative of the hostility that would face Unionists—real or suspected—in Confederate New Orleans. William Howard Russell, the English journalist who visited New Orleans early in the Confederate administration, reported that many British subjects in the city were forcibly conscripted into nominally volunteer Confederate military units and that the police arrested many people on charges of abolitionism merely for predicting northern victory. The assistant to New York–born dentist Anthony P. Dostie was arrested for asserting that President Abraham Lincoln would cut the levee at New Orleans if necessary to pre-

2. *Daily True Delta*, January 18, 1861; *Daily Delta*, April 28, 1861; *Bee*, June 21, 1861; *Daily Picayune*, October 1, 1861. Personnel Records of the Police Department, 1860–61, show numerous leaves of absence granted to policemen who went into military service.

serve the Union. Dostie was pressured to swear an oath of allegiance to the Confederacy in August, 1861, but this outspoken Unionist refused to take the oath and demanded and received a pass to depart the Confederacy. Some prominent men who hid their pro-Union sentiment managed to survive, but even failure to exhibit sufficient zeal for the secessionists' cause could mark one as a public enemy. Benjamin F. Flanders, a New Hampshire native and well-known New Orleans businessman for years, was expelled from the city despite his efforts to be discreet about his Unionist sympathies.[3]

The experiences of Flanders, Dostie, and Russell suggest that natives of the northern states or foreign countries were especially likely to be suspected of disloyalty to the Confederacy. A New York businessman was arrested as a possible spy in November, 1861, and an Irishman who made his home in New Jersey was arrested for expressing hostility to the Confederate States in March, 1862. A Unionist woman who struggled to restrain herself from voicing anti-Confederate feelings reported in her diary in October, 1861, that the "property of all Northerners and Unionists is to be sequestrated" and in January, 1862, noted that the "city authorities have been searching houses for firearms. It is a good way to get more guns, and the houses of those men suspected of being Unionists were searched first." On the floor of the Confederate Congress, Louisiana representative Charles M. Conrad proclaimed that there "were traitors in every State; in his own State there were, some of the biggest traitors in the land, and would be a disgrace to any nation. He alluded particularly to New Orleans. He was proud to say that in few instances were they natives of the State. They were of the nations of the North, of Europe, and of that fraternity of Germans who have never sympathized with us, and who are not only disloyal in sentiment, but traitors in conduct."[4]

Anyone, of whatever birthplace or social prominence, who publicly ex-

3. James Morris Morgan, *Recollections of a Rebel Reefer* (London, 1917), 40; Russell, *My Diary North and South*, 239, 250; Emily Hazen Reed, *Life of A. P. Dostie; or, The Conflict in New Orleans* (New York, 1868), 24, 28–29; George S. Denison to Salmon P. Chase, June 28, 1862, in *Annual Report of the American Historical Association for the Year 1902* (Washington, D.C., 1903), II, 307.

4. *Daily True Delta*, November 13, 1861, March 27, 1862; George W. Cable, ed., *Famous Adventures and Prison Escapes of the Civil War* (New York, 1893), 13, 15–16; "Proceedings of the Second Confederate Congress," *Southern Historical Society Papers* [First Session, House], LI (Richmond, 1958), 121.

pressed approval of the Union or disapproval of the Confederacy or its peculiar institution could expect to be denounced and arrested. Thus the police arrested a man who compared Lincoln favorably with Jesus, another for voicing sympathy for the North, one for alleged abolitionism, another for criticizing secession, and yet more whose offenses were reported by the newspapers simply as using treasonous or seditious language. Those convicted of sedition could expect to serve six months' imprisonment in the workhouse.[5]

The prospect of imminent invasion in the early months of 1862 placed a heavy strain on the city authorities. On February 20 the mayor and council created a Committee on Public Safety, whose sixty-plus members included two former mayors and a former police chief, to coordinate the efforts of the municipal government to defend the city with those of the state and Confederate governments. The Confederate military commander in New Orleans, Major General Mansfield Lovell, placed the city under martial law on March 15 and issued an order requiring all white males (except foreigners who were not naturalized) to take the oath of allegiance to the Confederacy or to leave the parish of Orleans. Mayor John Monroe canceled the celebration of Mardi Gras, and military patrols assisted the police in arresting merchants who sold liquor after 8:00 P.M., or kept other businesses open after hours, or violated the price limits set by the provost marshal. Even the chief of police ran afoul of martial law; he was arrested for interfering with an officer of the Second District provost marshal who was making an arrest for illegal liquor sales.[6]

Policemen faced the prospect of taking an active role in the shooting war when Governor Thomas Moore placed the 1st and 2d brigades of Louisiana Volunteers on alert to take the field on twenty-four hours' notice. According to Mayor Monroe, these brigades included "some fifty or more Police officers, who are not only willing but anxious to throw themselves

5. *Daily Picayune*, September 27, 1861; *Daily True Delta*, November 6, 1861; Reports of the Third District Police, March 7, 1862 (Night Watch).

6. *The War of the Rebellion: A Compilation of the Official Records of the Union and Confederate Armies* (130 vols.; Washington, D.C., 1880–1901), Ser. III, Vol. II, 728–29; John David Winters, Jr., "Confederate New Orleans" (Master's thesis, Louisiana State University, 1947), 122; *Daily True Delta*, March 5, 27, 29, 30, April 1, 1862; *Daily Delta*, March 30, 1862. See also Kenneth Radley, *Rebel Watchdog: The Confederate States Army Provost Guard* (Baton Rouge, 1989), 83, 190–92; William H. Robinson, *Justice in Grey: A History of the Justice System of the Confederate States of America* (Cambridge, Mass., 1941), 383–419, esp. 393–94.

into the breach, so to speak, and strike a blow in defence of the country, the State, the City, and their families." One of these policemen suggested that if they were called into service, their places on the force should be filled by men too old or unfit for the military.[7]

These ardent would-be soldiers never had to "throw themselves into the breach." The worst fears of Confederate New Orleanians were soon realized, though, when a federal naval task force commanded by Commodore David G. Farragut fought its way past the downriver forts, anchored in front of the city, and demanded the surrender of New Orleans to the Union. During the unsettled transition period after Farragut's arrival in late April, reinforcements temporarily expanded the police force by about one-third. The police were ably assisted by Paul Juge's European Brigade, composed of foreign nationals and including the staff members of the foreign consulates in New Orleans. Despite a food panic and apprehension over the federal occupation, the European Brigade and the police managed fairly well to keep peace in the city.[8]

A few days after Farragut's fleet arrived, ground forces under the command of General Benjamin F. Butler occupied the city, and Butler served as the head of military government in New Orleans until relieved of command in December, 1862. Among his first efforts to impose strict discipline was the prosecution and execution of William Mumford, who had defied Union authority by hauling down the U.S. flag raised over the Mint by Farragut's men. General Butler quickly closed down several newspapers for printing stories that offered support or even hope for the Confederate cause, forbade the city's churches to observe a day of fasting and prayer called for by Confederate president Jefferson Davis, and ordered that women showing disrespect to Union forces be treated as prostitutes. Several store owners were fined by Butler for failing to keep their shops open as ordered, and assemblies in the street were limited by his order to no more than three people. Dozens of New Orleanians were arrested and jailed for demonstrating opposition or animosity toward Union authorities, including Mayor John Monroe, former U.S. senator Pierre Soulé, and Eugenia Levy Phillips (she was alleged to have laughed at a public funeral

7. Messages of the Mayors to the City Council, February 25, 1862; *Daily Delta*, March 2, 1862.

8. Messages of the Mayors to the City Council, April 30, May 6, 1862; *Daily Delta*, April 27, 29, May 1, 2, 1862; *Daily Picayune*, May 15, 1862; Gerald M. Capers, Jr., *Occupied City: New Orleans Under the Federals, 1862–1865* (Lexington, Ky., 1965), 25–53.

procession for a deceased Union officer). Butler ordered the police to conduct a meticulous registration of all the people in every household in the city, indicating who had sworn loyalty to the Union and who had not, and to confiscate all firearms in private hands; any policeman failing in the former duty was to be fined and dismissed from the force.[9]

Early in his administration Butler took steps to ensure that the municipal police would be loyal to the Union. Captain Jonas French of the U.S. Army assumed the duties of chief of police, and on May 22 he visited the district stations to inform the policemen that they would have to swear an oath of allegiance to the United States to retain their positions on the force. One newspaper report suggested that many of the men feared that refusal to take the oath might lead to imprisonment as well as loss of employment, yet when faced with the choice, only eleven policemen swore allegiance. Loyalty to the Confederacy may have inspired much of this adamancy, but fear of reprisal by Confederate sympathizers probably also deterred men from taking the oath to the Union. As one police officer wrote in a letter to French on the day following his speeches to the force, "There was at least three fourths of these policemen ready to swere to be good and loyal citizen to the united states only for fear of the slung shot bowing knife and revolver that they would catch it in the dark."[10]

French dismissed the vast majority of the force, and while a new group of policemen was being organized, Union soldiers patrolled the streets. Federal troops under a provost marshal augmented the civil police until 1866. Although French was chief of the civilian force, Lieutenant Boyd Robinson of the First District performed much of the active work of command. Robinson was a native of New York but a longtime resident of New Orleans, having served on the police much of the time since 1839.[11]

9. Marion Southwood, *"Beauty and Booty," the Watchword of New Orleans* (New York, 1867), 21, 34, 44, 49, 50–51, 53–56, 63–64, 70, 120–22, 148–52, 184–85, 223; Winters, "Confederate New Orleans," 121–32; Capers, *Occupied City*, 54–97, 176–90; David T. Morgan, "Eugenia Levy Phillips: The Civil War Experiences of a Southern Jewish Woman," in *Jews of the South*, ed. Samuel Proctor and Louis Schmier with Malcolm Stern (Macon, Ga., 1984), 95–106. See also Joy J. Jackson, "Keeping Law and Order in New Orleans Under General Butler, 1862," *Louisiana History*, XXXIV (1993), 51–67.

10. Applications for Positions as Police Officers, 1862–65, for P. S. Nugent, RG 393, NA; *Daily True Delta*, May 22, 23, 1862; *Daily Picayune*, May 24, 31, June 1, 1862.

11. *House Reports*, 39th Cong., 2nd Sess., No. 16, pp. 105–108; Gilles Vandal, "The New Orleans Riot of 1866: The Anatomy of a Tragedy" (Ph.D. dissertation, College of William and Mary, 1978), 2–3.

Applications for the Unionist police poured in during the next few weeks, quickly exceeding a thousand despite the stigma of the turncoat. Unemployment in the city's depressed economy clearly stimulated recruiting. Many of the applicants cited financial distress as a motive and presumably a qualification for police service. One carpenter remarked on the nearly total cessation of business since the Union assault on the forts below the city before the occupation, resulting in his "great Distress and want at present," with "a Wife and Small family to Support." Another applicant claimed that a job on the police force "would save my poor helpless Familie from Starvation." Some men sought preferment on such grounds as old age, illness, or physical disability, apparently implying that police jobs should constitute a form of poor relief. "Being now an aged man," wrote one unfortunate fellow in his application, "I would solicit your generous aid, in procuring for me a place in the Police force or other occupation suitable for my age." Two other men classified themselves as "hardly fit to do any hard work."[12]

Despite the superannuated and infirm supplicants among the job seekers, the Union administration had good material from which to select the new police force. Some of the new applicants had valuable experience in military service or police work elsewhere than New Orleans. Three had formerly been British policemen, one a deputy U.S. marshal, one a Danish policeman, one a Texas Ranger, one a New York City policeman, and one a penitentiary guard. Twenty-two were veterans of the U.S. Army, three had seen service in the navy, one had been a marine, and one had served aboard a revenue cutter. Eight more had served in a German or French army. Fifteen were members of the European Brigade, which had helped secure the peaceful transition from Confederate to Union control. Two of the men seeking places on the detachment of river police cited experience as seamen.[13]

A prerequisite for establishing an applicant's character in the eyes of the Union administration was to demonstrate adherence to the Union cause. Because most of the police hopefuls had been living in a Confederate jurisdiction, proof of disloyalty to the Confederacy was an excellent reference. Thus one man claimed to have been summoned by Confederate

12. Applications for Positions as Police Officers for Ubrick Z. McKay, Joseph Heid, Patrick Tobin, William Daffenbach, and M. A. Huoty, RG 393, NA.

13. *Ibid.*

authorities three times for nonattendance at militia drill. Two applicants were self-proclaimed deserters from the Confederate army, and another avowed that he had led an entire company of eighty Confederate conscripts to enlist in the European Brigade. Two other men established their good faith by alleging that the Confederate authorities had imprisoned them for having expressed Unionist sentiments. Despite vigorous efforts to employ only loyal men, some covert Confederates and opportunists probably secured positions on the force.[14]

Evidence of disloyalty within the police department surfaced in the latter part of 1862. Three policemen accused Lieutenant Henry White of the Third District of subversive attitudes and other misconduct. White had been a policeman in New Orleans on and off since 1851. According to one of his accusers, he had declared when Union forces arrived that "it was a shame for the people of New Orleans he dont shot the God d—— son of the b——s Yankees." All of White's accusers alleged that he had recruited men onto the force who had never taken the oath of allegiance to the United States. Other charges against him included accepting a bribe and arbitrarily firing policemen under his command to open places for his friends. There is no apparent record of the resolution of White's case, but the incident suggests the difficulties inherent in purging the police department of Confederate sympathizers. As one man commented about a group of police candidates, there were "many very bad men who have the highest recommendations from *secesh*." [15]

The Union administration viewed with suspicion any organization that might harbor die-hard Confederate activists. One of the first acts of the occupation authorities in May, 1862, was to investigate the political sentiments of the city's volunteer fire companies. Of twenty-four companies, eleven were characterized by investigators as predominantly Confederate in sympathy and others partially so. One Union supporter in New Orleans wrote to Secretary of the Treasury Salmon P. Chase in June, 1862, that many middle- and working-class Unionists in the city were "afraid to come out openly for fear that even a temporary reverse to our arms might lead

14. Applications for Positions as Police Officers for James Geoghigan, Martin Duevel, C. H. Lea, George Fehn, Samuel H. Moreland, and John Rayne.

15. Applications for Positions as Police Officers for Harry White, Henry W. Bateman, Stephen Spellman, and Charles Duncan.

to a general massacre, especially the Germans, who are bitterly hated for their Unionism and their innate aversion to slavery."[16]

When General Nathaniel P. Banks took over command from Butler on December 14, 1862, the new administration was less firm in reining in Confederate sentiment. Shortly after assuming command, Banks released more than one hundred of the people jailed by Butler for disloyalty. A Treasury Department employee reported to Secretary Chase that "this is less a Union City now than when Gen. Banks came here. There is more manifestation of disloyalty" because "insufficient punishment follows offenses." The provost judge "is a mistake," for when a Confederate sympathizer "throws up his hat and hurrahs for Jeff. Davis in the street, Judge P[eabody] fines him five dollars. . . . Butler would have sent the offender to Ft. Jackson and neither he nor any acquaintance of his, would have committed the offense again." Banks imposed stricter controls beginning in late April, 1863, when he ordered all registered enemies to leave the Department of the Gulf within fifteen days and all persons remaining to take the oath of allegiance. Worried about political opinion in the 140 private schools patronized by Confederate sympathizers who had boycotted the public schools run under federal authority, Banks had the private schools investigated and discovered that many of them did not teach loyalty to the United States. In July, 1863, Banks banned all public assemblies except for religious worship supervised by a "commissioned priest" and ordered that all club rooms and gambling houses be closed. The police lieutenant of the Second District recommended that Chief French appoint a police officer to infiltrate the ranks of the Free Masons to ferret out rebel subversives. "I am informed," the lieutenant reported, "that there is something wrong going on in some of the lodges of the Free Masons, some plots or other against the United States." Observing that his nominee for the post of undercover agent was a Mason, the lieutenant closed with the ominous observation that "we must acknowledge there is many traitors among free Masons."[17]

16. Letters Received by the Chief of Police, Reports from Lieutenants Boyd Robinson, W. D. Miller, Henry White, and James Duane, Part IV, No. 1667, RG 393, NA; Max F. Bonzano to Salmon P. Chase, June, 1862, in Peyton McCrary, *Abraham Lincoln and Reconstruction: The Louisiana Experiment* (Princeton, 1978), 96.

17. Letters Received by the Provost Marshal, General Orders No. 18, 20, and 21 (July 3, 4, and 6, 1863), Part I, No. 1884, RG 393, NA; Applications for Positions as Police Officers, Lieutenant O. Bertin to Chief French; George S. Denison to Salmon P. Chase, February 26,

Anyone caught with tangible evidence of Confederate sympathy faced arrest, as one man discovered in May, 1863, when police arrested him for possession of two handkerchiefs with Confederate flags embroidered on them. A similar fate befell New Orleans artist J. E. Mondelli, who was arrested for painting a portrait of General Stonewall Jackson. Any hint of disrespect for the U.S. flag invited trouble as well, and businessmen were cautioned by the occupation authorities not to attach advertisements to the American flags flying from their establishments.[18]

Federal authorities in New Orleans not only had to install a politically reliable police force and maintain a secure hold on the city for the Union but also had to cope with changes in race relations. New Orleans was one of the areas not encompassed by the Second Confiscation Act of 1862 or the Emancipation Proclamation of January 1, 1863, inasmuch as it was already held by Union forces. Even though slavery remained legally intact until late 1863, black refugees from the countryside began arriving by the thousands, posing a major problem for public order. Fugitive slaves could legally be seized and restored to their owners, though Union officers so frequently declined to do so that noncompliance soon became the norm. Still, life for fugitive slaves was usually precarious. Many lived in squalid and pestilential "contraband" camps, often performing arduous labor for the government. In October, 1862, federal authorities began setting refugees to work on abandoned plantations. Black people in New Orleans were soon obliged to carry passes from their employers or the provost marshal. Those without passes were routinely dragooned into plantation labor— even some who were long-standing residents of the city.[19]

Black Orleanians, whether old residents or recent arrivals, often found themselves at odds with whites. Several times during the summer of 1862, groups of fugitive slaves fought with the police to retain their *de facto* freedom, for the police still captured, punished, and returned slaves to their masters. White citizens feared that the slaves would commit crimes, es-

1863, in *Annual Report of the American Historical Association for the Year 1902*, 362; Capers, *Occupied City*, 105–11, 188–89.

18. *Daily Picayune*, May 6, 1863; Mark E. Neely, Jr., Harold Holzer, and Gabor S. Boritt, *The Confederate Image: Prints of the Lost Cause* (Chapel Hill, 1987), 3; Letters Received by the Provost Marshal, Special Orders Extract, November 21, 1863, Part I, No. 1884.

19. John W. Blassingame, *Black New Orleans, 1860–1880* (Chicago, 1973), 25–32; Kate Mason Rowland and Mrs. Morris L. Croxall, eds., *The Journal of Julia LeGrand, New Orleans, 1862–1863* (Richmond, 1911), 206.

pecially rebellion. One schoolgirl confided her anxiety to her diary in May, 1862: "I fear more from the negroes than Yankees and an insurrection is my continual horror." Another white resident, Julia LeGrand, commented in December of the same year that rumors abounded of an impending insurrection. LeGrand noted soon afterward that there was chronic inter-racial conflict, sometimes involving black soldiers. "Even the Yankee police hate them," she wrote of the black population. An Irishman swore to a visiting English businessman that "thim d—— niggers will starve a poor white man out of house and home, if they sits them free, and be d——d to them." Similar hostility emerged in a court case in June, 1863. When a deputy constable referred to a slave woman in court as a "lady," one of the attorneys present protested his language. A "nigger," he said, ought not to be called a "lady."[20]

Slavery lost its legal foundation in October, 1863, as the result of a state court ruling. In December, General Banks recommended the removal by January 1, 1864, of all signs referring to slave sales, and he suspended slavery by military order on January 11, 1864. His initiative was confirmed by the state constitutional convention of that year and by the adoption of the Thirteenth Amendment in 1865.[21]

Though challenged by the difficulties inherent in occupying a hostile city, Union authorities were fairly successful in pacifying and managing New Orleans. Even the last Confederate chief of police, John McClelland, acknowledged the "kind treatment" and "sympathy" accorded him by Chief French. Policemen continued to be accused of wrongdoing, and some were dismissed from office, but delinquency was probably less frequent than it had been in the 1850s. Turnover of personnel hovered at levels comparable to those of the previous decade. The police force certainly worked at least as effectively as before the war.[22]

Other components of the federal administration in New Orleans ac-

20. Blassingame, *Black New Orleans*, 26–28, 31; Rowland and Croxall, eds., *Journal of Julia LeGrand*, 94; W. C. Corsan, *Two Months in the Confederate States, Including a Visit to New Orleans Under the Domination of General Butler* (London, 1863), 32; *Daily Picayune*, June 7, 1863.

21. Blassingame, *Black New Orleans*, 33; Vandal, "New Orleans Riot of 1866," 6–7; Capers, *Occupied City*, 223–24.

22. Orders and Circulars Issued by the Chief of Police at New Orleans, Circular to Lieutenants of Police (March 14, 1863) and General Order No. 6 (May 15, 1863), Part IV, No. 1669, RG 393, NA; Applications for Positions as Police Officers, John McClelland; turnover calculated from Personnel Records of the Police Department, 1862–65.

quitted themselves less favorably. A presidential investigative commission uncovered corruption reaching the highest levels, including the commanding general for New Orleans and the Department of the Gulf, Major General Stephen A. Hurlburt (who had succeeded Banks on September 23, 1864); the provost marshal general, Colonel Harrai Robinson; the assistant quartermaster, Captain Mahler; and A. A. Attacha, the provost judge. Under Attacha, the provost court handed down wildly disparate and inequitable punishments: six months in prison for murder, fifteen years for drunk and disorderly conduct, life imprisonment for larceny.[23]

A change in the city administration near the end of the war brought some turbulence in the police department. The last of the military mayors, the Irish-born former editor of the *True Delta*, Dr. Hugh Kennedy, was appointed to office in March, 1865, by Governor James M. Wells. In an attempt to strengthen the political power base of Governor Wells, Mayor Kennedy dismissed three police lieutenants, including Boyd Robinson, vaguely alleging that they were unfit for office. The total strength of the force was reduced from 450 to 400 men, and at least two dozen of the remaining policemen were dismissed to make room for Kennedy appointees. On the recommendation of the governor, Mayor Kennedy named M. D. Kavanagh the new chief of police. The mayor soon expressed dissatisfaction with Kavanagh when the chief refused to close the voter registry office in May. Governor Wells had declared the registry fraudulent and void—probably with good reason—and had ordered the mayor to close the registry office. Chief Kavanagh evidently thought the order conveyed to him by Mayor Kennedy was illegal.[24]

Although Mayor Kennedy was temporarily suspended from office by military order during the dispute with Chief Kavanagh, he quickly recovered his position. Within a few months, Kavanagh was replaced as chief of police by John Burke. Burke was a veteran of the U.S. Army, having seen service in the Mexican War, and had been a police officer in New Orleans for ten years before his appointment as chief. Under his leadership, the police earned praise from at least two newspapers in the city for improvements in efficiency and courtesy. This would soon prove to be a tran-

23. Final Report of the Smith-Brady Commission, 1–3, 126–27, 200–201, 296, Records of the Adjutant General's Office, No. 737, RG 94, NA.

24. *Times*, May 4, 5, 6, 11, 1865; *Daily Picayune*, May 9, 1865.

sitional phase presaging the restoration of conservative rule by former Confederates.[25]

The South was nominally peaceful but highly volatile in 1866. Racial tension led to violence in Norfolk, Virginia, in April, when whites attacked several hundred African Americans marching through the streets in a parade to celebrate passage by Congress of the Civil Rights Act. Five people died, three of them white and two black. The following month Memphis experienced even worse violence when white mobs, including policemen, attacked black people throughout the city over a three-day period, concentrating heavily on the black quarter of town and leaving forty-four blacks and two whites dead. In July, whites in New Orleans launched a murderous attack on black and white Republicans in which at least thirty-four blacks and four whites lost their lives. These episodes of violence helped bolster northern support for the Fourteenth Amendment and helped Republicans win enough seats in Congress to legislate Reconstruction policies more supportive of black civil rights than those favored by President Andrew Johnson.[26]

In March, 1866, the voters of New Orleans were permitted to elect their first slate of municipal officials since 1860. This election shifted control of the city government to conservative former Confederates in the Democratic party. Indicative of the rebel resurgence was the election of John Monroe as mayor, for Monroe had served in that capacity under the Confederate government and had then been imprisoned by General Butler for the duration of the war. Monroe's return to the mayoralty boded ill for the Unionists who had been serving on the police force. Indeed, one-third of that force signed a petition protesting his election.[27]

Monroe quickly used his mayoral authority to transform the police force into a bastion of conservative Democrats. As his chief of police, Monroe appointed Thomas E. Adams, who had filled the office in the late 1850s.

25. *Daily Picayune*, August 20, 1865; *Daily Crescent*, January 18, 1866; Applications for Positions as Police Officers, John Burke.

26. George C. Rable, *But There Was No Peace: The Role of Violence in the Politics of Reconstruction* (Athens, Ga., 1984), 31, 33–42; Jack D. L. Holmes, "The Underlying Causes of the Memphis Race Riot of 1866," *Tennessee Historical Quarterly*, XVII (1958), 195–221; Holmes, "The Effects of the Memphis Race Riot of 1866," *West Tennessee Historical Society Papers*, XII (1958), 58–79.

27. *Times*, January 28, March 5, 13, 1866; Vandal, "New Orleans Riot of 1866," 257.

Chief Adams had subsequently served as a colonel in the Confederate army. When Adams described the challenge he faced in policing the city in April, 1866, he characterized his 472 men as a force none too large to cope with "the immense congregation of bad men, the refuse of two armies, and . . . the idle and vicious portion of a population which was formerly controlled at home." The chief's oblique and pejorative reference to freedmen signaled the reactionary approach to race relations the police department would take under his leadership.[28]

The new police force appointed by the former Confederate mayor and commanded by the former Confederate chief was dominated by Confederate veterans. Chief Adams estimated that about two-thirds of his policemen were former Confederates, and Mayor Monroe conceded that more than half had served the South during the war. Although Monroe did not completely purge the force of Unionists, he allowed only a few to remain. About 15 percent of his appointees had first been appointed to the force under the Union occupation government and were thus probably Union men.[29]

It was this police force—all white, mostly formerly Confederate—that participated in the riot at Mechanics' Institute in New Orleans on July 30, 1866. A convention of Union loyalists had rewritten the state constitution in 1864, and by the summer of 1866 some of the convention delegates wanted to reconvene the constitutional convention. One faction of Louisiana Republicans, the moderates formerly led by Governor Michael Hahn, had lost badly in elections in late 1865 and early 1866. This faction sought a new session of the convention to secure the enfranchisement of black men and the disfranchisement of former Confederates. Thus the moderate faction hoped to rebuild their political strength on a foundation of black votes. At the same time, they wanted to ensure congressional recognition of Louisiana's state government.[30]

Opposition to the proposed convention coalesced in the month before

28. Reports of City Departments to the Board of Aldermen, 1866–69, Chief Thos. E. Adams to Mayor George Clark, April 12, 1866, NOPL; Vandal, "New Orleans Riot of 1866," 254.

29. Gilles Vandal has estimated that about 56 percent of the force were former Confederates ("New Orleans Riot of 1866," 253–56).

30. *Ibid.*, 165; Joe Gray Taylor, *Louisiana Reconstructed, 1863–1877* (Baton Rouge, 1974), 103–104; Donald E. Reynolds, "The New Orleans Riot of 1866, Reconsidered," *Louisiana History*, V (1964), 6–8; Rable, *But There Was No Peace*, 43–46.

it met. Most whites opposed admitting blacks to the political arena. Confederate veterans on the police force could lose their jobs if the convention movement succeeded. Some people also objected to the irregular—indeed, probably illegal—methods being used to recall the constitutional convention.[31]

Public tension mounted in July, when two small-scale racial brawls erupted. Controversy also swirled around the enforcement of the new Civil Rights Act, and Judge Edmund Abell of the First District Court in New Orleans was arrested for allegedly violating the new statute after he had advised the grand jury that the proposed convention session would be illegal. On July 24, Democrats held a mass meeting in Lafayette Square to condemn the constitutional convention. Three days later the Republicans responded with a rally of their own at Mechanics' Institute, the site chosen for the reconvocation of the convention. Dr. Anthony P. Dostie, a prominent Republican, who liked to call himself "the Robespierre of New Orleans," delivered a speech in which he apparently encouraged blacks to defend their rights with force if need be, advice sure to be deemed provocative by conservative whites. The Republican gathering ended in a torchlight parade, leaving the opposition in a heightened state of hostility and alarm during the next several days.[32]

Mayor Monroe and Lieutenant Governor Albert Voorhies opposed the recall of the convention but found that federal authorities would not stop the meeting. The temporary commander of federal troops in New Orleans, General Absalom Baird, advised the civil authorities that he would defend the conventioneers' right to assemble, though he did not endorse the validity of the convention's constitutional outcome. Monroe and Voorhies consequently scrapped their plans to arrest the convention delegates, and the mayor issued a proclamation calling for peace and good order, enjoining the people of New Orleans not to interfere with the convention.[33]

On July 30 the delegates gathered at Mechanics' Institute at noon, but because their number fell short of a quorum, they recessed to allow time

31. Vandal, "New Orleans Riot of 1866," 161–64, 173–74; Taylor, *Louisiana Reconstructed*, 105–106; Rable, *But There Was No Peace*, 46–48.

32. Vandal, "New Orleans Riot of 1866," 167, 177–81, 188–91; Taylor, *Louisiana Reconstructed*, 105–108; Reynolds, "New Orleans Riot of 1866, Reconsidered," 8–10; Rable, *But There Was No Peace*, 48–49.

33. Vandal, "New Orleans Riot of 1866," 192–203; Reynolds, "New Orleans Riot of 1866, Reconsidered," 8–10; Rable, *But There Was No Peace*, 48–49.

for absent delegates to be found. In the streets near Mechanics' Institute a large crowd of white men and teenaged boys milled about, among them many policemen and firemen. A procession of some 100 to 150 black men en route to the convention became embroiled in fisticuffs with white on-lookers. Though partisan reports afterward contradicted one another in explaining the proximate cause of the riot, evidently a white special officer of police fired the first shot, and the black marchers fired back. After the parade had arrived at Mechanics' Institute, a crowd of whites gathered, numbering perhaps between 1,000 and 1,500. Fighting began between the two crowds, and soon shooting erupted. The larger and better armed white crowd dispersed the black crowd after a brief street battle.[34]

The white mob, including many policemen, then besieged and eventually stormed the convention. They fired into the interior of the building, broke through the doors, and clubbed and shot unarmed delegates who vainly attempted to surrender. Dr. William Hire, one of the delegates, later testified that after witnessing a battle at close quarters inside the institute between the police-led mob and some of his fellow delegates armed only with chair legs, he endeavored to surrender to the police outside. He was severely clubbed by half a dozen officers but was more fortunate than others, whom he saw shot to death mercilessly by policemen. Hire was shot in the hand and stabbed in the chest before he was marched off and locked up at the station house. Two other victims, Stephen S. Fish and J. D. O'Connor, reported that when they agreed to let the police inside the institute after securing a promise of safe conduct, the policemen who had pledged them protection opened fire with their revolvers. Some convention members leaped from the windows to escape while others tried to fight their way to safety and were beaten, stabbed, or shot in the attempt. Even black people who were not connected with the convention were set upon by policemen at various points throughout the city.[35]

34. Vandal has estimated that the procession had about 50 to 60 marchers when it started and reached 100 to 150 by the time it reached Canal Street ("New Orleans Riot of 1866," 215, see also 214–20). Reynolds has put the number of marchers at 200 to 300 ("New Orleans Riot of 1866, Reconsidered," 11; see also 12). Rable has suggested that there were between 100 and 200 people in the parade (*But There Was No Peace*, 51; see also 52). See also Taylor, *Louisiana Reconstructed*, 108–109.

35. *House Reports*, 39th Cong., 2nd Sess., No. 16, pp. 6–10; Taylor, *Louisiana Reconstructed*, 109–10; Rable, *But There Was No Peace*, 52–54; Reynolds, "New Orleans Riot of 1866, Reconsidered," 11–12; Vandal, "New Orleans Riot of 1866," 221–23.

The arrival of federal troops between three and four o'clock in the afternoon brought an end to the violence. General Baird mistakenly believed that the convention was to meet at 6:00 P.M. and had not prepared his troops at Jackson Barracks—three miles from the city—to intervene as early as midday. His tardiness probably encouraged some federal authorities to excuse federal inaction by blaming the riot on a conspiracy of civil officials. Both contemporary and historical accounts have disputed whether there was a conspiracy to incite the riot; evidence against the conservatives is not completely persuasive, but it does cast considerable suspicion.[36]

Whether planned or spontaneous, the actions of the police force certainly merited censure. Even the most favorable interpretation of police involvement would at least indict a large number of policemen for murder, attempted murder, and assault and battery and would hold police commanders responsible for failure to control their men. Chief Adams was credited by the conservative press and by the Democratic minority report of a congressional inquiry with having risked his life repeatedly in efforts to check the violence. Nevertheless, Adams had earlier encouraged armed whites to gather at the site where the riot occurred, and Radical Republicans believed that he, Mayor Monroe, and Lieutenant Governor Voorhies had conspired to bring about the bloody assault.[37]

The human cost of this episode was considerable. At least thirty-eight people were killed (the death toll may have been higher), thirty-seven of them directly or indirectly associated with the convention forces; thirty-four of those who died were African Americans. Probably several hundred persons were wounded, most of them blacks or white convention delegates.

36. Members of each party charged the opposition with conspiracy, and although the evidence does not prove conclusively that either side had actually conspired to bring about the riot, certainly it is more plausible that conservatives may have done so. See Vandal, "New Orleans Riot of 1866," 227–34; Taylor, *Louisiana Reconstructed*, 110–11; Reynolds, "New Orleans Riot of 1866, Reconsidered," 13, 26–27; Rable, *But There Was No Peace*, 54–56, 208 n. 9.

37. *Times*, July 31, 1866; *Daily Picayune*, August 2, 1866; Vandal, "New Orleans Riot of 1866," 219. Governor James M. Wells, who was a convention supporter but had been absent from the city during the riot, accused the police of abetting the violence (*Times*, August 9, 1866). Henry Clay Warmoth, later a Republican governor of Louisiana, reported that he watched the uniformed police and white mob gather to storm the convention (*War, Politics and Reconstruction: Stormy Days in Louisiana* [New York, 1930], 48). One convention delegate, W. R. Fish, did thank three policemen by name for saving his life at hazard to theirs (*Times*, August 1, 1866).

Most of the casualties were convention supporters because their attackers were more numerous and better armed.[38]

Whoever was responsible for inciting or allowing the riot escaped punishment, for no one was prosecuted for complicity in the murders. Congress immediately appointed a select committee to investigate the riot. The committee's majority report attributed the riot to a premeditated conspiracy involving a large number of policemen, Mayor Monroe, and probably Lieutenant Governor Voorhies. The minority report exonerated Monroe, Voorhies, and Adams, characterized the recall of the convention as illegal, and blamed the violence on a spontaneous and localized outburst of feeling triggered by the alleged shooting of a police officer by a black man. The minority report ignored the abundant evidence of police misconduct.[39]

The select committee's majority underscored the suspicious dearth of prosecutions following the riot. Judge Abell of the First District Court explained away the failure to prosecute anyone for the violence by observing in his charge to the grand jury that the tumultuous nature of the event rendered the collection of evidence for prosecution very difficult. Ironically, the absence of prosecution and the notoriety the riot generated in the North helped stimulate Congress to impose Radical Reconstruction policies that would oust Louisiana Democrats from power.[40]

The riot at Mechanics' Institute in July, 1866, demonstrated the reactionary racism of the police department, yet less than a year thereafter New Orleans employed its first black policemen since 1830, making it in all likelihood the first American city to desegregate its police force after the Civil War. Among southern cities at the end of the war New Orleans had exceptional potential for the expansion of black opportunity and progress toward racial equality, in large part because of its extraordinary antebellum experience with race relations. Despite the many legal restraints on both slaves and free blacks, both groups found numerous ways to circumvent

38. *House Reports*, 39th Cong., 2nd Sess., No. 16, pp. 12–16; *Times*, August 3, 1866; Reynolds, "New Orleans Riot of 1866, Reconsidered," 13; Taylor, *Louisiana Reconstructed*, 110; Rable, *But There Was No Peace*, 54.

39. *House Reports*, 39th Cong., 2nd Sess., No. 16, pp. 1–36 (majority report), pp. 37–61 (minority report); Taylor, *Louisiana Reconstructed*, 113; Reynolds, "New Orleans Riot of 1866, Reconsidered," 16–17; Rable, *But There Was No Peace*, 56–57.

40. *Daily Picayune*, January 9, 1867; Taylor, *Louisiana Reconstructed*, 113; Reynolds, "New Orleans Riot of 1866, Reconsidered," 15, 27; Rable, *But There Was No Peace*, 57–58.

the laws. Many whites—including employers, policemen, grogshop keepers, and professional criminals—had a vested interest in helping blacks flout the law. The large number of white northerners in the city may have contributed to white toleration of black freedom because they had less investment in and commitment to slavery than white southerners did.[41]

Free blacks probably made the most important contribution to the special racial mixture of New Orleans. Of all Deep South cities, New Orleans had been home to the largest prewar population of free people of color, second in the nation only to Baltimore. The free black community of the Crescent City had a rich and dynamic tradition, especially distinctive because of the large number of mulattoes and the influence of French culture. Though separated from slaves by law and often by culture, free blacks forged links with the slave community by many means. They played a major role in manumitting slaves and became increasingly conscious of a racial bond with the enslaved, thus experiencing what one historian has called an "awakening of liberal conscience" as a result of the Civil War. Those blacks who had been free during the antebellum period expected to lead the black community after abolition, and most of the city's black leaders of the postwar period had been free before the war.[42]

These experiences helped make New Orleans a center of black progress

41. Wade, *Slavery in the Cities*, 83–89, 92, 145–46, 150–52, 156–58, 164–66, 178, 219–20, 223–25; Richard Tansey, "Out-of-State Free Blacks in Late Antebellum New Orleans," *Louisiana History*, XXII (1981), 369–86; Loren Schweninger, "A Negro Sojourner in Antebellum New Orleans," *Louisiana History*, XX (1979), 305–14; Berlin, *Slaves Without Masters*, 108–32, 172, 174, 262, 278; William W. Chenault and Robert C. Reinders, "The Northern-Born Community of New Orleans in the 1850s," *Journal of American History*, LI (1964), 232–47.

Census of 1860, Roll 418, p. 113, shows black policeman Marie Ursin, and Roll 419, p. 309, shows mulatto policeman R. Palio; Roll 419, p. 157 shows L. Badey, a black man whose occupation, nearly illegible, might be watchman. Ursin, Palio, and Badey do not appear in the Personnel Records of the Police Department for the years 1859–61.

42. Quotation from Ted Tunnell, "Free Negroes and the Freedmen: Black Politics in New Orleans During the Civil War," *Southern Studies*, XIX (1980), 28; Laurence J. Kotlikoff and Anton J. Rupert, "The Manumission of Slaves in New Orleans, 1827–1846," *Southern Studies*, XIX (1980), 172–81; David C. Rankin, "The Origins of Black Leadership in New Orleans During Reconstruction," *Journal of Southern History*, XL (1974), 417–40. Rankin has also argued that demographic and economic conditions, more than a "latin heritage," created a unique version of slavery and race relations in New Orleans; see "The Tannenbaum Thesis Reconsidered: Slavery and Race Relations in Antebellum Louisiana," *Southern Studies*, XVIII (1979), 5–31.

during Reconstruction. More African Americans lived there than in any other city in the country: 50,456 according to the 1870 census (followed by Baltimore with 39,558 and Washington, D.C., with 35,455). Despite white resistance, black New Orleanians gained some access to the city's streetcars, the New Orleans Opera House, the Boys' House of Refuge, the City Insane Asylum, and some of the city's social clubs, churches, saloons, steamboats, theaters, public schools, and colleges. As the state capital, New Orleans served as headquarters for a legislature with a substantial percentage of blacks and for three black lieutenant governors.[43]

But in the early months of 1866, such progress still lay in an uncertain future. The police department went through some changes in those months, but none of them dealt with issues of race. The Louisiana constitutional convention of 1864 had provided for several police reforms: a police board commission to be appointed by the governor, tenure of office during good behavior for policemen, uniforms with distinctions of grade, and pay increases, including a salary of eighty dollars per month for patrolmen. These were much like the provisions of the act passed by the legislature in January, 1862, but the occupation of the city by Union troops had prevented the implementation of that law. General George Shepley, acting as the military mayor of the city, had forbidden the election of police board commissioners because only one-fourth of the potential voters were registered, and those were registered by an oath to the Confederate government. The police operated without uniforms or a board of commissioners for the remainder of the war, even after the constitutional convention of 1864. It remained for the legislature to pass an enabling act in February, 1866, and the Common Council followed suit in April by implementing the constitutional and statutory reform provisions.[44]

These reforms, however, failed to address the persistent and pervasive racism in the police department. The board of commissioners of 1866 had the authority only to act as an administrative tribunal for cases of police

43. The best study of the black community in New Orleans during this period is Blassingame, *Black New Orleans*, esp. 173–210; see also Roger A. Fischer, *The Segregation Struggle in Louisiana, 1862–1877* (Urbana, 1974). Population data from *Ninth Census—Volume I. The Statistics of the Population of the United States* (Washington, D.C., 1872), 77–296.

44. Messages of the Mayors to the City Council, May 13, 27, 1862; *The Laws and General Ordinances of the City of New-Orleans, Together with the Acts of the Legislature, Decisions of the Supreme Court, and Constitutional Provisions Relating to the City Government*, comp. Henry J. Leovy (New Orleans, 1866), 366–76.

delinquency, leaving the power of appointment in the mayor's hands. The bloodletting at Mechanics' Institute was a clearer indication of the character of the police than the superficial appearance of the 1866 reforms. Mayor John Monroe used the power of appointment to create the heavily former-Confederate force that took part in the Mechanics' Institute riot.[45]

Some policemen complained of being hampered by the Civil Rights Act of 1866 in dealing with African Americans, and others discovered that they could not act with impunity in arresting freedmen. In September, 1866, two policemen were assailed by a crowd of black people, mostly discharged soldiers, when they attempted to arrest a black woman for disorderly conduct. A small party of police reinforcements was driven off by a hail of brickbats, and the sergeant at the scene withdrew his detachment to the station to avoid inciting a riot, whereupon the crowd dispersed. Seven months later, the police had to call in U.S. troops to disband a crowd of some five hundred black stevedores who had assembled to protest the loss of half of their wages to swindling contractors. A police sergeant intervened to save the life of a contractor who was about to be lynched by the mob, but otherwise the police refrained from action, even when two groups of laborers clashed the following day.[46]

Confederate hegemony in the police department came to an end in May, 1867, apparently because General Philip Sheridan, then commanding the district that included Louisiana under military Reconstruction, became convinced that the department would remain antagonistic to Reconstruction policies unless significant changes were made. Sheridan ordered Mayor Edward Heath, a Radical Republican appointed as mayor by Sheridan, to reduce from five years to two the residence requirement for policemen, which had excluded former Union soldiers from the force. Sheridan also directed the mayor to "adjust the present police force so that at least one half of said force shall be composed of ex-Union soldiers."[47]

During the week following Sheridan's order to admit former Union soldiers to the ranks of the police, Chief Adams reluctantly bowed to fed-

45. The mayor had difficulty getting the entire force into uniform in the first months after uniforming was officially adopted, largely because supernumerary policemen could not readily afford to pay for their own uniforms; each policeman bore the cost of his own uniform (*Times*, August 25, 1866).

46. *Daily Picayune*, September 13, 1866; *Tribune*, May 17, 1867; *Times*, August 18, 1866.

47. Sheridan issued Special Order No. 33 on May 2, 1867. *Tribune*, May 3, 10, 11, June 4, 1867.

eral authority and issued an order forbidding interference with black people aboard streetcars, for the police would henceforth enforce the law that prohibited the ejection of passengers on the grounds of their color. Although the appointment of white Unionists to the police force pushed the department in a direction more to the liking of black Republicans, it fell short of satisfying their full expectations. The editor of the black-managed New Orleans *Tribune* appealed for the inclusion of African Americans on the force, arguing that it was morally obligatory given the large population of blacks in New Orleans, and denying that fear of murderous attacks on black policemen could justify their continued exclusion from policing.[48]

Under pressure from the black community, from the Republican party, and probably also from the military government, Mayor Heath responded on May 30, 1867, by appointing Dusseau Picou and Emile Farrar as policemen in the Second District. They were the first black men to serve as police officers in New Orleans in more than a generation. The next week, the mayor appointed more than a dozen black policemen, and others followed later. Governor James M. Wells initiated the appointment of black men to the board of police commissioners with the selection of Charles J. Courcelle. Chief Thomas Adams was criticized by the *Tribune*, which advocated his removal from office to rid the department of rebel influence. The former Confederate chief lasted for two months before General Sheridan dismissed him at Mayor Heath's request. In his stead, Major J. J. Williamson of the U.S. Army became chief of police.[49]

Despite the appointment of black and white Unionists to the police force, black New Orleanians still faced formidable challenges. Many white Republicans lacked commitment to achieving racial equality. When President Andrew Johnson ordered the enforcement of a state law excluding blacks from jury service, the *Tribune* asserted that his action triggered open hostility to the Republican party and racial equality by white members of the police department. The result for black and white Republicans on the force was, the *Tribune* said, that "every means is resorted to [to] make them abandon their position." The inconsistency of Mayor Heath put pressure on black policemen, too. The mayor proclaimed that white businessmen had a right to refuse service to African Americans, and one black policeman found himself in the awkward situation of being assigned to duty at a ballroom catering to whites only. The mayor feuded with Chief Williamson

48. *Tribune*, May 8, 10, 1867.
49. *Tribune*, May 28, 31, June 1, 2, 4, 6, 11, 1867; *Daily Picayune*, August 1, 9, 10, 1867.

over his authority to make duty assignments for policemen and vacillated in supporting his black appointees.[50]

Heath reluctantly left the mayor's office after the Democrats swept the municipal election of April, 1868. Although he protested that the election had been illegal, he was forced to surrender the office to Hugh Conway; both sides accused their opponents of interfering in the electoral process. Chief Williamson refused to honor Conway's selection of a new chief of police, threw a protective cordon of police around his own office, and, unlike Heath, retained his position with the sanction of the military.[51]

Although the Democrats won the mayoral race in 1868, the Republicans held the governor's office and dominated the state legislature. To assure their advantage, Republicans in the legislature devised a bill that combined the parishes of Orleans, Jefferson, and St. Bernard into a single metropolitan police district. Complete authority over the police force for this district, including the power of appointment, was vested in the Board of Metropolitan Police Commissioners. The governor would appoint the commissioners for a term to run concurrently with his own.[52]

New Orleans Democrats loathed the Metropolitan Police law as another form of invasion and protested their impending loss of authority over policing the city. The Common Council adopted a resolution in August, 1868, condemning the law as "a direct encroachment upon the liberty of the people," declared the tax provision to support the Metropolitan Police an excessive burden, and appointed a five-man committee to convey their protest to the governor and the legislature. Despite their opposition, the legislature passed the Metropolitan Police bill in September, and the new force prepared to go on duty the following month under the command of Superintendent J. J. Williamson, who had been serving as the municipal chief of police.[53]

The Common Council's August resolution coalesced local opposition. When the Metropolitan Police attempted to assume their duties, they ran headlong into resistance from local officials that soon escalated into violence. In the city of Jefferson, which bordered on the Fourth District of New Orleans, Metropolitans were arrested by local authorities and the Jefferson city council made a formal protest against the new force. During

50. *Tribune*, June 19, December 18, 1867; *Daily Picayune*, April 4, 5, 10, 1868.

51. *Daily Picayune*, April 15–18, 21, June 11–13, 1868.

52. *Acts of Louisiana*, 1868, pp. 3, 85–98; *Daily Picayune*, July 4, December 30, 1868.

53. *Daily Picayune*, July 11, 1868; Ordinances and Resolutions of the Common Council (New Series), No. 986, August 19, 1868.

the next week rioting in the parish of St. Bernard and in New Orleans imperiled the viability of the Metropolitan organization.[54]

African Americans initially constituted half of the Board of Metropolitan Police Commissioners and 65 percent of the force. The federal military commander in New Orleans succinctly summarized the opposition to the Metropolitans when he observed that the "community at large refused to recognize or uphold the authority of a body thus constituted." Although Superintendent Williamson attempted to mollify white conservatives by suspending the black policemen, the Common Council of New Orleans declared the Metropolitan Police Act unconstitutional and directed Mayor Conway to organize another force under the old law. When Williamson resigned, Conway reappointed the former chief, Thomas Adams, but the federal military authorities warned the mayor that the city government would not be permitted to establish a police force of its own, nullified Adams' appointment, and made George L. Cain the acting superintendent. The city government brought suit in court in an effort to have the Metropolitan Police Act voided, but failed.[55]

The temporarily all-white Metropolitans stood their ground, and their board returned enough of the black policemen to duty to give them representation on the force roughly proportional to the black share of the general population. Most white New Orleanians continued to oppose this force because it was racially integrated and run by a Republican state commission. Experiments with a metropolitan system of policing in other southern cities during Reconstruction also faced vigorous objections, and such opposition eventually destroyed them all. In New Orleans the Metropolitan Police survived only as long as the Republicans controlled the state government and received federal support under military Reconstruction.[56]

54. *Times*, October 27, 28, 1868.
55. *Times*, October 29–31, November 1, 5, December 4, 1868.
56. State-controlled police boards were introduced in several U.S. cities before the Civil War (New York in 1857, Cincinnati in 1859, Baltimore in 1860, Chicago and St. Louis in 1861) as partisan reforms designed to wrest control of urban police forces from one political party and give it to another, usually giving Republicans at the state level power at the expense of Democrats at the municipal level. After the war, Republicans in Tennessee imposed state-run systems on Memphis, Nashville, and Chattanooga, but the Democrats regained control of the police in those cities in 1869. Indeed, most such reforms in the North were eventually repealed, too. See Ketcham, "Municipal Police Reform," 126–28, 139–40; Fogelson, *Big-City Police*, 14; Robert Thompson Mowrey, "The Evolution of the Nashville Police from Early Times to 1880" (Senior thesis, Princeton University, 1974), 35, 47–48.

# 5

## CRISIS OF LEGITIMACY
### The Metropolitan Police, 1868–1877

A SMALL event can sometimes yield an incisive insight into a larger phenomenon. In 1870 the Metropolitan Police swapped their old flimsy badges, numbered in a separate series for each precinct, for a new model. The badge was round in shape, unlike the crescents of the former city police, and the new numbers ran in a single continuous series for the entire force. Each policeman's badge thus had a unique number.[1]

The adoption of new badges symbolized two important characteristics of the Metropolitan Police: a willingness to depart from tradition and an appreciation of rational and efficient organization. Police reform flourished in the years 1868–1877. The state government under Republican administration increased the size of the force, expanded Metropolitan Police jurisdiction to encompass the entire state with primary responsibility for Orleans Parish and two contiguous parishes, mounted a substantial contingent of police on horseback and deployed other men on boats, instituted medical screening of recruits and imposed strict medical discipline on active members of the force, provided more on-the-job instruction and drill, offered pensions for long service, sharply reduced arrests for vagrancy, and gave the police larger public health and social service roles. The racial and ethnic composition of the Metropolitan Police force was diverse, including blacks in numbers roughly proportionate to their share of the general population in New Orleans and overrepresenting the Irish and natives of the northern states.

But the Metropolitan force was controlled by the Republican party and

---

1. *Annual Report of the Board of Metropolitan Police to the Governor of Louisiana, for the Year Ending September 30, 1871* (New Orleans, 1872), 32. The year of record for this series of annual reports (hereafter cited as *Annual Report*) ended September 30 in 1869, 1870, 1871, 1872, and 1873; the last extant report covered the period from October 1, 1873, to December 31, 1874.

included black policemen, which made it illegitimate in the eyes of most white New Orleanians. Conservative opposition to the Metropolitans took the form of protracted litigation, tax delinquencies, and organized violence, including a sizable battle in New Orleans in September, 1874, that resulted in more than one hundred dead and wounded. When the federal government withdrew support for military Reconstruction in Louisiana after the federal election of 1876, conservative Democrats took control of the streets of New Orleans and installed their own police force in place of the Metropolitans, partially or wholly undoing many of the reforms instituted by the Republicans.

Republican efforts at police reform were numerous and varied. One of their goals was to hire more capable men as police officers. During the Metropolitan administration, prospective policemen underwent a more rigorous evaluation of their physical fitness, educational background, and character than had been customary in the past. The screening process for candidates included a medical examination by the police surgeons. During the 1850s the police department had contracted for the services of a physician to perform a variety of duties, mostly caring for prisoners, but he did not ordinarily evaluate police candidates' physical qualifications. The police surgeons of the Metropolitan force, however, routinely examined recruit candidates and policemen who were under consideration for promotion. More than six hundred men per year were examined by the two surgeons, about one-fourth of them up for promotions. The compulsory examination made it more difficult for the infirm to obtain positions on the force.[2]

The police surgeons played an important role in enforcing stricter medical discipline on the force. In earlier years policemen who were ill or injured had had to rely on private physicians or Charity Hospital for treatment. Under the Metropolitan administration the police surgeons cared for their ailments. This reform not only helped sick or wounded men but also discouraged malingering. Tighter medical discipline resulted in a substantial reduction in absenteeism. In 1855 the absence rates had been 20 percent for the day force and 28 percent for the night watch, and in 1860 the rates were 13 percent for the day police and 15 percent for the night

2. *Annual Report*, 1868/69, pp. 39–43, 1869/70, pp. 68–71, 1870/71, pp. 49–51, 1871/72, pp. 33–35, 1872/73, pp. 43–45, 1873/74, pp. 47–50.

watch. In contrast, the Metropolitans' rate of absence averaged just 1.7 percent from 1868 through 1874.[3]

The police surgeons treated more than five hundred police cases each year, inspected the stations and prisoners, administered medical examinations, and made recommendations for improving the health of the force. Noting the high incidence of malaria among the police, the surgeons pointed out that many of the men lived near standing water and that relocating their places of residence would save much of the cost of sick time. They also advised the department to adopt waterproof capes for protection against the wet weather and pleaded for more welfare services for the homeless indigents of the city.[4]

Another innovation during the Metropolitan administration was the enactment of a pension plan for policemen. Any member of the force who became disabled in the line of duty or who became superannuated after ten years of service was eligible for annual payments of up to $150. The widow and children of any policeman who was killed in the discharge of his duty or who died after a decade of service also became eligible for the $150 annuity. This was a pittance, but it was the first systematic pension provision for the New Orleans police. Pensions had been granted occasionally by the city council as special rewards as far back as the 1820s, but only a tiny fraction of the men who worked on the police force ever received one, and each case required a special allocation by the council. The prospect of a regular pension would be an inducement for policemen to maintain a record of good behavior and make policing a career.[5]

Another Republican reform promoted a more rational and efficient territorial distribution of police personnel. Since the consolidation of the city in 1852 the police had been organized on a four-district pattern, with a headquarters station in each district and one or more substations in the larger districts. Appointments were ordinarily made by district, and transfers to other districts were infrequent. Even the qualifications for the job varied by district because men who served in the districts with many French-speaking citizens were required to speak both French and English. The Metropolitan Police Act abolished the old system in favor of precincts, each to contain not more than one hundred policemen and to constitute a

3. *Ibid.*
4. *Ibid.*
5. *Acts of Louisiana*, 1868, p. 93; *Annual Report*, 1870/71, pp. 17, 19, 1871/72, pp. 11, 22, 1873/74, pp. 18, 28–31.

captain's command. This formula eventually yielded nine precincts and six substations, thus substantially increasing the total number of police stations and making the coverage of territory more thorough and efficient.[6]

Another territorial reform was embodied in the Metropolitan Police Act. By including Jefferson and St. Bernard parishes in the Metropolitan District, the new law struck down the arbitrary barriers that had obstructed police operations in outlying areas, especially urban areas contiguous with New Orleans but beyond the city's administrative limits. Thus Jefferson City, the urbanized southeastern corner of Jefferson Parish bordering on the old Fourth District of New Orleans, and the city of Algiers, located across the Mississippi River from New Orleans, were incorporated into the district.[7]

Although the Metropolitan District encompassed only three parishes, the Metropolitan Police had statewide authority. The law empowered members of the Metropolitan Police to execute criminal process throughout Louisiana with the full power of constables (though they were not to serve civil process). Thus police could go beyond the Metropolitan District if they operated under a warrant issued by any magistrate. The broadening of police jurisdiction reached its peak with the Metropolitan Brigade law of March, 1873. This act authorized the governor to muster the Metropolitan Police as a militia brigade whenever he deemed it necessary for public safety, thus allowing the police to act as a small army and navy to enforce Reconstruction policies throughout the state. This militia act provided a loyal force to protect black and white Republicans in the countryside from the violence of conservative vigilantes. The Metropolitans took the field in a military capacity only a few times outside their home district and proved not very effective in protecting their friends and allies in the countryside, but nonetheless this practice excited the animosity of conservatives.[8]

A sanitary company established as a special unit of the Metropolitan force and composed of about a dozen men broadened police operations by including the inspection of "all ferry boats, manufactories, slaughter houses, tenement houses, hotels and boarding houses, and edifices suspected of or charged with being unsafe." In one year (1868/1869), the

6. *Acts of Louisiana*, 1868, pp. 85–98; *Annual Report*, 1868/69, pp. 5–6, 1869/70, pp. 6–7.
7. *Acts of Louisiana*, 1868, pp. 85–98; *Annual Report*, 1868/69, pp. 5–6, 1869/70, pp. 6–7.
8. *Acts of Louisiana*, 1868, p. 88, 1873, p. 76.

sanitary company inspected 34,828 premises and investigated 7,737 complaints. Its inspections resulted in the issuance of 6,810 work orders, most of which were complied with by the owners who received them. The company also compelled the cleaning of 6,092 privies and arranged for the removal of 1,332 dead animals and 32,850 loads of "night soil." The sanitary company was dissolved as a separate unit in July, 1870, but its men were individually detailed to serve the inspectors of the newly created Board of Health and continued to operate in that capacity.[9]

The efficacy of the Metropolitan Police was also enhanced by new technology. Responding to innovations in weaponry and escalating violence against the Republican government, the Metropolitans adopted new weapons. Police commanders issued Winchester repeating rifles to their men on several occasions when they anticipated riot or battle, and in some instances the Metropolitans employed cannon and Gatling guns. Such armament did not guarantee success, but it did give the Metropolitans a rough technological parity with their opponents.[10]

The Metropolitan Police also increased their tactical mobility. For the first time since 1805–1806, a portion of the men were put on mounted service. The expense of horses had become a serious objection to the mounted Gendarmerie early in the century, but the relatively large budget of the Metropolitan Police permitted some thirty-six men (about 5 percent of the force) to be deployed on horseback during 1870, primarily in the suburban periphery of the city. In 1873, the number of mounted men increased to about seventy, and when the size of the total force was reduced, the horse patrol represented more than 10 percent of the police. In addition to horses, the police made use of boats to patrol the river, including a steam launch, and rented steamboats to carry expeditionary forces into the

9. *Acts of Louisiana*, 1868, pp. 91–92; *Annual Report*, 1868/69, pp. 38–39, 1869/70, pp. 29, 65–67, 1870/71, p. 54, 1871/72, pp. 39–40, 1872/73, pp. 49–50, 1873/74, pp. 57–58. One of the sanitary company's cases resulted in a U.S. Supreme Court decision in 1873, which interpreted the privileges and immunities clause of the Fourteenth Amendment. The Crescent City Livestock Landing and Slaughterhouse Company enjoyed a licensed monopoly in the meat market and obtained an injunction barring the sale of meat by the Cavaroc Slaughterhouse in June, 1870. The Supreme Court declined to intercede in what it construed as intrastate commerce and left the monopoly intact.

10. *Daily Picayune*, December 14, 1872; *Republican*, March 6, 1873, Stuart Omer Landry, *The Battle of Liberty Place: The Overthrow of Carpet-Bag Rule in New Orleans, September 14, 1874* (New Orleans, 1955), 123, 129.

countryside. Horses and boats served the broadened scope of the police in the Metropolitan District and the state at large.[11]

During the first four years of the Metropolitan administration, the police were stronger numerically than they had been since the Know-Nothings had decreased the size of the force from about 450 to 265 men (as a ratio of policemen per 10,000 of population, from approximately 31 to 19). From 1860 through 1867, the force had remained roughly stable at about 500 or slightly less, and the police/population ratio declined slightly in that time from 30 to 28 per 10,000. The Metropolitans enjoyed a substantial increase in personnel in their early years. The police force reached its greatest size of the nineteenth century in 1870, when its ranks included 679 active duty officers and 55 support personnel (almost 36 active duty policemen per 10,000 of population).[12]

The numerical strength of the Metropolitan Police allowed the force to patrol in pairs in the most densely populated parts of the city. One-man foot patrols had been the previous rule, except for detectives and day policemen on special assignment. In the face of a more frequently hostile public, the two-man teams made considerable sense. After 1870, however, a policy of fiscal retrenchment in state government compelled the Board of Police to scale down the force, and the police/population ratio dropped considerably. By 1874 the entire organization counted only 455 men (about 24 police per 10,000 of population). Not surprisingly, the number of annual arrests peaked in 1870, falling each year thereafter.[13]

Police commanders sought to improve the job performance of their men by providing more on-the-job training and drill. Under the command of Superintendent George L. Cain and later A. S. Badger, the Metropolitans drilled regularly in military style to instill discipline. The men also received more instruction in techniques of policing than had been the practice before, and their appearance was inspected frequently and rigorously. The Civil War experiences of the superintendents and some of their men evidently provided the impetus for this approach.[14]

11. *Acts of Louisiana*, 1868, p. 96; *Annual Report*, 1869/70, p. 7, 1870/71, p. 55, 1871/72, pp. 10, 40, 1872/73, pp. 10, 30–31.

12. *Annual Report*, 1868/69, pp. 6, 20–21, 1869/70, pp. 9, 36–37, 1870/71, pp. 5, 18–19, 1871/72, pp. 5, 10–11, 1872/73, pp. 20–21, 1873/74, pp. 7, 17–18.

13. *Annual Report*, 1868/69, pp. 6, 20–21, 1869/70, pp. 9, 36–37, 1870/71, pp. 5, 18–19, 1871/72, pp. 5, 10–11, 1872/73, pp. 20–21, 1873/74, pp. 7, 17–18; *Daily Picayune*, August 25, 1869; see also note 20.

14. *Annual Report*, 1870/71, pp. 31–32.

In their efforts at police reform the Republicans emphasized social service as opposed to crime control and maintenance of order. Destitute and homeless transients had formerly been subject to arrest on charges of vagrancy or suspicion and upon conviction were sentenced to terms of labor in the city workhouse. A change in the state vagrancy law after the Civil War resulted in less repressive treatment of the homeless. The tremendous increase in unemployment during and after the war, especially among urban blacks, made it necessary to redirect policy to help ameliorate the plight of the needy. Antebellum laws had aimed to suppress black vagrancy, but the abolition of slavery, the invalidation of the postwar Black Codes, and the virtual suspension of the state's law against vagrancy largely restrained the police from arresting both black and white vagrants. Vagrancy and suspicion had constituted 17.8 percent of total arrests in the mid-1850s, but between 1868 and 1874 they amounted to just 4.8 percent of the total. Superintendent A. S. Badger complained about the new policy, describing the floating population of thieves as a serious danger to the city and beseeching the Board of Metropolitan Police Commissioners to press the legislature for a more stringent law. A new law passed in 1871 permitted somewhat more arrests for vagrancy, but it still kept police from jailing vagrants with the frequency common in the 1850s.[15]

The police were one of the most important agencies in the relief of poverty. Publicly administered poor relief was nearly nonexistent in New Orleans, and the Metropolitan Police provided a rudimentary shelter for the homeless by lodging them in the precinct stations. Sheltering the needy had been a significant police function even in the 1850s, and it increased enormously in scale under the Metropolitan administration. Between 1868 and 1874, the Metropolitans housed an average of just under 15,000 people per year, 90 percent of whom were male—a fifteenfold increase over the number of stationhouse lodgers in the mid-1850s. The resident population of the city had not doubled in the interim, rising from 169,000 in 1860 to 191,000 in 1870 and 216,000 in 1880. Stationhouse accommodations for lodgers were better than no protection at all, but the stations were often

---

15. *Acts of Louisiana*, 1865, Extra Session, pp. 16–20, and 1867, pp. 205–207; *Report of the Attorney General to the Legislature*, 1869, p. 6; *Daily Picayune*, November 29, 1869, May 11, 1875, March 11, 14, 1877; *Annual Report*, 1868/69, pp. 12–13, 44, 57–58, 1869/70, pp. 42, 57–58, 1870/71, pp. 7, 22, 36, 1871/72, pp. 7, 26, 1872/73, p. 34, 1873/74, p. 37. See also Charles Vincent, *Black Legislators in Louisiana During Reconstruction* (Baton Rouge, 1976), 108–10.

in dilapidated condition, with too much or too little ventilation, and the lodgers slept on a bare board without blanket or pillow. After 1871, the conditions improved somewhat, when the police designated separate rooms in the First Precinct station for the purpose and adopted more stringent measures for cleaning the facility.[16]

Political leaders regarded stationhouse lodging as especially inhospitable for women, and the city established a women's lodging house to serve both adult women and their children. When the onset of economic depression in 1873 intensified the need for poor relief, the city began to operate a soup house adjacent to the women's lodging facility. It provided a meal of boiled beef, soup, and bread between 10:00 A.M. and 2:00 P.M. each day. The soup house clients were disproportionately female and black, but men and women of both races were welcome.[17]

Other social services the police performed included returning an average of 150 lost children each year to their families, transporting accident victims to the hospital, and assisting the Board of Health in fighting disease. During 1873 the sanitary police engaged in public health programs against successive epidemics of smallpox, cholera, and yellow fever. They located epidemic victims, conveyed them to the hospital—often in the face of resistance from victims and their families—and fumigated and disinfected the residences and contiguous streets.[18]

A novel feature of policing in this period was the view shared by Superintendents George L. Cain and A. S. Badger that prostitution should be legalized and regulated. Cain had the unusual distinction of being a supporter of the women's rights movement. When Dr. Mary E. Walker, the only female surgeon in the U.S. Army during the Civil War, visited New Orleans in 1870, she lectured as an advocate of women's rights and paid a call on Superintendent Cain. In three successive annual reports to the legislature, Cain and Badger proposed the decriminalization of pros-

16. *Annual Report*, 1868/69, pp. 35, 43, 1869/70, pp. 47, 71, 1870/71, pp. 33–34, 41, 50–51, 1871/72, pp. 29, 35, 1872/73, p. 38, 1873/74, p. 42; *Population of the United States in 1860*, 195; *Statistics of the Population of the United States at the Tenth Census (June 1, 1880)* (Washington, D.C., 1883), 418. See also Gilles Vandal, "The Nineteenth-Century Municipal Responses to the Problem of Poverty: New Orleans' Free Lodgers, 1850–1880, as a Case Study," *Journal of Urban History*, XIX (1992), 30–59.

17. *Daily Picayune*, June 21, 1874, March 15, 1875.

18. *Annual Report*, 1868/69, pp. 34–35, 1869/70, pp. 47–48, 1870/71, pp. 41–42, 1871/ 72, p. 30, 1872/73, pp. 39, 49–50, 1873/74, p. 43.

titution so that the government might ameliorate its evils. Both men argued that prostitution was inevitable, and they cited the experiences of European cities and of St. Louis, which had begun to regulate the business in 1870. The police superintendents, however, made no headway with the legislature. Prostitution remained subject only to *de facto* regulation by corrupt policemen and other government officials who prospered personally from the trade in flesh.[19]

Women constituted a larger proportion of all arrestees during Reconstruction than they had before the Civil War. In the mid-1850s, 17.1 percent of all arrestees had been women, but for the years 1868–1874 their proportion was 27.6 percent. Women's arrest rates rose across all categories of crime except for vagrancy and suspicion. Female arrestees differed from males by being slightly younger (mean ages were 31.6 for men and 29.7 for women), slightly less likely to be married (64.0 percent of men were single versus 68.8 percent of women), and much more often illiterate (65.8 percent of females were illiterate but only 41.4 percent of males).[20]

The rise in the proportion of women arrested from the 1850s to 1868–1874 probably can be attributed to a slight rise in the female percentage of the city's population (from 49.5 percent in 1860 to 52.8 percent in 1870) and particularly to the increased percentage of African Americans (26.4 percent in 1870 compared with 14.3 percent in 1860). The percentage of females among black arrestees was probably higher than among white arrestees, reflecting both greater deference by policemen to white women than black women and a higher rate of real offenses—especially minor public order offenses—among black women than white women. It is also possible that the rate of offenses rose for white women and that white policemen became somewhat more willing to arrest them—changes in behavior and attitude possibly caused by the Civil War experience. Unfortunately, no evidence from either period differentiates arrests by both race and gender, and the real rates of criminal offenses for any demographic group (as opposed to arrest rates) must remain largely conjectural.[21]

19. *Annual Report,* 1869/70, pp. 51, 58–59, 1870/71, p. 33, 1871/72, p. 23; *Daily Picayune,* February 23, 1870; *Times,* February 8, 1870. The police kept mug books of women in "closed albums," while men's pictures were in open frames (*Daily Picayune,* September 29, 1873). See also John C. Burnham, "The Social Evil Ordinance—A Social Experiment in Nineteenth Century St. Louis," *Bulletin of the Missouri Historical Society,* XXVII (1971), 203–17.

20. *Annual Report,* 1868/69, pp. 23–35, 1869/70, pp. 40–46, 1870/71, pp. 34–41, 1871/72, pp. 24–29, 1872/73, pp. 32–38, 1873/74, pp. 35–42.

21. *Population of the United States in 1860,* 195; *Ninth Census—Volume I,* 629.

Although the Metropolitan administration failed to persuade the legislature to decriminalize prostitution, it did achieve a variety of other reforms. Some of those were anathema to white conservatives, who would bitterly resist any change that prevented them from controlling the police in New Orleans or challenged the traditional system of white supremacy.

New Orleans' rich yet contentious and burdensome tradition of racial and ethnic diversity posed peculiar problems for the criminal justice system, and the police themselves imperfectly mirrored the diversity of the city's population. During the Reconstruction era, African Americans joined the police force in numbers roughly proportional to the black share of the urban population and enjoyed basically the same powers and opportunities as white policemen. Racial tension within the police force occasionally surfaced in public view, but such incidents were minor compared with the white public's racist hostility to the integrated police. Despite these tensions, the Metropolitan Police seem to have dealt with both the black and white communities rather evenhandedly, though evenhandedness could never placate white New Orleanians who opposed racial equality.

Northerners and immigrants also contributed to the diversity of the city and the police. By 1870 the Irish had recovered from the nativist onslaught of the late antebellum period and were once again the most overrepresented ethnic group on the police force. Natives of the northern states were also substantially overrepresented. White southerners and Germans were only moderately underrepresented, and in absolute numbers they contributed the third and fourth largest nativity contingents on the force. Although interracial conflict dominated the news of the day (and has dominated historians' accounts of the period), ethnic identity still mattered among whites, and ethnic rivalry and animosity appeared from time to time.

When the Metropolitan force first went on duty in 1868, it was 65 percent black. Because of fierce white resistance, Superintendent J. J. Williamson suspended all of the black policemen, but black men were eventually employed again. In 1870, the black share of police jobs was 28.1 percent, roughly equal to the black proportion of the city's population, 26.4 percent. Although the Metropolitan Police constituted the largest integrated force in the urban South and included the largest contingent of black policemen (182 men in a total force of 647 in 1870), several other southern cities employed black policemen in 1870, most of them in proportions close to the percentage of blacks in the local population (see Table 14).

Local political considerations rather than any national or regional policy determined the employment of black policemen, reflecting both the decentralized structure of the American criminal justice system and the importance of local politics during the Reconstruction period. Savannah and Charleston, for example, were not greatly different in population size (49,000 in Charleston in 1870 and 28,000 in Savannah). Both had large concentrations of African Americans (54 percent in Charleston and 46 percent in Savannah) and almost the same proportion of immigrants in the white adult male population (42 percent in Charleston, 43 percent in Savannah). Located not far apart, they shared much the same flora, fauna, geography, and climate, and each served as a commercial outlet for an agricultural hinterland producing a great deal of cotton and rice. Yet Charleston's force was racially integrated and Savannah's was all white, dressed in Confederate gray and under the command of a former Confederate officer.[22]

Savannah and Charleston were separated by a state boundary, but even within the jurisdiction of a single state the racial composition of urban police forces could vary widely. In Virginia, the Petersburg force was integrated, but Richmond had no black policemen. Norfolk had only token integration on its force, yet its twin city of Portsmouth was almost fully integrated. The struggle for integration was thus largely local. In some places, conditions and forces within the individual city determined the outcome; in others, such as Tennessee and Louisiana, the involvement of the state government in municipal politics shaped the course of change.[23]

Winning jobs on the force did not end the struggle for black policemen. One historian of race relations in the post–Civil War South has suggested that in some cities black policemen were prevented from officially interacting with whites by law, administrative order, or custom, but black policemen in New Orleans evidently experienced much the same opportunities as white policemen and exercised the same powers. Black men held positions on the Board of Metropolitan Police Commissioners and

22. Edward King, *The Great South: A Record of Journeys in Louisiana, Texas, the Indian Territory, Missouri, Arkansas, Mississippi, Alabama, Georgia, Florida, South Carolina, North Carolina, Kentucky, Tennessee, Virginia, West Virginia, and Maryland* (Hartford, 1875), 369; Census of 1870, RG 29, NA; *Statistics of the Population of the United States at the Tenth Census*, 416–56.

23. Mowrey, "Evolution of the Nashville Police," 35.

## TABLE 14
## Percentage of Blacks in Police and Total Population
## in Twenty Southern Cities,
## 1870 and 1880

| | 1870 | | 1880 | | | | 1870 | | 1880 | |
| | Police | Total Population | Police | Total Population | | | Police | Total Population | Police | Total Population |
|---|---|---|---|---|---|---|---|---|---|---|
| New Orleans | 28 | 26 | 7 | 27 | | Galveston | 8 | 22 | 13 | 24 |
| Charleston | 42 | 54 | 19 | 55 | | Washington, D.C. | 4 | 33 | 5 | 33 |
| Mobile | 37 | 44 | 0 | 42 | | Savannah | 0 | 46 | 0 | 51 |
| Montgomery | 50 | 49 | 0 | 59 | | Nashville | 0 | 38 | 0 | 38 |
| Vicksburg | 50 | 55 | 14 | 49 | | Richmond | 0 | 45 | 0 | 44 |
| Petersburg | 37 | 54 | 0 | 54 | | Atlanta | 0 | 46 | 0 | 44 |
| Portsmouth | 29 | 35 | 0 | 34 | | Memphis | 0 | 39 | 23 | 44 |
| Norfolk | 3 | 46 | 0 | 46 | | Louisville | 0 | 15 | 0 | 17 |
| Augusta | 2 | 42 | 0 | 46 | | St. Louis | 0 | 7 | —[a] | —[a] |
| San Antonio | 13 | 16 | 12 | 15 | | Baltimore | 0 | 15 | —[a] | —[a] |

*Source:* Censuses of 1870 and 1880, RG 29, NA; *Statistics of the Population of the United States at the Tenth Census (June 1, 1880)* (Washington, D.C., 1883), 416–56.

[a]Not included in the research.

commanded precincts. As ordinary cops on the beat, they wore uniforms, carried guns, and otherwise had the full authority of police officers. No formal rules restrained them from arresting whites, nor is there evidence of any informal or covert efforts within the force to apply a segregationist policy. Indeed, in a city only partially desegregated, the police were among the pioneers of integration.[24]

Black policemen had and exercised the power to arrest whites. Whether they arrested proportionately more blacks than whites remains unknown because for most arrests it is not possible to ascertain the race of both the policeman and the arrestee. At least some interracial arrests did occur. For example, during the months of June, July, and August, 1870, black policemen arrested whites on at least sixteen occasions and possibly on many more.[25]

Black men also held important police leadership positions. Several black men served on the Board of Metropolitan Police Commissioners. At the outset African Americans held three of the six seats (counting the *ex-officio* seat of the lieutenant governor). Among the black commissioners were Charles J. Courcelle, J. B. Gaudette, James Lewis, J. W. Quinn, C. C. Antoine, Oscar J. Dunn, and Thomas Isabelle. Although no black man ever held the post of superintendent, blacks did serve at the next level, as precinct commanders. At least seven African Americans commanded either a precinct or a precinct substation. Four of these men held the rank of captain: Octave Rey, James Lewis, Eugene Rapp, and Peter Joseph. Three

24. Rabinowitz, *Race Relations in the Urban South*, 41–43.

25. *Daily Picayune*, June 2–August 31, 1870; *Graham's Crescent City Directory* (New Orleans, 1870); *Edwards' Annual Directory* (New Orleans, 1871–73). No official arrest books from the period survive. The only records of arrests are the newspaper reports, but these did not often indicate the race of police and arrestees. Many of the published arrests did not even report the names of the persons involved. When the newspapers did report names, the police were often cited by surname, and although the arrestees' full names were usually given, they were only occasionally accompanied by a designation of race. No official police rosters for the period are available, but one can be reconstructed for the summer of 1870 from the population schedules of the federal census, and this list includes policemen's racial identities. Some of the arrestees can be found in the city directories for 1870 and 1871, which showed African Americans as "colored," but most of the arrestees did not appear in the directories (probably because of their transience or social marginality). One further complication was the sharing of surnames by some white and black policemen. Thus, although some positive identification of black-on-white arrests can be made, an accurate estimate of frequency or proportionality by race is impossible.

other precinct or substation commanders were sergeants: H. E. deFuentes, J. B. Gaudette, and Ernest Chaumette. Black officers headed at least two precincts during most years and held command in three precincts in 1872 and 1873.[26]

Black policemen participated fully in their work, and they carried firearms on duty. During one of the early battles in which the Metropolitan Police participated, the New Orleans *Times* mentioned that black policemen were armed with Enfield rifles as well as the usual revolvers. In more peaceful times, a traveler to New Orleans visited the state legislature and observed that at "the doors stand negro policemen, armed with clubs and revolvers."[27]

In interracial households, policemen—both black and white—were disproportionately represented. Of 205 interracial couples in the 1870 census schedules for New Orleans, seven included a policeman. In three households white policemen—a German, an Italian, and a Spaniard—lived with black or mulatto women. Perhaps more remarkable, in four other households mulatto policemen lived with white women (in only 29 interracial unions in the city did African American men live with white women). Three of these men were Louisianans with French surnames, and the fourth was a native of Spain; the white women were natives of Ireland, England, New York, and Louisiana. Policemen accounted for only 1.3 percent of all employed males over the age of sixteen, yet 3.4 percent of all interracial unions included a policeman. Although African American policemen constituted only 0.4 percent of the male work force in New Orleans, 13.8 percent of all interracial unions with white women involved black policemen.[28]

Other illuminating details about black policemen can be gleaned from the census records. Most were fairly young men; 77 percent of white policemen were forty years old or younger. Black policemen were younger still; 92 percent were no older than forty, and their mean age was three years below that of their white counterparts (32.4 compared with 35.5).[29]

Black policemen were more likely to have been native-born than their white counterparts. A large percentage of white policemen in New Orleans were immigrants, notably Irish; black policemen were mostly Louisianans

26. *Tribune*, May 28, 1867; *Times*, May 9, 1872; Blassingame, *Black New Orleans*, 157; Census of 1870, RG 29, NA.

27. *Times*, October 20, 1868; King, *Great South*, 95.

28. Census of 1870, RG 29, NA; Blassingame, *Black New Orleans*, 206–207.

29. Census of 1870, RG 29, NA.

by birth. Of the 182 African American policemen in the 1870 census, only 3 (1.6 percent) were foreign-born (in Spain, Denmark, and the West Indies). Of the native Americans, 130 (71.4 percent) came from Louisiana, while 42 (23.1 percent) were from other former slave states. Only 7 (3.8 percent) had migrated to Louisiana from the northern states.[30]

Though more often native than their white colleagues, most of the black policemen shared the same socioeconomic niche with white policemen. Most policemen of both races owned less than $100 of personal property and no real estate. About one-sixth of each racial group surpassed the $100 level of personalty, and about one-tenth owned some realty. Black policemen were considerably more likely to own $100 or more of property, either real or personal, than the general black adult male population of New Orleans. Thus black policemen were spread over the middle and lower classes.[31]

30. *Ibid.* By 1870 most black Americans were natives of the United States, but some foreign-born blacks had been brought into the country as slaves legally through South Carolina as recently as 1807, and by special congressional exemption refugees from St. Domingue via Cuba were allowed to bring slaves into the United States in 1809–10. The illegal slave trade brought in many throughout the antebellum period—perhaps an average of a thousand per year or more—and some free foreign-born blacks immigrated to the United States of their own volition. See Dwight F. Henderson, *Congress, Courts, and Criminals: The Development of Federal Criminal Law, 1801–1829* (Westport, Conn., 1985), 161–207; Warren S. Howard, *American Slavers and the Federal Law, 1837–1862* (Berkeley, 1963); W. E. B. Du Bois, *The Suppression of the African Slave-Trade to the United States of America, 1638–1870* (1898; rpr. New York, 1965).

31. Census of 1870, RG 29, NA. Property values for the white and black adult male populations of the city are based on random samples consisting of 2,378 whites and 856 blacks. Calculations for police property values are based on complete enumerations of 465 white and 182 black policemen. Roughly the same fraction of white and black policemen owned over $100 in personalty: 17.9 percent of black policemen, 16.3 percent of whites. But among the one-sixth of blacks and whites who exceeded $100 of personal property, whites held substantially more. The mean value of personalty for that 16.3 percent of white policemen was approximately $428, while for the 17.9 percent of blacks, it was only $255. Few policemen owned real estate: 8.7 percent of blacks, 10.3 percent of whites. For this minority of police real property owners, the mean value was higher for whites than blacks: $1,203 in contrast to $972 for blacks.

Only 5.7 percent of the black adult male population owned personal property worth more than $100, while the figure for black policemen was 17.9 percent. The mean value for policemen who had such property was less, however, than for the black population: $255 (police), $487 (population). The same was true for real estate. More black policemen owned real estate than was true for the population of adult black males (8.7 versus 6.8 percent), but their mean

In one sense, black policemen held a higher economic position than white policemen. White policemen were less likely to own either personal or real property than the general white public. Yet black policemen were more likely than the black public to own both kinds of property, suggesting relatively high status in the black community.[32]

Though most policemen came from fairly humble economic circumstances, a minority of them were in the middle of the class structure. About one-tenth of the black policemen can be traced back to earlier years through the city directories to determine their previous occupations. Of seventeen men, two had low white-collar jobs, seven worked in skilled blue-collar trades, six were semiskilled or service workers, and two were employed as unskilled laborers.[33]

The city directories provide another link to black policemen's pasts, for about one-tenth of the 1870 African American policemen can be traced backward to determine their status as free men before the Civil War. That would not, however, be an accurate measure of how many black policemen of the Reconstruction era had been free or slave before the war. City directories would have included only a few free black laborers, thus underrepresenting free men of color. Moreover, blacks who migrated to New Orleans during and after the war obviously would not have been in New Orleans city directories in the antebellum period.[34]

It seems likely, though, that the African American policemen of 1870 came disproportionately from the ranks of antebellum free men of color rather than from the prewar slave population. A hint of this was the relative number of African American policemen designated as "mulatto" by the census enumerators as opposed to "black." Census marshals described 75.8 percent of the African American policemen as mulatto, but in the adult African American male population of the city, only 34.5 percent appear on the returns as mulatto. The antebellum community of free people of color

---

value was less ($972 for black policemen, $1,879 for black adult males). Of the white adult male population, 31.9 percent owned $100 or more of personalty, and 17.6 percent held realty. Among white policemen, only 16.3 percent possessed $100 or more of personal property and just 10.3 percent owned real estate. Differences in property ownership between the police and the general population of adult males persist even in age-specific analysis.

32. *Ibid.*

33. *Gardner's Commercial and Business Registry of New Orleans* (New Orleans, 1860).

34. *Ibid.*

had been heavily mulatto (77.3 percent), but the slave population had been predominantly black (75.2 percent).[35]

The extent to which the black policemen of 1870 had participated in the Civil War is difficult to gauge, but some of the men had seen military service. Approximately one-tenth (eighteen men) of the 1870 black police contingent can be identified as Union soldiers from Louisiana units. Others may have served under different names or in units from other states. The Louisiana black veterans all served with one of two regiments, the 6th and 7th Louisiana Colored Infantry.[36]

Perhaps the most distinguished of the black policemen with Civil War service was Jordan B. Noble. Noble gained fame in antebellum New Orleans as a veteran of three wars. Born free in Georgia, he joined the 7th U.S. Infantry in 1813 at the age of thirteen. He served as a drummer in the battle of New Orleans in January, 1815, and again during the Seminole War in Florida in the 1830s and the Mexican War of the 1840s. In a parade in 1860 commemorating the victory over the British, Noble delivered a short speech to the crowd and received a special medal at the order of General Winfield Scott. During the Civil War, the former drummer held the rank of captain, commanding C Company, 7th Louisiana Colored Infantry. The 1870 census described Noble as "mulatto" and noted that he held real estate valued at $1,500. He held the highest rank in the Union army of the black police veterans.[37]

The next highest ranking black veteran on the police force was Octave Rey. Born in New Orleans in 1837, Rey was the youngest of three brothers and the son of Barthelemy Rey, a member of the first school board of an institution for indigent orphans. Octave Rey, a cooper by trade, married Louise Belleme in 1859 at St. Augustine Catholic Church, and the couple had at least six children. Rey joined the Union army during the Civil War, serving as a lieutenant in E Company, 6th Louisiana Colored Infantry, and

35. Census of 1870, RG 29, NA; *Population of the United States in 1860*, 194.

36. Index to Compiled Service Records of Volunteer Union Soldiers Who Served in Organizations from the State of Louisiana, Records of the Adjutant General's Office, 1780s–1917, RG 94, NA.

37. Census of 1870, RG 29, NA; Roland C. McConnell, *Negro Troops of Antebellum Louisiana: A History of the Battalion of Free Men of Color* (Baton Rouge, 1968), 74, 85, 114–15. Noble was also active in the colonization movement in the 1850s (Joseph Logsdon and Caryn Cosse Bell, "The Americanization of Black New Orleans, 1850–1900," in *Creole New Orleans: Race and Americanization*, ed. Arnold R. Hirsch and Joseph Logsdon [Baton Rouge, 1992], 215).

sustaining a leg injury while on an extended march. Rey resigned his commission in 1863 because "concord does not exist among the officers of the army and . . . the difference of race [was] the cause of it."[38]

Rey joined the Metropolitan Police and became a captain commanding the Fourth Precinct. After losing his position as a result of the conservative "Redemption" in 1876–1877, Rey remained a respected member of the community and property owner (he held $500 worth of personalty and $500 of realty in 1870). He served as chief of special election marshals for the First Congressional District in the November election of 1882. When he was involved in a shooting incident in 1886, the *Daily Picayune* referred to his service during Reconstruction and described him as a "tall, fine looking man." At 6 feet 2½ inches, Rey was described by a fellow black New Orleanian as a "tall man of herculean proportions—energetic, powerful, and dynamic in his thinking." Although not highly educated, Rey was reputed to have a "prodigious memory for names and people," a trait that must have served him well as a policeman. He received a federal pension for his military service and died in 1908.[39]

Black policemen found that integration caused racial friction, not only with the white public but also with white policemen. After the Republicans integrated the force, some white policemen expressed open hostility toward them, preferring "to be 'damned' rather than give their votes to a party which recognizes *negro equality*." In an argument in 1872, a white police captain called his white sergeant a "nigger." The sergeant then shot the captain. The racist epithet was obviously seen as a grievous insult to a white man's honor. Some blacks evidenced prejudice, too. In 1869, an African American secretary of the Board of Metropolitan Police Commissioners called a citizen, P. V. J. Kennedy, a "d——d Irish——" and stated that Kennedy had been "transported to this country, and every foreigner like him."[40]

Neither the Civil War nor the Thirteenth Amendment produced enough solidarity among white New Orleanians to erase old ethnic animosities. In

38. Records of the Veterans Bureau, Military Service and Pension File of Octave Rey, RG 15, NA; Rodolphe Lucien Desdunes, *Our People and Our History* ed. and trans. Sr. Dorothea Olga McCants (Baton Rouge, 1973), 114–20.

39. Desdunes, *Our People and Our History*, 114–20; *Daily Picayune*, November 7, 1882, April 21, 1886; Census of 1870, RG 29, NA.

40. *Tribune*, December 18, 1867; *Daily Picayune*, October 3, November 20, 28, 1872; *Times*, May 13, 1869.

one post–Civil War incident, a police sergeant was accused by his men of "oppressing the Irish members of the force." In another episode, policeman James Gleason quarreled with police corporal Beaseler, whom he called a "Dutch——," and shot him in the arm. Regional origin among U.S. natives also proved a subject of conflict, and some men viewed the term *Yankee* as a serious provocation. In 1872, a white Louisianan on the force was shot to death by another white policeman he had called "a d——d Yankee ——."[41]

Although anti-Irish sentiments persisted, by 1870 the Irish had returned to the position of strength they enjoyed on the police force before the Know-Nothings purged the force in the mid-1850s. White natives of Louisiana and the other southern states were somewhat underrepresented on the Metropolitan Police in 1870, but the Irish were overrepresented, as were natives of the northern states and British immigrants (see Table 15). The Irish were overrepresented on the police forces of many southern cities in this period, including thirteen of the seventeen cities shown in Table 16 for 1870 (their representation was nearly proportional in two more), and thirteen of sixteen for 1880 (their representation was roughly proportional in the other three). In New Orleans the Irish contingent was the largest of any nativity group among whites. The Irish were influential, too; among those holding leadership positions were Captains William McCann, Thomas Flannigan, James Gibney (who had served as a Confederate army officer during the war), and Leonard Malone (who had first joined the New Orleans police in 1847 and became chief of detectives in 1889), and Sergeants Thomas Wing and James Scaret.[42]

White northerners' share of police jobs was almost double their percentage of the white adult male population; they accounted for 11.7 percent of the Metropolitan force but only 6.7 percent of white adult males. Northerners, however, were not widely overrepresented on southern urban police forces during Reconstruction. Of the seventeen cities shown in Table 16, northerners were overrepresented in only four, and in just two (Galveston and San Antonio) were they heavily overrepresented. Not only were north-

41. *Daily Picayune*, October 5, 1866, September 20, 1876, October 3, 1872. Obviously the provocation included the deleted expletives as well as the ethnic epithets.

42. *Gardner's New Orleans Directory* (New Orleans, 1869); *Graham's Crescent City Directory* (New Orleans, 1870); *Edwards' Annual Directory; Soards' Directory* (New Orleans, 1874–77); *Bee*, February 21, 1871; Census of 1870, RG 29, NA; New Orleans Death Certificates, LI, 401.

## TABLE 15
### NATIVITIES OF WHITE POLICE IN 1870

| | Police | | White Adult Males (sample) | |
| | % | No. | % | No. |
|---|---|---|---|---|
| Native-born | 32.3 | 150 | 33.3 | 793 |
| Louisiana | 15.1 | 70 | 20.3 | 483 |
| Other slave states[a] | 5.6 | 26 | 6.3 | 149 |
| Pa., N.J., N.Y | 6.9 | 32 | 4.2 | 100 |
| New England | 2.6 | 12 | 1.6 | 39 |
| Midwest | 2.2 | 10 | 0.8 | 19 |
| Other | 0 | 0 | 0.7 | 3 |
| Foreign-born | 67.7 | 315 | 66.7 | 1,585 |
| Ireland | 37.0 | 172 | 14.2 | 338 |
| Germany | 17.0 | 79 | 22.2 | 528 |
| France | 2.6 | 12 | 15.2 | 361 |
| Spain | 0.9 | 4 | 1.9 | 46 |
| Italy | 0.2 | 1 | 3.3 | 78 |
| Britain | 4.7 | 22 | 3.7 | 88 |
| Other | 5.4 | 25 | 6.1 | 146 |
| Totals | 100.0 | 465 | 100.0 | 2,378 |

*Source:* Census of 1870, RG 29, NA.

[a]Slave states as of 1860.

erners overrepresented on the Metropolitan force in New Orleans, but they contributed a disproportionate number of leaders on that force, including Board of Police treasurer S. N. Burbank (of New York), Sergeant William Duncan (from Massachusetts), Captains Boyd Robinson (New York), D. C. Woodruff (New York), and R. B. Edgworth (New Hampshire), and Superintendent A. S. Badger. Badger held the superintendency longer than any other man, from 1870 to 1874. A native of Boston, Badger first came to New Orleans in 1862 as a lieutenant in the U.S. Army and at war's end, having attained the rank of colonel, he settled in the Crescent City. There he married and, as a loyal Republican, secured posts as state tax collector and harbormaster before joining the Metropolitan Police. In 1870 he was promoted from captain to superintendent and continued in that command until he was severely wounded in the battle of Liberty Place in September, 1874. Thereafter he served successively as postmaster,

TABLE 16

PERCENTAGE OF IRISH NATIVES IN POLICE AND CONTROL SAMPLES IN SEVENTEEN SOUTHERN CITIES, 1870 AND 1880

| | 1850 | | 1860 | |
|---|---|---|---|---|
| | Police | White Adult Males (sample) | Police | White Adult Males (sample) |
| Savannah | 55 | 24 | 45 | 16 |
| Charleston | 54 | 17 | 51 | 10 |
| Mobile | 33 | 20 | 34 | 12 |
| St. Louis | 27 | 20 | —[a] | —[a] |
| Montgomery | 42 | 10 | 20 | 6 |
| San Antonio | 23 | 5 | 27 | 5 |
| Galveston | 8 | 11 | 39 | 8 |
| Vicksburg | 44 | 17 | 50 | 10 |
| Atlanta | 15 | 8 | 5 | 5 |
| New Orleans | 37 | 14 | 22 | 11 |
| Memphis | 51 | 20 | 50 | 15 |
| Louisville | 20 | 14 | 25 | 12 |
| Augusta | 37 | 20 | 23 | 11 |
| Nashville | 7 | 13 | 17 | 8 |
| Lexington | 21 | 16 | 40 | 14 |
| Petersburg | 0 | 5 | 4 | 2 |
| Richmond | 8 | 7 | 4 | 5 |

Sources: Censuses of 1870 and 1880, RG 29, NA.

[a]Not included in the research.

collector of the port, U.S. appraiser, special deputy collector of customs, and U.S. appraiser of merchandise.[43]

Other ethnic groups added to the diversity of the police. The Germans outnumbered every group except the African Americans and the Irish in 1870, but they were moderately underrepresented on the Metropolitan force in 1870, as they were in every southern city shown in Table 16 in that year except Vicksburg (in Galveston and Mobile they were only slightly underrepresented). They apparently did not hold any major leadership positions, although one captain was a native of Switzerland with a Germanic surname. White Louisianans had much the same profile; they were moderately underrepresented and evidently held only one police captaincy. British immigrants, though a bit overrepresented, constituted only a small percentage of the force. The French, Spanish, Italians, and other foreign-born groups were both proportionately underrepresented and absolutely few in number, though one Spaniard did achieve the rank of captain.[44]

Although an ethnic and racial microcosm of the city's population, the police were an imperfect, disproportional microcosm. They exhibited considerable ethnic and racial diversity, as did the public with which they interacted. One of the few quantitative measures of the interaction between police and citizenry, the record of arrests, shows a striking symmetry between the police and arrestees. African Americans constituted 28.1 percent of the police force, almost identical to the black share of arrestees, 27.2 percent. Among white nativity groups, the Irish were the most overrepresented group both on the police force and among the arrestees. Similarly, British immigrants were the only other foreign-born group overrepresented both on the police and among arrestees. The Spanish, French, Italians, and other immigrants were considerably underrepresented among arrestees as well as on the Metropolitan force (see Table 17).[45]

43. City directories cited in note 42; Census of 1870, RG 29, NA; New Orleans Death Certificates, CXXXV, 255; *Daily Picayune*, May 10, 1905. Badger's successor as superintendent, William F. Loan, also hailed from Massachusetts. Loan had served as an ensign in the U.S. Navy during the Civil War and had settled in New Orleans at the end of the war. Like Badger, Loan received appointments to patronage positions, including harbormaster and deputy U.S. marshal, and, after his service with the Metropolitan Police, custom house inspector at Algiers (New Orleans Death Certificates, LXXXIX, 78; *Daily Picayune*, April 14, 1886).

44. City directories cited in note 42; Census of 1870, RG 29, NA.

45. *Annual Report*, as cited in note 20.

## TABLE 17
### Incidence of Arrest by Nativity Group,
### 1868–1874 (Whites Only)

| | No. of arrests | A<br>Arrests as %<br>of Total White<br>Arrests | B<br>% of 1870<br>White Adult Male<br>Population in<br>Nativity Groups | Ratio<br>A/B |
|---|---|---|---|---|
| Ireland | 38,903 | 30.5 | 19.3 | 1.58 |
| Britain | 5,104 | 4.0 | 3.0 | 1.33 |
| United States | 54,038 | 42.4 | 35.2 | 1.20 |
| Germany | 14,806 | 11.6 | 20.4 | .57 |
| Spain | 1,525 | 1.2 | 2.2 | .55 |
| France | 6,706 | 5.3 | 10.0 | .53 |
| Italy | 1,937 | 1.5 | 3.7 | .41 |
| Other | 4,357 | 3.4 | 6.3 | .54 |
| Totals | 127,376 | 99.9 | 100.1 | — |

*Sources: Annual Report of the Board of Metropolitan Police* 1868/69, p. 33, 1869/70, p. 45, 1870/71, p. 39, 1871/72, p. 28, 1872/73, p. 37, 1873/74, p. 41.

*Note:* The annual reports did not cross-tabulate arrests by race and nativity, except the report for 1868–69, which subdivided U.S. natives by blacks and whites. No foreign-born groups were shown by race, but only a tiny fraction of foreigners would have been black. Using the 1868–69 black percentage of U.S. native arrestees as an estimate to subtract from U.S. native arrestees for other years and assuming no blacks among the foreign-born (which introduces an error of only very slight magnitude), this table presents estimates of the number of white arrestees by nativity.

Because the real crime rate for each of these demographic groups is unknown and arrest records identifying both the arrestee and the arresting officer by race and nativity are lacking, the racial and ethnic similarities between the police and those they arrested cannot be explained. One may only suggest that such symmetry makes a poor *prima facie* case for concluding that police systematically discriminated by race and ethnicity in making arrests.[46]

46. Unfortunately, only one of the annual reports of the Board of Police included arrest data by race (1868/69). John Blassingame has suggested that blacks had a relatively high crime rate, citing their percentage of all arrestees in October and November, 1867 (38 and 35 percent). He has also observed that 30 percent of the inmates in the parish prison in the 1870

✳

Most white New Orleanians never accepted the legitimacy of the Metropolitan Police because the Metropolitans were a racially integrated arm of the Republican state government. Conservative whites might laud the behavior of individual policemen and the effective leadership of the Metropolitan superintendents, but the force was founded on a government that lacked the consent of the racist conservatives it governed. The New Orleans *Times* summarized the conservative case against the Metropolitans in an editorial in 1873: "There are plenty of good men and brave among the police, and we are not unmindful of the fact. Our quarrel is not with them, but with the law which compels us to support them and yet allows us no voice in their management; which reduces our city officers from their rightful attitude of masters to that of clerks and servitors; which foists upon us a body of men who, whatever may be their virtues or efficiency, are yet by the terms of their creation placed in false relations with the community they are ostensibly intended to serve." As a consequence, the Metropolitans were forced to struggle against bitter conservative opposition in the forms of litigation, tax resistance, and organized violence.[47]

Opposition to the Metropolitan Police coalesced very quickly. Local officials in the cities of Jefferson and New Orleans and a theater owner in New Orleans immediately contested the legality of the Metropolitan Police

---

census were African Americans and 43 percent in September 1874. Although he has acknowledged the problem of inferring crime rates from arrest reports, he has not commented on the difficulty in inferring crime rates, or even arrest rates, from static jail population figures. Even if blacks and whites had identical arrest rates, it is quite possible that fewer black arrestees would have been able to make bail, secure release on their own recognizance, or win their cases in court because of economic inequality or discrimination by judges or juries (Blassingame, *Black New Orleans*, 162).

Roger Fischer has noted a pattern of racial segregation of prisoners in the state penitentiary and the Orleans Parish Prison; neither institution was under the control of the Metropolitan Police (*Segregation Struggle in Louisiana*, 84).

When the arrest data are analyzed according to arrestees' occupations, the rather unsurprising result shows that New Orleanians with high occupational status had low arrest rates, and those with low status occupations had high arrest rates. The average annual arrest rates per 100 of population by occupational status group were 9.8 for high white-collar workers, 14.9 for low white-collar workers, 24.2 for skilled blue-collar workers, 53.4 for semiskilled and service workers, and 53.4 for unskilled and menial workers.

47. *Times*, April 7, 1873, May 7, 1868, June 9, 1870; *Daily Picayune*, August 12, 1869, February 11, 1870, June 7, September 2, 28, 1871, October 4, 1872, March 3, December 18, 1873, September 6, 1874, November 5, 1875, September 7, 1876, March 17, 1877.

Act, seeking injunctions to bar the deployment of the new force. This tactic failed because the courts upheld the Metropolitan statute.[48]

Withholding taxes proved a more fruitful tactic of resistance. The jurisdictions within the Metropolitan District were annually assessed for their proportionate shares of the total cost of the police. Jefferson, Carrollton, Algiers, St. Bernard, and New Orleans refused to pay on numerous occasions. In fact, New Orleans began to renege on its financial obligations even earlier, when former Union soldiers and black men joined the city police force. The tax delinquencies of the local governments exacerbated the state's burdensome debt problem and entangled the Metropolitan force in lengthy and troublesome court battles, seriously hampered the payment of police salaries, and eventually forced retrenchment of many police jobs.[49]

Paying the policemen became a major problem. Even before the Metropolitan Police Act took effect, impoverished police officers who had gone unpaid for months had staged a protest and threatened more serious action as early as September, 1868. Because the Board of Metropolitan Police Commissioners was often unable to raise the necessary cash through tax levies, it resorted to issuing salary warrants. An alternative to cash payments was necessary to allow the police to operate, but the issuance of warrants in lieu of hard money worked economic hardship on the policemen. Warrants were issued in several different series denoted by colors; they had a market value of at best 80 to 85 percent of face value, and at times they dropped to a mere 50 percent of their nominal worth. Despite a face value of approximately $83 per month, the actual value of a patrolman's warrant was rarely more than $50 per month in the 1850s.[50]

The Board of Police tried to stabilize and secure the funding of police operations by getting the legislature to tinker with the mechanics of collecting taxes, but these efforts met with little success. An act of 1870 made police warrants receivable for taxes and license fees. Legislation in 1870, 1874, and 1875 attempted to enforce tax collection for the payment of Metropolitan Police appropriations. To protect the Metropolitan organi-

48. *Annual Report*, 1868/69, pp. 44–48; *Daily Picayune*, June 16, 1869; *Republican*, June 15, 1869.

49. *Acts of Louisiana*, 1867, pp. 171–73; *Annual Report*, 1868/69, pp. 7–8, 1869/70, pp. 10–16, 1870/71, pp. 7–8, 1872/73, p. 8, 1873/74, pp. 11–12; *Report of the Attorney General*, 1869, p. 7; *Daily Picayune*, May 1, 7, June 19, 20, 1868.

50. *Annual Report*, 1868/69, pp. 8–9, 1869/70, p. 15; *Times*, September 16–18, 1868, May 28, 1870.

zation from its creditors, the legislature passed a bill in 1869 to prohibit justices of the peace in New Orleans from issuing processes of garnishment against the Board of Police. An act of the legislature in 1869 addressed the underpayment of policemen by adding 30 percent to their salary for the year as compensation for the devalued warrants, but this was merely a stopgap. The actions of the legislature failed to put the police on a consistently sound financial footing.[51]

Financial constraints were so severe that in 1874 and 1875 the legislature enacted two laws to reduce the level of taxation, cut back police expenditures, and pare down the payroll by discharging a substantial number of policemen. From a high of about 735 personnel in 1870, the force was reduced to about 450 men in 1874 and to about 350 by 1876. A force smaller than that of 1860 was compelled to patrol a geographically enlarged jurisdiction with a population roughly twice that in 1860.[52]

Resistance through the courts and through tax delinquencies drained the Metropolitan Police purse, but still more damaging was violent opposition to police authority, both from individuals and from organized groups. The custom of carrying deadly weapons continued to plague the peace of the city, for the war had exacerbated an already extreme proclivity for personal violence among New Orleanians. Organized violence reached an extraordinary level; in eight and one-half years the Metropolitan Police fought at least four small battles and quelled several riots. The toll on policemen ran high: they suffered an average of twenty-two gunshot wounds and twenty other wounds each year.[53]

The inauguration of the Metropolitan organization had been ominously violent. When the police first went on duty in October, 1868, riots in New Orleans and St. Bernard and legal resistance by Jefferson City officials had endangered the viability of the force and led to the suspension of all black policemen. An attempt by city officials in New Orleans to form their own police was thwarted when the U.S. military commander threatened to use troops to enforce the law.[54]

51. *Acts of Louisiana*, 1869, pp. 42, 65, 1870, Extra Session, pp. 213–14, 1874, pp. 68–72, 1875, pp. 35–39; *Annual Report*, 1869/70, p. 15.

52. *Acts of Louisiana*, 1874, p. 109, 1875, p. 10; *Annual Report* as cited in note 12; *Daily Picayune*, March 16, 1876.

53. *Daily Picayune*, May 6, 1871, May 15, 1877; *Report of the Attorney General*, 1869, pp. 3–4.

54. *Annual Report*, 1868/69, p. 7.

In May, 1869, the Metropolitan Police fought the local officials and municipal police of Jefferson City in a successful attempt to install Metropolitan officers in that jurisdiction. The mayor and police chief of Jefferson City refused to allow the Metropolitan detachment to go on duty and had the men arrested and charged with carrying concealed weapons and with illegally trying to carry out police functions. The Metropolitan policemen, commanded by Captain Gustave Schrieber, were then released on their own recognizance. Superintendent Cain of the Metropolitans obtained warrants for the Jefferson City mayor and chief of police, which he tried to serve by marching on the Jefferson City city hall with some three hundred Metropolitan policemen. The Jefferson City force fired on the Metropolitans, who returned fire for a short while and then retreated to the Carrollton railroad depot. One Metropolitan was killed and at least eleven wounded. When federal troops with artillery arrived to assist in assaulting the city hall, it had been abandoned by the local forces. The Metropolitans occupied the hall and began operations as the sole police in Jefferson City.[55]

The Metropolitans' next serious confrontation did not take place until after the hotly contested and much disputed election of November, 1872. The race for control of the state legislature and the governor's office that year began with five contending parties but eventually narrowed to two. The Republicans ran William P. Kellogg, a white Vermonter, as their gubernatorial candidate and a black, C. C. Antoine, for lieutenant governor. The opposing Fusion ticket was headed by Democrat John D. McEnery for governor and Liberal Republican D. B. Penn for lieutenant governor and backed by a coalition of Democrats and Republican followers of former governor Henry Clay Warmoth. Both sides resorted to chicanery, and both claimed electoral victory. The U.S. Grant administration in Washington supported Kellogg as the winner, but the Fusionists established their own competing state government in January, 1873. Thus rival state governments contended for power. When Kellogg ordered a change in command of the state militia, a group of white militiamen refused to turn over control of the Carondelet Street armory in New Orleans. Superintendent Badger of the Metropolitan Police, who recognized Kellogg as the lawful governor, led policemen from four precincts, armed with Winchester rifles, to seize the armory. The militiamen were unwilling to surrender to the

55. *Times*, May 18–20, 1869; *Annual Report*, 1868/69, p. 7.

Metropolitans but peacefully turned over the armory to the police when ordered to do so by a delegation of U.S. Army officers. The intervention of federal officers allowed the militiamen to surrender gracefully and averted the possibility of a bloody resolution to the confrontation but did not resolve the struggle between the rival state governments of Kellogg and McEnery.[56]

This struggle reached its climax in March, 1873, when McEnery supporters staged a massive assault on the Metropolitan Police. After ransacking a gun store on the night of March 5, a party of McEnery adherents armed primarily with revolvers joined with rifle-bearing compatriots to attack the police station in the Cabildo on Jackson Square. Following an exchange of shots, the situation on the square stabilized with the McEnery force of at least two hundred men considerably outnumbering the Metropolitans. When the action at Jackson Square reached an impasse, parties of police were stopped and disarmed by McEnery followers around the city, and McEnery's men captured the police station in Jefferson City.[57]

Superintendent Badger tipped the balance by bringing up reinforcements armed with rifles and accompanied by a twelve-pounder Napoleon cannon. They dispersed the opposition at Jackson Square, and shortly thereafter the Metropolitans recaptured the station at Jefferson City. The police took possession of McEnery's office and the chambers of his legislature and other state offices at the Odd Fellows' Building, arresting several legislators in the process. U.S. troops helped the police to patrol the streets after the struggle was over.[58]

Scarcely a month elapsed before the Metropolitan force was deployed again as a military unit. The police were called out of the city in April to the town of Colfax, some two hundred miles from New Orleans, where an intense battle between blacks and whites had resulted in a massacre of the black contingent, leaving as many as one hundred African Americans dead.

56. *Daily Picayune*, December 14, 20, 1872; Taylor, *Louisiana Reconstructed*, 253–55; Rable, *But There Was No Peace*, 122–24.

57. *Daily Picayune*, March 6–8, 1873; *Times*, March 6, 1873; *Republican*, March 6–7, 1873; Taylor, *Louisiana Reconstructed*, 254–55; Rable, *But There Was No Peace*, 125. The mob at Jackson Square may have been considerably larger than two hundred; Rable has placed it at six hundred.

58. *Daily Picayune*, March 6–8, 1873; *Times*, March 6, 1873; *Republican*, March 6–7, 1873; Taylor, *Louisiana Reconstructed*, 254–55; Rable, *But There Was No Peace*, 125.

The Metropolitans arrived too late to stop the violence, but they did arrest several whites.[59]

Almost immediately the police were pressed into service again in their capacity as the Metropolitan brigade of militia. An expedition to keep the peace in a tense racial confrontation in the town of Amite proved uneventful, perhaps because the appearance of the police was sufficient to prevent any outbreak of violence. Two weeks later, in May, 1873, some 125 Metropolitans encountered more formidable opposition in the town of St. Martinville, which also lay outside the Metropolitan District. There the police faced an organization of whites who were resisting the authority of the state government to collect taxes. For several days the Metropolitan detachment was besieged in the courthouse by the tax resisters, who numbered somewhere between four hundred and six hundred men. The skirmishing resulted in few lives lost, and the arrival of police reinforcements brought the violence to an end about a week after it had begun. Back in New Orleans, the remaining elements of the police were alerted and stationed to guard the legislature against a rumored coup. The Orleans Parish grand jury protested the use of the Metropolitan Police outside the city, asking the district court judge to have the governor and Superintendent Badger indicted for usurpation of powers not properly belonging to their offices. No indictment was forthcoming, but the police were not obliged to do service outside the district again.[60]

The uneasy truce between the police and their conservative antagonists endured for a little more than a year. It ended on September 14, 1874, in the bloodiest struggle of the Metropolitan administration, the battle of Liberty Place. Beginning at Opelousas in April, 1874, Democrats throughout the state formed local groups called White Leagues to assert white supremacy and destroy the Republican government of William Kellogg. In New Orleans an organization that had been known as the Crescent City Democratic Club in the 1868 and 1872 elections served as the nucleus in

59. *Times,* April 7, 13, 16, 1873; *Republican,* April 22, 1873; Taylor, *Louisiana Reconstructed,* 267–73; Rable, *But There Was No Peace,* 126–29. The *Times* alleged that several policemen opposed being mobilized as militia, but the *Republican* denounced that claim as a "fabrication" (*Times,* April 23, 27, 30, May 1, 1873; *Republican,* April 26, 1873).

60. *Times,* May 6–11, 1873; *Republican,* April 22, 1873. The Board of Metropolitan Police contended that the deployment of the police as a militia unit was detrimental to their role in policing the Metropolitan District and asked the legislature to repeal the Metropolitan Brigade law (*Annual Report,* 1873/74, pp. 12–13).

forming the city's White League. John McEnery, regarded by Democrats as the legitimate winner of the 1872 gubernatorial race, became the state-wide leader of the loosely affiliated White Leagues. The White League in New Orleans prepared for possible military action against the Kellogg administration by drilling secretly and ordering arms from outside the state. The Metropolitan Police became aware of the arms shipments and began seizing guns, some already in the city and others as they arrived by steamer, on September 8, 9, and 10.[61]

McEnery left the city, probably to protect himself against criminal charges in the likely event of a White League coup against the Kellogg regime, and his lieutenant governor, D. B. Penn, and militia commanders Frederick N. Ogden and John B. Angell prepared to seize the statehouse (the former St. Louis Hotel) and to use force if necessary to ensure that guns aboard a recently arrived steamer were unloaded and used to arm members of the White League. On September 13, the White League called for a mass rally at the Henry Clay statue on Canal Street for the following day. As a crowd of perhaps five thousand whites gathered on Canal Street on September 14, White League military units set up barricades along Poydras Street (roughly parallel to and four blocks upriver from Canal) all the way from Carondelet Street to the river (a distance of about twelve blocks).[62]

Most of the federal troops stationed in New Orleans had been sent out of the city to avoid the seasonal risk of yellow fever (an epidemic of the disease had ravaged New Orleans the previous year). To deal with the White League insurgency, the Kellogg administration could call on a force of black militiamen under the command of General James Longstreet, adjutant general of the state militia, and between five hundred and six hundred Metropolitan policemen under Superintendent Badger. With two Gatling guns and a battery of artillery, Longstreet and Badger led the Metropolitans from the Cabildo station on Jackson Square and the militia from the statehouse to Canal Street, establishing a line along Canal running about four blocks from the Custom House (at Canal and Decatur) to the levee. From the levee end of the line Badger led about half of the policemen toward the White League position, but detachments of White Leaguers

61. *Daily Picayune*, June 24, September 9–13, 1874; Taylor, *Louisiana Reconstructed*, 290–92; Rable, *But There Was No Peace*, 137–38.

62. *Daily Picayune*, September 10–13, 1874.

had sneaked onto the levee and were able to enfilade Badger's force, which received fire from its front and left flank. The Metropolitans did not make good use of their cannon and Gatling guns, and the White League fired effectively enough so that the police soon retreated, leaving Badger lying wounded in Canal Street. As the police retreated, the militia followed their example and fled. Many of the policemen threw down their guns and stripped off their uniform coats and hats. The armed forces of the White League had carried the day, losing sixteen killed and forty-five wounded to the Metropolitans' eleven killed and sixty wounded.[63]

The White League and its supporters celebrated their victory, mourned their dead, occupied the statehouse, and installed a new city police force under Chief Thomas Boylan, whose experience in law enforcement extended back to the 1850s. Their rejoicing was cut short, though, when they learned that on September 15 President Grant ordered the insurgents to lay down their arms within five days. They complied with the order, refraining as usual from direct confrontation with the federal government, and the Republican government was quickly restored. After only four days of forced retirement, the Metropolitan Police returned to duty.[64]

The battle of Liberty Place did not give Democrats control of the state and city governments, but it did vividly demonstrate the vulnerability of the Republicans and the Metropolitan Police. A few months later, in January, 1875, the Democrats attempted a legislative coup in the statehouse, using strongarm tactics but refraining from the sort of overt military action that had led President Grant to intervene on behalf of the Kellogg administration the previous September. A bloodless show of force by federal troops shored up the Republican regime once more, but the incident again showed that if the federal government failed to provide military support for the Republicans in Louisiana the Democrats might prevail. The Metropolitan Police grew weaker because financial problems forced retrench-

63. *Daily Picayune*, September 15–24, 1874; *Republican*, September 15–26, 1874; Taylor, *Louisiana Reconstructed*, 293–94; Rable, *But There Was No Peace*, 138–40; Landry, *Battle of Liberty Place*, 96–132. The number of militia under Longstreet's command is not clear; Taylor suggested three thousand, but the number near the battle certainly had to have been far fewer. Landry has estimated four hundred.

64. *Daily Picayune*, September 15–24, 1874; *Republican*, September 15–26, 1874; Taylor, *Louisiana Reconstructed*, 293–94; Rable, *But There Was No Peace*, 138–40; Landry, *Battle of Liberty Place*, 96–132.

ment and reduced the number of policemen still further, by some one hundred between 1874 and 1876.[65]

Louisiana Republicans entered the 1876 election with serious handicaps. Under Kellogg, the Republicans had relied largely on black voters, but many Louisiana African Americans believed he had appointed too many whites to political office and resented his failure to provide schools for their children. The Democratic candidate for governor, Francis T. Nicholls, had not been active in politics long enough to make many enemies, and he repeatedly assured blacks that he would protect their rights and interests. The Democrats succeeded in persuading some blacks to support Nicholls and intimidating many black and white Republicans into not voting. Both Nicholls and the Republican gubernatorial candidate, Stephen B. Packard, claimed victory, and they established rival state governments in New Orleans in January, 1877. Nicholls kept his supporters from resorting to violence, and both the lame duck president Grant and the incoming president Rutherford B. Hayes declined to intervene to support Packard. The Nicholls government gathered strength and money and spread its influence over the state, while the Packard government, barricaded in the statehouse, shrank away to nothing.[66]

The commander of the Democratic city police, Thomas Boylan, took possession of the Metropolitan Police stations and put his own force on duty on January 9, 1877. By February 1, only seventy-five Metropolitans remained at the statehouse to support the Republicans. On April 6, Packard received official word from a commission sent by Hayes to New Orleans that his administration would not be sustained by the federal government, and on April 24 the last of the U.S. troops boarded a steamer and left the city.[67]

Meanwhile, the Nicholls legislature considered a bill to return the police in New Orleans to the control of the municipal government and adopted it on March 31, 1877, after some debate. Restored to its former preeminence in law enforcement matters, the Common Council enacted an ordinance on April 26 to restructure the police. Thus ended a period of

65. Taylor, *Louisiana Reconstructed*, 304–305.

66. *Daily Picayune*, January 10, 11, 1877; *Republican*, January 10, 11, 1877; Rable, *But There Was No Peace*, 180–83; Taylor, *Louisiana Reconstructed*, 487–99.

67. *Daily Picayune*, February 1, April 25, 26, 1877.

fifteen years almost to the day since the U.S. Navy had appeared before the city in 1862 and initiated an era of unusual federal influence over policing. The city commanded its own police once again, and conservatives controlled the city.[68]

68. *Acts of Louisiana,* 1877, pp. 57–58; *Daily Picayune,* March 3, 7, 20, April 27, 1877; Ordinances and Resolutions of the Common Council (Administrative Series), No. 3914, April 26, 1877, and No. 3964, May 31, 1877.

# 6

# "THE WONDER IS THAT THIEVES DON'T PICK UP THE TOWN AND CARRY IT OFF"
## The Crescent City Police, 1877–1889

W HEN Mark Twain visited New Orleans in 1882, he saw much to praise. He found the city "well out-fitted with progressive men," and the bustle of economic activity he observed led him to call it "a driving place commercially." New Orleans impressed Twain as "the best-lighted city in the Union, electrically speaking"; telephones were to be found "everywhere," and its newspapers were first-rate.[1]

Indeed, despite the Civil War, the huge municipal debt accumulated both before and during Reconstruction, and three terrible yellow fever epidemics in the 1870s, New Orleans boosters could point with pride to signs of civic achievement. The city's educational institutions included 3 colleges, 42 high schools, and 145 elementary schools; it could boast of two opera houses with 3,800 seats, two theaters with a seating capacity of 4,600, and an academy of music that accommodated 2,200 people. The municipal infrastructure included 140 miles of street railroad served by 373 cars and coaches, a waterworks pumping an average of 8 million gallons daily through 71 miles of pipe, and a gasworks producing almost 600,000 cubic feet per day.[2]

But neither residents nor visitors commented favorably about the New Orleans police. A sweeping descriptive survey of more than two hundred U.S. cities published as part of the 1880 census report commented that in New Orleans "the entire force is ill-paid, and at times not paid; it is there-

---

1. Quoted in Joy J. Jackson, *New Orleans in the Gilded Age: Politics and Urban Progress, 1880–1896* (Baton Rouge, 1969), 5.

2. George E. Waring, Jr., *Report of the Social Statistics of the Cities* (2 vols.; Washington, D.C., 1887), II, 273–75, 290. Although boosters would have found these quantitative measures impressive in comparison with earlier phases of the city's history, they would have appeared unfavorable in the light of other cities' achievements as of 1880.

fore deficient in *morale*, and is totally inadequate in point of numbers." The English traveler George A. H. Sala also found the police of the Crescent City a disappointment. "The New Orleans policeman is apt to be . . . attired on the 'go-as-you-please' principle. . . . It is the business of a policeman to inspire awe; and how can you expect to be awe-stricken by a personage who wears a turn-down collar and a Byron tie, who carries a gold watch and chain at his fob, and who smokes a cigar while on duty?" Local journalists routinely found the police woefully unsatisfactory. One such editorialist asserted that the police department was "a discredit to the city . . . the force has been deteriorating until it is doubtful if it can become much worse." Another editorial assessment of the shortcomings of the police concluded in disgust, "The wonder is that thieves don't pick up the town and carry it off."[3]

Critics had good cause to fault the police of the Crescent City. As the city government struggled to deal with its debt burden, it reduced the size of the police force until it was indeed "totally inadequate in point of numbers" and kept salaries so low that recruiting good men was difficult. Police involvement in politics increased, provoking well-founded charges of voter intimidation, and the patronage system of appointments too often bestowed favor on the incompetent and corrupt. Black New Orleanians were greatly underrepresented on the police force and faced more abuse by white policemen. The police also suffered from an internal power struggle between the increasingly independent detective squad and the chief of police, a struggle marked by a murderous gun battle in 1881 which left one detective dead and another severely wounded.

Indeed, irresponsible shooting by policemen was a serious problem. The district attorney in 1885 tried to offer guidance toward the development of a sensible policy on police use of deadly force but made virtually no headway. The state legislature did not exempt police officers from the prohibition on carrying concealed weapons, and most policemen continued to violate that law; the mayors offered inconsistent and conflicting advice ungrounded in statutory and decisional law; the chiefs of police apparently made few—if any—suggestions to the men on the beat about the use of force; and when policemen shot and killed citizens, the courts declined to

---

3. *Ibid.*, 292; George Augustus Sala, *America Revisited: From the Bay of New York to the Gulf of Mexico, and from Lake Michigan to the Pacific* (5th ed.; London, 1885), 281–82, *Times*, August 15, 1879, April 27, 1880.

hold them accountable for their actions. Without official policy direction or legal education, lacking any training in firearms safety and marksmanship, policemen made their own individual policy regarding deadly force, with very destructive results.

Improvements in policing in these years were few. In 1886 the city initiated a fast response system, installing telegraph boxes in scattered locations to allow patrolmen on their beats to call the station for rapid reinforcement by horse-drawn patrol wagons. The state legislature adopted a law in 1888 which mandated a civil service system for New Orleans, thereby curbing some of the blatantly partisan political activities of the police force. Yet the civil service reform could not extricate the police from politics entirely, and it helped redefine the role of the police by narrowing it to crime control and the maintenance of order, sacrificing some of the social service that had long been part of policing.

*Redemption* was the word conservative white Democrats in Louisiana and elsewhere in the South used for the undoing of Reconstruction. For a people who had already apotheosized the Civil War as a glorious Lost Cause and who had condemned Republicans as venal and vindictive carpetbaggers and scalawags, Redemption served as the denouement of a three-act morality play. Conservatives regarded the fall of the Reconstruction government as a happy ending. But the return of the Democratic party to power in Louisiana changed the course of race relations, for after 1877 African Americans made few gains and suffered considerable losses. Black men in New Orleans won few police appointments, and police treatment of the black population became more abusive. Policing also suffered from municipal penury—and parsimony—as the manpower shortage of the late Reconstruction era worsened and police salaries fell to antebellum levels.

Retrenchment dramatically affected the police after 1877. The budget of the Metropolitan Police had reached a peak of about $840,000 in their first year of operation, falling thereafter to about $600,000 by 1874. The latter figure closely approximated the cost of the pre-Metropolitan city police in 1867, when the municipal budget allocated just under $600,000 to the police. When the legislature abolished the Metropolitan force in 1877 and turned control back to the city authorities, it placed a ceiling of $325,000 on the police budget, but in fact the Common Council never availed itself of the maximum allowable appropriation.[4]

4. *Annual Report of the Board of Metropolitan Police*, 1869/70, pp. 8–11, 1873/74, p. 8; *Acts of Louisiana*, 1877, pp. 57–58.

Police budgets after 1877 started small and shrank rapidly. The Common Council allowed only $250,000 for the police in 1879 and even less in subsequent years. By 1883 the council had whittled the cost of policing down to $183,000, and the police budget for 1888 amounted to just $171,000. Thus the Crescent City Police (as this organization was called) received an annual appropriation that was at most about 40 percent of the smallest Metropolitan budget and at its lowest ebb was a mere 20 percent of the largest Metropolitan budget. Although the Metropolitan force had served an area embracing three parishes, roughly nine-tenths of its assessments had been in and for the city of New Orleans. Even allowing for the change in jurisdictional territory, the post-Reconstruction police operated on one-half to one-fourth the sums allotted to the Metropolitan force.[5]

Financial hardship led immediately to serious manpower shortages. The first city ordinance to organize the police in April, 1877, was amended by the Common Council just one month later to lower police salaries so as to employ a greater number of patrolmen for beat duty. Just under 400 men were appointed at the outset, but this number fell as allocations for the police declined. By 1887 there were only 230 active-duty policemen on the force. The ratio of policemen to 10,000 of population never rose above 15 in the years 1877–1889 and dropped as low as 11 per 10,000. During the tenure of the Metropolitan Police, that ratio had never fallen below 24 and had reached a high of 36 active-duty policemen for every 10,000 people. No doubt the Metropolitan force needed more men to deal with the organized resistance of white conservatives, but the Crescent City Police were certainly undermanned. This was a common problem in the post-Reconstruction South, as retrenchment led to police manpower reductions in many southern cities (see Table 18).[6]

The city government's penny-pinching produced not only an understaffed police force but an underpaid one as well. The salary of Metropolitan policemen had been a nominal $80 per month, which meant about $50 to $65 of buying power after their pay warrants had been discounted. Patrolmen earned only $50 per month after 1877, except for a brief period during which they received $60. Payment of salaries of the Crescent City Police was often overdue. During the yellow fever epidemic of 1878, many

5. *Times*, August 15, 1879; *Daily Picayune*, January 5, 1883, January 1, 1885, December 28, 1887.

6. *Times*, August 15, 26, 1879; June 7, 1880; *Daily Picayune*, January 26, 1887.

## TABLE 18
### Number of Policemen per 10,000 of Population in Eighteen Southern Cities in 1870 and 1880, with Net Change

|  | 1870 | 1880 | Net Change (%) |  | 1870 | 1880 | Net Change (%) |
|---|---|---|---|---|---|---|---|
| Galveston | 9.4 | 13.5 | +43.3 | Nashville[a] | 11.2 | 8.1 | −27.7 |
| Petersburg | 10.0 | 10.6 | + 6.0 | San Antonio | 12.2 | 8.3 | −32.4 |
| Charleston | 16.1 | 16.6 | + 3.1 | Richmond | 19.8 | 13.1 | −33.8 |
| Lexington | 9.5 | 9.0 | − 5.3 | Savannah | 32.2 | 18.9 | −41.3 |
| Vicksburg | 14.5 | 11.9 | −18.1 | Memphis | 16.2 | 9.2 | −43.2 |
| Augusta | 26.6 | 21.6 | −18.8 | New Orleans | 33.8 | 15.4 | −54.4 |
| Norfolk | 17.7 | 13.7 | −22.6 | Mobile | 35.6 | 14.1 | −60.4 |
| Atlanta | 15.1 | 11.2 | −25.8 | Montgomery | 22.7 | 9.0 | −60.4 |
| Louisville | 14.7 | 10.8 | −26.5 | Portsmouth | 16.2 | 4.4 | −72.8 |

*Sources:* Censuses of 1870 and 1880, RG 29, NA.

[a]Data are for change in administration in 1869.

of the city's taxpayers fell into delinquency, and the Common Council was consequently delayed in paying the police. The exigency of the moment compelled many policemen to sell their pay certificates to speculators for less than face value. This became the common practice whenever the municipal government could not meet the payroll with cash.[7]

The minuscule salaries of policemen were frequently the subject of public complaint because low salaries made it difficult to attract good men to the force. In 1879 the New Orleans *Times* advocated higher salaries to improve the police force, whose flaws it attributed to politically motivated appointments and to the "miserable and shameful manner in which the men are paid, or, rather, *not* paid, the effect of which is to drive away nearly every man who can make a living at any other occupation and to leave only those who cannot better even the wretched pittance they receive from the City." The following year the *Times* observed that the police department could recruit a good man only when he was out of work, and "as soon as he finds something else to do he resigns. The consequence is the force is being constantly changed and, as a rule, only those who have some sinister

7. *Daily Picayune*, August 15, 1878; *Times*, April 27, 1880.

purpose in view, or whose services, for various reasons, are not in demand remain." Regular policemen often took leaves of absence to work at other jobs when the city treasury was empty. Appeals from the newspapers and the mayors fell on unsympathetic ears in the chambers of the Common Council. In the course of one debate over police salaries in 1879, a member of the council remarked that policemen were paid more than day laborers, had an easy job, and ran no more risk than laborers in industry. The councilman wanted to reduce the fifty-dollar-per-month compensation.[8]

The city government's debt burden also weakened the pension system because the city declined to make appropriations for the pension fund. Members of the force created a police relief fund in 1878 to care for sick and indigent policemen during the yellow fever epidemic of that year. Contributions from other police forces around the country, including those of New York, Detroit, and Cincinnati, helped to establish the fund, but by 1882 the police were resorting to the sale of tickets for a benefit performance of the Hess Acme Opera Company to replenish the coffers. By April, 1883, the fund had dwindled to a mere $215 so the precinct captains met with the chief and resolved to ask several amateur dramatic clubs to do more benefit performances. The only consistent source of money for pensions came from the fines levied against policemen for delinquencies. This money, however, was reserved for widows and orphans. To make matters worse, the practice of paying policemen for time lost to job-related illness or injury was discontinued.[9]

The city's financial difficulties caused it to have nearly the weakest police force of America's major cities in these years. New York, Boston, Baltimore, St. Louis, and Washington all had higher police-to-population ratios. Other cities with police manpower proportionate to that of New Orleans, such as Louisville, Cincinnati, Detroit, and Philadelphia, or with lower ratios, like Cleveland, Chicago, and Milwaukee, had less severe crime problems and were easier to patrol because of their high population density. Not only was the New Orleans force scattered over an unusually large territory, but it also had the lowest compensation of any big-city police in the country. Patrolmen in New York, Boston, and San Francisco made twice as much as their Crescent City counterparts (sometimes for fewer hours on the job), and the great urban places of the southern periphery—

8. *Times,* March 12, August 26, 1879; *Daily Picayune,* January 5, 1883.
9. *Times,* June 13, 1879; *Daily Picayune,* November 28, 1882, April 4, 1883, July 25, 1889.

St. Louis, Baltimore, and Washington—paid their patrolmen 50 to 80 percent more than did New Orleans. Among other southern cities, only Mobile offered less compensation (a trifling forty dollars monthly) to its patrolmen. Norfolk, Memphis, Atlanta, Savannah, and Montgomery had salary scales 10 to 20 percent higher than New Orleans, while Chattanooga and Charleston paid their patrolmen the same fifty dollars per month earned by officers in New Orleans.[10]

Because it was undermanned, the police force had increasing difficulty in preserving the peace during the labor-management troubles of the late 1870s and 1880s. Strikers complained of inequitable police tactics, especially when black workers were involved. Although the police were not consistently brutal or repressive in handling strikers, striking workers sometimes had cause to complain that the police were trying to "bulldoze" them. During a teamsters' strike in September, 1881, several policemen shot indiscriminately into crowds, and one officer was subsequently indicted for murder. Despite the temporary addition of one hundred extra policemen for the duration of the strike, the police proved inadequate and the militia was mobilized to maintain order. When the city streetcar drivers struck in December, 1884, the police again performed ineffectually. Even though the police put in a great deal of overtime, the city had to employ temporary special policemen during the crisis.[11]

The inadequacy of the municipal police led business interests to rely more on private security forces. A harbor patrol of some thirty to forty men, paid out of a private fund collected from wharf lessees, was placed under the command of the chief of police, and its men were commissioned with the same powers as municipal policemen. The Cotton Exchange employed a private police force to check pilferage at the cotton presses and yards and on steamboat landings and ship wharves. Other private security arrangements supplemented the city police, too. A night watch patrol for the business district operated on a subscription basis, and detective agencies provided their services for hire.[12]

10. *Times*, August 15, 1879; Waring, *Report*, I, 116–20, 385–86, 484–87, 591–92, 614, 675, 834, 870, II, 23, 47–49, 69, 103, 128, 139, 149, 162, 167, 179, 197, 203, 210, 372–73, 385, 508–509, 590–91, 614, 675, 811–12.

11. *Daily Picayune*, March 19, June 3, 1878, September 3, 11–15, 1881, October 19, 1883, November 7–9, December 30, 31, 1884, January 1, 1885, April 15, 1886, October 31, November 6–8, 1889; *Times*, October 29, 30, 1879, January 24, February 10, April 6, September 7, 10, October 20, November 7, 24, 1880.

12. Waring, *Report*, II, 292–93; *Daily Picayune*, October 9, 1881, June 14, 1884, January

A vigilante organization, the Committee of Public Safety, was formed in the late summer of 1881 to compensate for deficiencies in the police department. This was a secret, avowedly nonpartisan body divided into eight branches or companies and led by a Grand Council. The committee proclaimed that its purposes were to protect life, liberty, and property and to do so impartially; to coerce public servants to do their duty and protect them from abuse when they did so; to monitor the expenditure of public funds to ensure that they were not misused; to ferret out unwilling witnesses and suppressed evidence; and to prevent undue personal or political influence on the issuance of pardons. Its members apparently did not resort to violence, instead focusing their energies on assisting in the prosecution of suspected criminals, and they were praised for their work by the *Daily Picayune*, the district attorney, and Chief of Police Thomas Boylan. The committee's relationship with the police department seems to have been impartial, for it actively aided the prosecution of persons accused of assaulting policemen, yet it also sponsored cases against policemen implicated in abuses of authority, including the clubbing of black people by white officers. In the spring of 1882 the committee ran into increasingly frustrating resistance, and it eventually faded into oblivion.[13]

The most daring effort to harness private resources for the maintenance of order was a scheme to establish an illegal licensing system for gambling. Mayor Joseph Shakspeare formulated the plan and put it into effect in 1882, and for about five years it worked with some success to regulate gambling and provide funds for social services. The great triumph of the Shakspeare plan was that it generated money to construct and operate the city's first almshouse. Despite its illegality, the Shakspeare plan gained the approval of the grand jury and the city council because it reduced the number of gambling establishments and placed them under a rudimentary system of control. Though the almshouse was its most tangible product, the system also seems to have reduced police graft because the open toleration of licensed gambling houses removed much of the incentive for gamblers to bribe policemen or yield to police extortion. In effect, graft money went directly to the city government.[14]

7, 1885; Ordinances and Resolutions of the Common Council (Administrative Series), No. 6715, November 1, 1880 (Council Series), No. 3762, May 21, 1889.

13. *Daily Picayune*, August 3, 10, 14, September 4, October 30, December 8, 9, 1881, January 17, March 16, April 2, 1882.

14. *Daily Picayune*, December 2, 1882, August 14, 1883, March 6, 1884.

Another important manifestation of regressive change in policing was the increasingly racist behavior of the overwhelmingly white police force toward the African American community. In 1880, African Americans held only 6.6 percent of police jobs (they constituted 26.7 percent of the city's total population), and among its white members, natives of Louisiana accounted for a majority of white policemen; of the foreign-born groups, only the perennial Irish were overrepresented (see Table 19). The leaders of the city government signaled the resurgence of racism as policy. In 1885 Mayor Joseph Guillote ordered the police to make blanket arrests of African American men who congregated around gambling houses; levee laborers (many of whom were black) were on strike at the time, and the mayor announced that he wanted any black man who "did not want to work" to be sent to jail. On another occasion a squad of policemen dispersed an orderly and peaceful meeting of black Republicans who were forming a Blaine and Logan club for the 1884 election and who offered no provocation to the police. In the election of November, 1884, the chief of police had his men arrest some five to six hundred black men before the polling to prevent their voting against the regular Democratic ticket.[15]

Black people encountered trouble with the police individually, too. One black man refused an arbitrary order from two white policemen to "move on" and was shot to death; the two policemen were tried for murder but were acquitted. In another instance, a white policeman arrested a black man who had been knifed by several white men; at his hearing the judge elicited the facts, recognized the injustice of the arrest, and released the wounded man. Faced with such abuse from the police, black New Orleanians became reluctant to call on the police when they were victimized by crime. White policemen were not invariably the enemies of African Americans; on some occasions white officers arrested other white members of the force for abusing blacks. Yet the adversarial relationship between black citizens and the police certainly intensified after 1877.[16]

Partisan politics increasingly corrupted the city police after 1877. Black voters were prime targets for mass arrests and police intimidation, and white opponents of the regular (conservative) Democratic administrations also found themselves subject to police harassment. When an election in

15. Census of 1880, RG 29, NA; *Daily Picayune*, August 8, November 4, 5, 8, 9, 23, 1884, October 28, 1885.

16. *Daily Picayune*, March 11, April 17, November 8, December 3, 1884.

## TABLE 19
### NATIVITIES OF WHITE POLICE IN 1880

|  | Police | | White Adult Males (sample) | |
| --- | --- | --- | --- | --- |
|  | % | No. | % | No. |
| Native-born | 65.3 | 203 | 51.5 | 1,079 |
| Louisiana | 55.6 | 173 | 37.9 | 793 |
| Other slave states[a] | 3.9 | 12 | 6.8 | 142 |
| Pa., N.J., N.Y. | 3.5 | 11 | 3.3 | 69 |
| New England | 1.0 | 3 | 1.5 | 32 |
| Midwest | 1.3 | 4 | 2.0 | 41 |
| Other | 0 | 0 | 0.1 | 2 |
| Foreign-born | 34.7 | 108 | 48.4 | 1,014 |
| Ireland | 22.2 | 69 | 10.8 | 226 |
| Germany | 8.0 | 25 | 15.3 | 321 |
| France | 1.3 | 4 | 9.8 | 205 |
| Spain | 0 | 0 | 2.3 | 48 |
| Italy | 0 | 0 | 2.3 | 48 |
| Britain | 1.6 | 5 | 2.9 | 61 |
| Other | 1.6 | 5 | 3.9 | 82 |
| Totals | 100.0 | 311 | 99.9 | 2,093 |

*Source:* Census of 1880, RG 29, NA.

[a]Slave states as of 1860.

December, 1883, was marred by voter intimidation, one of the city tax collectors who opposed the regular Democrats observed that the actions of the police indicated that the force was "against us." Probably even more abusive than the municipal police were the officers of the civil sheriff's department. A grand jury report in 1884 recommended that the sheriff's department be barred from officiating at elections because they frequently interfered in a partisan fashion. Two sheriff's deputies stood trial that year for committing murder at the polls, but they were acquitted.[17]

An integral part of the politicization of the police was partisan favoritism in the appointment of policemen. When the legislature abolished the Metropolitan organization, it also restructured the police board. Instead of empowering the governor to appoint the commissioners, that power was

17. *Times,* September 3, December 4, 1879, November 3, 1880; *Daily Picayune,* November 6, 1878, December 15, 1883, February 28, April 29, May 30, June 5, November 4, 1884.

vested in the mayor. The police board's only function was to adjudicate cases of alleged police misconduct and remove policemen. Even this shrunken jurisdiction of the Board of Police Commissioners came under fire, for in 1881 Mayor Shakspeare vetoed an ordinance that would have turned out the incumbent commissioners and the entire police force. Such resistance to partisanship in appointments was rare, however, and the force was "reorganized" to allow new favorites into the ranks in 1883, 1884, and 1887. A new city charter abolished the police board in 1883.[18]

Despite the statute making police appointments permanent on condition of good behavior, the reorganizations rendered appointments temporary and partisan. Candidates for the police received favorable consideration for appointment and promotion on the basis of their party affiliations, their ethnic backgrounds, their kinship ties, and their memberships in fire companies and militia units. When journalists advocated police reform, they singled out such practices as particularly pernicious. The New Orleans *Times* in 1879 attributed the poor performance of the police to low salaries and to the "system by which the policemen are appointed, and by which appointments are distributed as political rewards instead of by the standard of efficiency." When the *Daily Picayune* called for reorganization of the force in 1882, it cautioned that reorganization should mean "something more than turning out one man's friends in order to furnish another man's friends with place and salary. . . . The very moment that a policeman learns that he is expected to serve his patron rather than the public, he becomes an active politician, to the detriment of his efficiency as an officer."[19]

Another problem afflicting the Crescent City Police derived from the increasing independence of the detectives on the force. Detectives had been a part of the police at least since the early 1850s, when they were called special officers and served directly under the chief of police. The detectives of the Crescent City Police held positions of considerable status and power. They earned twice as much as patrolmen and almost as much as captains (each of whom commanded a precinct); their work was more varied and

18. *Times*, March 12, 1879; *Daily Picayune*, January 26, February 2, 13, April 27, May 4, August 30, 1881, November 23, 1882, January 8, 24, 31, May 7, 14, 1884. Although the law granted the power of appointment jointly to the mayor and the Board of Administrators, in practice the mayor seems to have made most of the appointments.

19. *Times*, January 4, 1879; *Daily Picayune*, November 20, 1882, January 8, 1883, September 17, 1885, September 3, 1886.

interesting than beat patrol duty and offered more opportunity for graft; and their intimate connection to the highest circle of the police elite made them influential and powerful.

The extent of the detectives' power can be gauged by their effort to establish virtual autonomy from the chief of police. In 1881 the Common Council created the post of chief of aids (detectives were known at the time as aids to the chief of police), which established a post virtually equal to that of the chief of the whole department; under this ordinance detectives would report to the chief of aids rather than to the chief of police. Although the mayor vetoed the ordinance, the council passed it over his veto. Later in the year, the Board of Police Commissioners requested that the office be abolished and that detectives be patrolmen detailed to that duty, rather than separate and distinct appointees. The council repealed its chief of aids ordinance for a while but subsequently reestablished the office, and the conflict over the detectives' aspirations for autonomy persisted for most of the 1880s. In 1888, Mayor Shakspeare recommended the abolition of the detective squad, and when the legislature enacted the civil service law the following year, detective duties were assigned to patrolmen detailed for the purpose and subject to reassignment to beat patrol.[20]

The conflict over the detective squad assumed special intensity because of the dubious character of some of the men who served as aids, especially two of the chiefs of aids. The first man to hold the office, Thomas Devereaux, had a checkered career marked by violence, but this did not prevent his becoming a leading contender for the post of chief of police. As a detective of the Metropolitan Police, Devereaux shot and killed an escaped convict under circumstances that led another policeman to allege that the homicide was premeditated murder. Though he was not convicted of any crime, Devereaux lost his place on the force because of a personal conflict with Superintendent W. F. Loan in 1875. Shortly thereafter he was arrested for the murder of former detective Robert Harris, who had evidently been an accessory to an attempt to kill Devereaux. When Harris was shot to death in February, 1876, the grand jury indicted Devereaux, but the petit jury acquitted the future chief of aids. After the end of Reconstruction Devereaux received an appointment as superintendent of the Boys' House

20. *Daily Picayune*, April 6, 8, October 5, 19, 27, 1881, February 20, 1883, August 18, 1885, February 10, 24, 1886, May 9, 1888.

of Refuge. He was soon elected to the legislature, and not long thereafter he became chief of aids.[21]

As chief of aids and still a member of the legislature, Devereaux preferred charges against Chief of Police Thomas Boylan when Boylan attempted to issue orders directly to the detectives rather than transmit them through Devereaux. Devereaux missed a chance to become chief of police himself when Mayor Shakspeare vetoed a reorganization ordinance in 1881; had the ordinance been implemented, the mayor asserted that the Board of Administrators would have overridden his wishes and named Devereaux chief. Devereaux' rivalry with Boylan played an important role in embroiling the chief of aids in a dispute with two of his detectives, Mike and David Hennessy, who had aligned themselves with Boylan rather than Devereaux.[22]

In October, 1881, Devereaux filed charges with the Board of Police Commissioners, accusing the Hennessys of several offenses. Both of the Hennessys (who were cousins) asserted that the accusations were malicious and unfounded. The police commissioners placed enough credence in the Hennessys' claims that they suspended Devereaux and charged him with disrespect to the board and Chief Boylan. While this case was in process, Devereaux and the Hennessys got into a fight, during which Devereaux shot Mike Hennessy in the jaw and was himself fatally wounded by David Hennessy. Both of the Hennessys were dismissed from the force. Mike lingered near death for a long time but survived to stand trial with his cousin for murder. The two were acquitted, probably in part because Chief Boylan testified on their behalf. David Hennessy was reappointed a detective, then resigned to become assistant and then head of a private detective agency. He returned to the city police in 1888 as chief of the department. Mike became head of a private detective agency in Houston, where he was murdered in 1886, shot five times by unknown parties while returning home from the theater. David was murdered in 1890 in New Orleans, apparently because of his investigation of shootings in the Italian-American community.[23]

Another chief of aids, Theodore J. Boasso, achieved notoriety a few

21. *Daily Picayune*, November 3, 1875, February 26, March 2, 1876, October 14, 1881. Robert Harris had once been accused of attempted murder.

22. *Daily Picayune*, January 20, July 2, October 14, 1881.

23. *Daily Picayune*, October 11, 14, November 8, 1881, April 25–28, 1882, May 28, 1884, September 8, 1885, October 1, 1886.

years after the killing of Thomas Devereaux. In 1885, Boasso obtained a false marriage license and used it to seduce a young woman named Catherine Kuhn. After the chief of aids had abandoned the woman and assaulted her brother, he was arrested, tried, and sentenced to fourteen years in the penitentiary.[24]

Special officers also represented a problem in these years. The term had originally been used to designate detectives, but the special officers of the Crescent City Police were not detectives. Just what they were was an issue disputed by the mayors, the council, and several newspapers. The mayors consistently held that special officers were plainclothes policemen—neither detectives nor beat patrolmen—assigned to special duties. Critics claimed that they were nothing more than deadheads, political favorites rewarded with a policeman's salary and clothed in official authority but without responsibilities. Evidently there were two classes of special officers, one group chosen by the precinct commanders to do special duty as plainclothesmen and another group appointed directly by the mayor. The precinct special officers seem to have had legitimate duties, but the mayor's special officers may well have been mere holders of sinecures. The number of special officers was also a matter of debate and conjecture. The mayors insisted that the number was rather small, but in 1887 a member of the Common Council determined, with the advice of police commanders, that nearly one-fourth of the force were special officers. Special officers seem to have been involved in an unusual number of shootings, including the murder of Administrator of Police Patrick Mealey in 1888 by special officer Louis Clare.[25]

Throughout the dozen years following Reconstruction, the Crescent City Police continued to be plagued by problems. Austere budgets left them undermanned and underpaid; racial discrimination prevented black men from gaining full representation on the force and subjected black citizens to abuse by white policemen; and partisan politics encouraged policemen to violate their nominal role of neutrality in elections. To make matters worse, policemen carried and used guns although there was no system to train them to minimize the possibility of misusing deadly force.

24. *Daily Picayune*, July 19, August 18, October 27, 31, 1885.
25. *Daily Picayune*, November 2, 1881, June 7, 1882, June 14, 1884, January 23, October 20, 1885, June 29, July 11, 1887, January 2, May 22, September 11, November 7, 1888, May 27, 1889.

✻

On the evening of May 2, 1887, five uniformed city policemen sat down to share supper at Fabacher's restaurant in New Orleans. A quarrel soon broke out between two precinct commanders, Lieutenant Thomas Reynolds and Sergeant Michael McLaughlin. As all five men remained sitting Sergeant McLaughlin drew his revolver and fired one round into the floor. Both the lieutenant and the sergeant then stood up at the table and, with their respective revolver muzzles nearly touching, blazed away with four shots each. Customers and restaurant employees dived for cover, narrowly escaping wounds or death. McLaughlin and Reynolds, unscathed by the fusillade, were then subdued and disarmed by their colleagues. After a fast trip to police headquarters, where they were suspended by the chief of police, the sergeant and the lieutenant returned to Fabacher's to finish their meal, their firefight apparently mutually forgiven if not forgotten.[26]

As a paradigm of police use of deadly force, the McLaughlin-Reynolds incident underscores several salient themes: the policemen involved irresponsibly discharged their revolvers; they recklessly endangered not only their own lives but those of several bystanders; and they demonstrated abysmal marksmanship by missing each other in an exchange of nine shots. The administrative and judicial outcome is equally instructive. Lieutenant Reynolds escaped punishment, whereas Sergeant McLaughlin received a stern reprimand from the mayor, along with a suspension of twenty-seven days that was later rescinded with back pay.

The McLaughlin-Reynolds shooting was in many ways exemplary of a problem that had long beset New Orleans. The city's leaders had feared capricious use of force by the police from early in the century but had never found an effective way to translate policy into practice. Certainly they had tried to devise policies to restrain police use of force. In 1809 the mayor and city council had instructed the police not to use force in making arrests unless they encountered resistance, and even then they were supposed to warn the individual three times before resorting to force; the policemen guarding the prison and powder magazine were eventually instructed that they, too, were to issue three warnings before firing upon anyone attempting to break in or escape. The state legislature adopted a statute in 1834 forbidding the New Orleans police to use arms in making arrests unless necessitated by self-defense, and two years later the city government deprived the police of their swords, leaving them with only a

26. *Daily Picayune*, May 3, 1887.

spontoon or club. Further legal guidance came in 1851, when the Louisiana courts restrictively defined the conditions for justifiable homicide. One ruling held that homicide could not be justified if committed only to prevent a misdemeanor but seemed to suggest that killing might be justified to prevent a violent felony. The other important appellate decision that year stipulated that to justify homicide as self-defense the killer had to be able to show that a "known felony was attempted on his person," that he had committed the homicide out of "necessity to avoid immediate death, or at least an insupportable outrage," and that the killer had faced an assault that was "eminently perilous, and unavoidable but by the death of the assailant."[27]

The law allowed greater discretion to use force against slaves and convicts. In the 1820s, the city council authorized policemen to use force to make the prisoners on the city chain gang work. Beginning in 1817, the council permitted militiamen—who, unlike city guardsmen, routinely carried muskets when on patrol duty—to fire upon any slave "who shall refuse to halt when pursued." The state legislature expanded this authority in 1855 to grant any freeholder the right "to make use of arms" to arrest the flight of any slave who, when not at his or her usual place of work or residence, ran from interrogation. The wording of this statute was somewhat ambiguous, for even though it authorized the use of arms, it enjoined the freeholder "to avoid killing the slave." A court ruling the following year clarified the situation by asserting that statutory authority to make use of arms in arresting fleeing slaves necessarily carried a risk of killing.[28]

The law also imposed a partial constraint on police use of arms by forbidding the carrying of concealed weapons throughout the state, granting no exception to policemen. A report in the 1880 census noted of New Orleans that the "law against carrying concealed weapons applies in full force to policemen. But this law is not enforced as against the police." Nothing in the law forbade policemen or private citizens to bear arms openly in the city. When the police first began carrying revolvers in the

27. *Ordinances Issued by the City Council of New-Orleans*, 38–64; *Acts of Louisiana*, 1834, pp. 139–41; Messages of the Mayors to the City Council, January 21, 1836; *Digest of Ordinances*, 105–15; *Carmouche* v. *Bouis*, 6 Louisiana Annual Reports 95 (1851); *State* v. *Brett*, 6 Louisiana Annual Reports 652 (1851).

28. Ordinances and Resolutions of the City Council, December 18, 1817, September 1, 1828; *Acts of Louisiana*, 1855, p. 386; *Duperrier* v. *Dautrive*, 12 Louisiana Annual Reports 664 (1856).

1850s, the mayor had objected and called it an illegal practice because the weapons were usually concealed. Private citizens frequently carried concealed weapons, too; the term *pocket pistol* was not only an advertising gimmick but also a description of common practice. Carrying a pistol in a pocket was unequivocally illegal, for even partial concealment of a pistol violated the law, according to Louisiana appellate decisions in 1856 and 1885. In the latter case a man was arrested for carrying a revolver with the barrel and cylinder stuffed into his pants, with the grip, trigger guard, and hammer exposed to view, which the court construed as illegal concealment.[29]

Actual police practice in the manner of carrying deadly weapons varied somewhat, but certainly much of the time those weapons were concealed in violation of the law. In 1874 the *Daily Picayune* noted that "the pistols that they have been tacitly permitted to carry in times gone by are no longer flourished in the faces of the people, but worn peacefully and secretly." In January, 1885, Mayor Joseph Guillote tried to get policemen to carry their guns openly and therefore legally by ordering them to wear their weapons outside their coats. Frustrated by less than perfect compliance, Guillote repeated these instructions in April, professing that "he would see them enforced." At the same time, the chief of police advised his force that when carrying a revolver each man "should carry it in a holster attached to his belt and baton." Some men probably persisted in concealing their weapons to avoid paying for a holster or to protect them from rain. Not until 1898 did the state legislature exempt police officers from the general ban against carrying concealed weapons.[30]

While Mayor Guillote was trying to order the police to carry their weapons openly in 1885, he also offered directions to the men about using their guns. His prescriptions were published in the newspapers along with policy recommendations and comments from District Attorney Lionel Adams and Chief of Police Zach Bachemin. The most sophisticated guidelines, and the most soundly grounded in law, were those offered by Adams. Drawing upon a diverse body of decisional and statutory law—a mixture of English common law, American state court rulings, an influential treatise on homicide by an American jurist, and a Louisiana statute—Adams pre-

29. Waring, *Report*, II, 293; *State v. J. T. Smith*, 11 Louisiana Annual Reports 633 (1856); *State v. Lucy Bias*, 37 Louisiana Annual Reports 259 (1885).

30. *Daily Picayune*, September 22, 1874, January 20, 1885; *Daily States*, April 24, 1885; *Acts of Louisiana*, 1898, pp. 158–59.

sented his interpretation of the prevailing law respecting police use of deadly force to the press in April, 1885.[31]

The two broadest and most basic rules of law in the district attorney's guidelines were derived from nineteenth-century American state appellate decisions. According to the district attorney, an arresting officer was not permitted to use force or violence unless the arrestee resisted or fled. This rule was drawn from an 1839 Alabama case in which a shopkeeper had committed assault and battery on a man he suspected of stealing from his store. When an arrestee did offer resistance, the officer was bound to employ only such force as was "necessary to overcome the resistance and accomplish the arrest," an interpretation propounded by a judge in Maine in an 1853 case involving a constable's deputy accused of using excessive force in making an arrest.[32]

To define the circumstances of justifiable homicide, Adams relied largely on the English common law as interpreted by the preeminent seventeenth-century chief justice of the King's Bench, Sir Matthew Hale, and by Sir Michael Foster, an eighteenth-century King's Bench magistrate. If a police officer attempted to make a legal arrest and had to use force to overcome resistance by the offender, and if in doing so the officer killed the offender, the homicide was justified—so long as the arrest was legal. But if the officer killed the arrestee while making an illegal arrest, the officer was guilty of manslaughter. Thus, in overcoming resistance during an arrest, the police officer need not worry about the gravity of the offense, only the legality of the arrest.[33]

When an offender fled rather than resisted, the police were held by law—if not in practice—to a stricter standard in using force. In situations involving flight, the gravity of the offense was also important, not just the legality of the arrest. If the alleged offender was subject to arrest for a felony, then the officer was permitted to kill the offender in flight if killing

31. *Daily States*, April 24, 1885; *Daily Picayune*, April 22, 1885.

32. *Findlay* v. *Pruitt*, 9 Porter 195 (Alabama, 1839); *Murdock* v. *Ripley*, 35 Maine Reports 472 (1853).

33. Adams' citation was to 2 Hale 218, which was an error. It should have been to 2 Hale 118, that is, Sir Matthew Hale, *The History of the Pleas of the Crown* (2 vols.; London, 1736), II, 118. Adams also cited Foster 318, that is, Sir Michael Foster, *A Report of Some Proceedings on the Commission of Oyer and Terminer and Goal [sic] Delivery for the Trial of the Rebels in the Year 1746 in the County of Surry, and of Other Crown Cases. To Which Are Added Discourses Upon a Few Branches of the Crown Law* (Dublin, 1767), 318. Foster in turn cited 1 Hale 490.

was the only means to arrest the flight. But when a police officer killed a fleeing suspect, the burden of proof was upon the officer to establish three facts: that the decedent had indeed committed a felony, that the officer had made clear to the offender his intention to make the arrest, and that he could not otherwise effect the arrest than by slaying the felon. Thus the wise and just officer would not shoot at a fleeing suspect unless the policeman carried a felony warrant for the individual's arrest or had personally witnessed the commission of a felony. Furthermore, he would not shoot without attempting vigorous pursuit and ascertaining that the felon would escape unless deadly force were invoked.[34]

If the fleeing offender was guilty only of a misdemeanor, the police officer who committed the homicide was guilty of murder. An exception to this rule held the police officer guilty only of manslaughter if it was apparent that the use of force was not intended to be fatal. Should the fleeing misdemeanant be wounded and survive, the officer was indictable for assault with a deadly weapon.[35] In sum, then, a policeman might legally kill to make any legal arrest when resistance was offered. If the offender took flight, the officer could kill only if the fleeing individual was a demonstrable felon.

At the same time that District Attorney Adams offered these guidelines to the police, Mayor Guillote gave the force different and contradictory advice. The mayor's directions were even more stringent in limiting the police than the district attorney's. Only "in necessary self-defense if attacked," and then not unless "their lives were in peril," were police officers supposed to resort to their guns, according to Mayor Guillote. The mayor's

34. Adams' citations included 2 Hale 118, 119. Though he made no reference to Louisiana decisional law on this point, an antebellum case had enunciated the same principle: *Carmouche* v. *Bouis*, 6 Louisiana Annual Reports 95 (1851). The district attorney also cited Wharton on Homicide, section 213. Francis Wharton authored a specialized treatise on homicide, *The Law of Homicide in the United States* (Philadelphia, 1855), and a broader work which included a treatment of homicide, *On the Criminal Law of the United States* (3rd ed.; Philadelphia, 1855). Both works were published in several editions. The same principles of law can be found in 2 Hale 118, 119.

35. The district attorney cited 2 Hale 217 (it should have been 2 Hale 117), and section 791, Revised Statutes, which had been enacted in 1855; see *The Revised Statute Laws of the State of Louisiana from the Organization of the Territory to the Year 1869, Inclusive, with the Amendments Thereto. Enacted at the Sessions of the Legislature up to and Including the Session of 1876, and References to the Civil Code, the Code of Practice, and the Decisions of the Supreme Court of the State of Louisiana*, ed. Albert Voorhies (New Orleans, 1876), 215.

instructions were a distillation of the two Louisiana court decisions of 1851 which had defined justifiable homicide for all citizens and a restatement of the 1834 statute that had limited police use of sidearms to instances of self-defense. On the question of shooting at persons who took flight to avoid arrest, the mayor disagreed with the district attorney, asserting that the police were "not to fire their pistols at any fugitive, but are to arrest them by other means." Unlike Adams, Guillote drew no distinction between accused felons and misdemeanants, thus offering a personal judgment more restrictive than the existing law mandated.[36]

Chief of Police Bachemin did nothing to resolve the potential confusion for police officers in the contradictory advice of the district attorney and the mayor. When asked if he had any instructions for his men about the use of their weapons, Chief Bachemin replied: "No, sir; they have no instructions from me." Perhaps the chief was derelict in telling his men nothing; yet he came very close to an accurate summation of the preceding three decades of police experience with handguns when he stated that the "use of the revolver is left entirely to a policeman's own discretion."[37]

The best-informed source of guidance for police officers who did want to abide by the letter of the law was the district attorney's office. But the district attorney's synopsis of the rules of law called for a delicately judicial use of discretion by policemen who had no training in the law or the use of weapons except what they acquired on the beat. About four months after the district attorney published guidelines for the use of force, Mayor Guillote ordered Acting Chief of Police Thomas Reynolds to have the police manual and city ordinances read to the police semiweekly. This modest effort was the most intensive training yet attempted. Under the stress of confrontation, how could a policeman so ill-trained quickly make a sensible decision to shoot or withhold fire? The burden of choice was considerable, and the discretion of the policeman on the scene was sure to be profoundly

36. *Daily States*, April 24, 1885. Mayor Joseph Shakspeare helped confuse the issue in 1890 by recommending a broader mandate for using deadly force. "The Mayor has recently more than once declared the right of the police to shoot down offenders against the laws, and we fear that this dangerous doctrine has been at the bottom of the unfortunate killing referred [a slaying by police in 1890]. If the case should ever come to trial it is hoped that the Judge of the Criminal Court will charge the jury on the rights and privileges of the police to kill citizens. The recent deliverances of the Mayor on the subject have doubtless done much to confuse the public mind on the subject" (*Daily Picayune*, October 16, 1890).

37. *Daily States*, April 24, 1885.

influenced by his fears, his personal convictions about taking life, and his awareness of the presence—or absence—of supervisors or witnesses.[38]

Thus the legal education of policemen had not significantly improved since the introduction of the revolver as a standard sidearm in the 1850s. One small improvement had come about over that span of years. The revolvers manufactured in the 1880s were mechanically superior to the cap-and-ball models of the antebellum period. Ammunition had evolved into the self-contained cartridge, in which bullet, propellant, and primer constituted one unit, and it was less prone to accidental discharge, less corrosive of the handgun, and easier and faster to load. Moreover, the revolver itself had been refined, with stronger steels used in construction, better sights affixed, and more convenient overall size and configuration than had formerly been true. The widespread use of double-action mechanisms made it possible to fire a revolver merely by squeezing the trigger, whereas previously, cocking the hammer and firing the piece were separate operations.

Technological marvels though they may have become, the improved revolvers of the 1880s in no sense conferred technical virtuosity on their users. Lacking any training in safety or marksmanship, members of the police force had no claim to technical mastery of their guns. Accidental shootings cut short the lives of policemen and private citizens from the 1850s through the 1880s; deliberate shootings cost many more.

Far from showing expertise, police marksmanship proved abysmal. A sample of ninety cases of police involvement in shootings amply demonstrates their limitations in the use of guns. Although most of the shootings seem to have taken place at short range, policemen nonetheless had a hard time hitting what they aimed at. Accounts with details allowing an estimate of distance suggest that four-fifths of the shootings occurred at a range of about ten feet or less. Yet only 46 percent of the policemen actually struck their antagonists. No more than 25 percent of the shots fired found their intended targets, and the figure was probably closer to 15 percent or even

---

38. *Daily Picayune*, August 7, 1885. In 1898 the superintendent of police recommended "the building of ranges for target practice, and that a competent officer be detailed to instruct the men in the handling and firing of their pistols, so that poor marksmanship and awkwardness may be overcome. Men who are used to handling and firing guns usually display more caution and accuracy in the use of firearms than those who are not familiar with them" (*Annual Report of Board of Police Commissioners and Superintendent of Police*, 1898, p. 39).

less. The result was that of the people fired on by these officers, a maximum of 38 percent were wounded or killed.[39]

By contrast, the citizens who fired at policemen showed greater accuracy. Fully 74 percent of these shooters struck their police antagonists (compared with 46 percent for police). Moreover, 41 percent of the targeted individuals (that is, policemen shot at by citizens) became casualties, as against 38 percent for policemen shooting citizens.

Citizen shooters also proved less dangerous to bystanders. Not one of the ninety cases involved a bystander shot by a citizen, yet policemen shot an average of one bystander for every six intended antagonists they shot.

Perhaps the most ironic conclusion to be derived from these data is that policemen were their own worst enemy. Although intrapolice shootings constituted only 10 percent of all cases, they accounted for 36 percent of policemen killed. Even when allowance is made for the doubling effect of police officers being at both ends of the exchange of gunfire, the disproportion in fatalities still remains.[40]

39. In 55 percent of the cases, there was no indication of distance between the antagonists. The sample of shootings covered the years 1863–89 and was drawn from the following sources: Record of Inquests and Views, Coroner's Office, XX, 42, 121, 209, XXI, 64, 136, XXII, 204, XXIII, 118, 205, 337, 366, XXIV, 191, XXV, 58, 67, 128, 228, 262, 334, XXVII, 119, XXVIII, 26, 79, XXX, 103, 368, XXXIII, 3, 230, 264, XXXIV, 9, 95, 155, 637, XXXV, 26, 53; First District Court, Minute Books, Cases 485, 517, 848, 1035, 3912, 4766, 4858, 5648, 5686, 5895, 5899; Superior Criminal Court, Parish of Orleans, Minute Books, NOPL, Cases 104, 322, 509, 547, 840, 860, 2666; Criminal District Court, Parish of Orleans, Docket Books, NOPL, Cases 512, 1701, 1838, 2394, 3712, 4152, 5070, 5611, 5701, 6098, 9017, 10327; Register of Convicts Received, Feb. 13, 1866, to Dec. 29, 1889, Louisiana State Penitentiary, Angola, Convicts 2444, 4292, 7365; Arrest Books, New Orleans Police Department (microfilm, NOPL), September 10, October 13, 1881, April 22, 1883, November 7, 1884, April 15, July 6, 1885, October 8, December 25, 1886, April 16, May 2, October 2, December 27, 1887, January 1, 2, 15, March 4, 1888; *Biennial Report of the Board of Control of the Louisiana State Penitentiary for the Years 1890 and 1891, to His Excellency, the Governor of Louisiana, Baton Rouge, La., April 14, 1892* (Baton Rouge, 1892), Convict 9078; *Biennial Report of the Board of Control of the Louisiana State Penitentiary for the Years 1894 and 1895 to His Excellency Murphy J. Foster, Governor of Louisiana* (Baton Rouge, 1896), Convict 9078; *Annual Report of the Board of Metropolitan Police*, 1868/69, p. 41, 1869/70, p. 69, 1871/72, p. 35, 1872/73, p. 45, *Daily Delta*, January 15, 1863; *Times*, May 5, 1869, April 9, May 14, July 13, August 29, November 4, 1879, May 15, October 10, December 8, 1880; *Daily Picayune*, various dates from June 14, 1863, to September 24, 1890; *Times-Democrat*, June 26, 1884. Shootings in the Mechanics' Institute riot of 1866 and the battle of Liberty Place in 1874 have been excluded from this sample.

40. The inferiority of police marksmanship remains evident even after elimination of

Why were police such poor marksmen? Their lack of training in the use of firearms, combined with the stress of quick and often unpredictable combat, seem the most important explanations. Of distinctly secondary importance were the poor lighting conditions in which most shootings occurred. About four-fifths of the cases took place at night, twilight, dawn, or in the rain. Mechanical inadequacy of the firearms may also have contributed to the problem. Even as late as 1898, 15 percent of the police force carried mechanically useless guns. The traditional concept of marksmanship was scarcely appropriate in most cases, for the leisurely assumption of a one-handed shooting stance followed by the precise alignment of sights and target were grossly unsuited to swift violence at short range.[41]

Even more appalling than policemen's inaccuracy with their weapons was their poor judgment in deciding under what circumstances to shoot. Three-fourths of the sample cases involved alleged self-defense and/or the effort to effect an arrest by police officers, but the remaining one-fourth were clear-cut abuses of authority.

Many of the instances in which policemen alleged self-defense must be regarded with skepticism. In the twenty-five cases of self-defense (or defense of third parties), the degree of peril to the officer's life was questionable in several instances. Twice policemen fired when—they claimed—a citizen appeared to be drawing a weapon. The use of force may have been legitimate, but the allegation of menacing would have been the easiest to invent as an excuse. In two other cases, policemen fired after being manually assaulted by lone citizens; again the severity of the assaults may have been less than claimed by the policemen.[42]

The cases of alleged self-defense were too beclouded to allow any definitive conclusions about the validity of police resort to firearms. Shooting at fleeing suspects was another story. Many of these cases (nearly half) consisted of policemen firing at persons they believed to be burglars. Anyone found near an open door in a dark house or store at night or in the

---

shootings in which policemen were fired upon but never fired a shot themselves. The disparity was not, therefore, attributable to citizens taking easy shots in point-blank ambuscades.

Policemen also fired their revolvers to kill dogs. In one instance, a policeman alleged that he had shot at a dog, but other policemen testified that he had fired merely to relieve the monotony on his beat. See *Times*, August 10, 1881; *Daily Picayune*, November 9, 1881, June 27, August 8, 1882, January 19, July 21, 1883, July 8, 1884.

41. In 49 percent of the cases, there was no basis for judging the quality of the light.

42. *Daily Picayune*, September 27, 1866, September 5, 1882.

yard of an unlighted home might have seemed to the officer on the beat to be a likely burglary suspect, especially if that individual took flight. But for a policeman to fire under such conditions when not assaulted or menaced was an assumption of juridical powers beyond the bounds allowed by the formal law or good sense. Some policemen showed restraint in dealing with suspects who took to their heels; in four cases the only shots fired by the police were directed into the air to intimidate the runners, and in another instance, an officer fired a warning shot in the air before taking actual aim at the suspect. But the problem of poor judgment in shooting at fleeing suspects was still a major one, as evidenced by the case of a policeman who opened fire at night on a man who turned out to be a lamplighter going about his duties. Even when the person in flight was known to be a felon, the use of force could reasonably be questioned. In one instance, a policeman shot an escaped convict to death and claimed the man had fled to avoid arrest, but another officer accused the shooter of premeditated murder.[43]

The last class of shootings left no doubt about the misconduct of the men who used the guns. One officer took a shot at his wife during a domestic quarrel; another slew a man for merely ignoring a "move on" order; two cases were unprovoked police assaults on citizens; another incident stemmed from a crowd having jeered at a policeman; and nine shootings were disputes among policemen. Together these cases constituted one-fourth of the total.[44]

Thus, at an absolute minimum, one-fourth of all cases involved police misuse of force. When other cases of apparent misjudgment or wrongdoing are added, about half of all police shootings involved probable or certain violations of the formal law by the police. And that conclusion does not even consider that many—probably most—police officers broke the law by carrying their guns in a concealed manner.

These shootings exacted a terrible human cost—a cost determined in part by the level of violent crime among the general public (especially the adult male public) and compounded by the poor judgment of so many policemen. The butcher's bill for these cases included thirty-three people

43. *Daily Picayune*, December 17, 1863, March 27, November 3, 1875, July 25, 1882, April 2, 1885, April 15, July 11, 1887.

44. *Daily Picayune*, October 3, November 20, 1872, June 18, 1874, September 22, 1875, March 14, September 20, 1876, May 25, 1877, September 11, October 14, 1881, November 8, 1884, January 18, 1885, October 7, 1886, May 3, 1887, January 2, 1888.

dead (fourteen policemen, seventeen targeted citizens, and two bystanders) and another forty-one wounded (twenty-four police officers, twelve targeted citizens, and five bystanders).

The judicial outcome of these shootings varied considerably according to the status of those killed and those doing the shooting. Of twenty-two policemen who killed private citizens, not one was convicted of murder, manslaughter, or a lesser offense (six were indicted, tried, and found not guilty of murder or manslaughter). The results of the cases involving nine private citizens who killed policemen proved quite a contrast. All nine were indicted and tried for either murder or manslaughter; of these, four were convicted of murder, and one other was shot to death at the courthouse by the son of the policeman he had been accused of killing (the policeman's son was subsequently acquitted of murder). Of the four citizens convicted of murdering policemen, all were sentenced to life in the penitentiary with hard labor. One, however, was pardoned and released after barely a year's imprisonment, and another received a pardon after seven years in the penitentiary. The other status category of shootings involved policemen shooting other policemen. Of the four policemen who killed colleagues, one was convicted of murder and sentenced to life in the penitentiary, one was convicted of manslaughter and sentenced to three years with hard labor, and two were indicted, tried, and found not guilty of murder. The policeman sentenced to three years at hard labor was pardoned after eleven months in the penitentiary, and the policeman sentenced to life was pardoned after four and a half years of imprisonment.[45]

Thus, although people who killed policemen stood a substantial chance of receiving some punishment, policemen killed members of the general public with something close to impunity. Some policemen lost their jobs on the force for shooting citizens to death, and some endured the stress and cost of a trial, but none—at least in these cases—was ever convicted and punished for a criminal offense.

The paucity—or absence—of criminal penalties for police misuse of force roughly paralleled the prospect for civil penalties; a citizen injured by improper police resort to force had a very limited chance of collecting damages in a civil action. Municipalities enjoyed considerable, though not total, immunity against suits regarding the actions of their police officers

---

45. Data derived from court cases and penitentiary records cited in note 39. In several cases, two policemen were charged with killing one citizen.

and other employees. In an 1854 case, New Orleans police officers pursued a fleeing slave they had found illegally enjoying the comforts of a cabaret; they overtook the fugitive and beat him to death with clubs even though he offered no resistance. The slave's owner sued the city government for compensation, but the state supreme court decision disallowed any award—even though it acknowledged the unnecessary use of force by the police—because the city was not liable for damages ensuing from the actions of city employees. In 1873, a New Orleans woman, Helen M. Barnes, initiated a suit against the city and the Board of Metropolitan Police, charging them with neglect of duty for not preventing the death of her husband at the hands of rioters. The judge found for the defendants, though his reasons were "orally assigned" and thus not in the historical record.[46]

Injured parties could sue police officers as individuals, but even if a judgment could be won, collection was problematic. Policemen were bonded, but even as late as 1890 only in the amount of $1,000 for patrolmen (in the Helen Barnes case in 1873 the plaintiff had sought an award of $20,344). Only a small minority of policemen owned any real property, and only a slightly larger minority accumulated more than $100 of personal property. The small salaries of most policemen guaranteed that garnishment of wages would be a very slow method of collecting any sizable judgment.[47]

Although the criminal and civil consequences for policemen who resorted to force seem to have been practically negligible, the effects of such incidents on the personality and character of policemen is much more difficult to gauge. Some men probably enjoyed the sensation of having conquered a foe and survived, but some policemen showed a distaste for violence, as evidenced in a shooting involving policeman John Griffin. In June, 1887, Griffin responded to a black woman's cry for help during an assault by endeavoring to arrest her assailant, Willie Taylor, a black eighteen-year-old seaman. After Griffin laid hands on Taylor, the latter wrenched free and shot Griffin in the left arm and chest. As Taylor cocked his gun for a second shot, the policeman grabbed him with one hand, trying to take away the gun, while drawing his own revolver with the other hand.

46. *Samuel Stewart* v. *The City of New Orleans*, 9 Louisiana Annual Reports 461 (1854); *Helen M. Barnes* v. *City of New Orleans and Board of Metropolitan Police*, Superior District Court, Orleans Parish, Case No. 9240, NOPL.

47. *Manual of the City Police Adopted by the Board of Police Commissioners January 1st, 1890* (New Orleans, 1889), 24.

They fell to the ground together, struggled, and Griffin fired three shots, striking Taylor in the head and killing him. Seriously wounded, the policeman was quoted by a newspaper reporter as having said with tears in his eyes, "I have never harmed a flea willfully in my life, and I am sorry I had to shoot the negro, but it was his life or mine."[48]

Other policemen refrained from using deadly force even when the law would clearly have sanctioned their doing so. In April, 1884, a policeman approached a drunken black man who was flourishing a revolver, whereupon the drunk placed the muzzle of the gun against the abdomen of the officer. Grabbing the muzzle in his hand, the policeman diverted the gun just as it discharged, wounding and burning his hand. The officer wrestled the man and with the aid of others brought him into custody. Five years later another policeman interrupted a robbery in progress and knocked a gun away from his belly in a brief struggle with the robbers. One robber fled, but the officer pursued and captured the man without resort to gunplay. In other instances, policemen wrestled handguns away from drunks and brawlers and effected arrests merely with manual force. In November, 1888, two policemen tried to arrest a fugitive who had fired a shot at them in an earlier arrest attempt half a year before. On this occasion, the fugitive cut both officers with a knife, bit them, and kicked one of them in the stomach and groin. With this provocation, one policeman used his revolver, but only to club the man into submission.[49]

A gun battle also offered a chance for a policeman to win glory. In 1885, Corporal Thomas Duffy attempted to arrest three men who had committed a slungshotting and robbery. When he approached them, they fired at him at point-blank range and struck him with a slungshot. Wounded in the chest, the officer opened fire and killed one of the assailants. When the case came before the recorder for a hearing, Duffy was honorably discharged from any further legal proceedings and complimented by the mag-

48. *Daily Picayune*, June 22, 1887, January 16, 1890. A group of citizens subsequently awarded Griffin a medal for his effort.

49. *Daily Picayune*, March 9, 1882, April 11, 1884, May 13, 1887, November 15, 1888, October 23, 1889. Some policemen did not even carry revolvers. An inspection of revolvers owned by policemen in November, 1898, showed that 15 percent of the men owned none and another 15 percent owned worthless ones. The remainder were distributed among the following manufacturers: Colt, 40 percent; Smith and Wesson, 26 percent; Mervin and Hulbert, 2 percent; less than 1 percent each for Webley, Hopkin and Allen, and Ives and Johnson (*Annual Report of Board of Police Commissioners and Superintendent of Police*, 1898, p. 11).

istrate for his gallant conduct. Duffy emerged a hero, but at the cost of a wound and a close brush with death.[50]

Dishonor and opprobrium could also be the lot of a policeman who used his revolver. A police sergeant named McCabe fired three shots at an African American man who, McCabe alleged, had struck him with a bottle. The sergeant then sought out two black policemen and told them to make the arrest, referring to his assailant as "some —— nigger." The black policemen declined to do so, fearing that the sergeant would murder the man once he was in custody, whereupon Sergeant McCabe proclaimed that "niggers were not wanted on the force anyhow." In addition to McCabe's obvious expression of racial prejudice, the provocation of being struck with a bottle may well have been insufficient justification for his resort to the gun. The sergeant tried to have the two black policemen punished; Superintendent David Hennessy vouched for the black officers' good character in their hearing before the Board of Police Commissioners, and the board dropped the charges against them.[51]

Racial prejudice very likely helped precipitate some police shootings. At least two cases during the 1880s—aside from the McCabe incident—seem to have involved wholly unnecessary resort to deadly force by white policemen who victimized black citizens. In three other shooting incidents policemen fired into crowds of African Americans under circumstances that cast doubt on the legality of the use of potentially deadly force. In one episode, a white police sergeant, Thomas Reynolds, shot to death a black teamster, James Hawkins, who had resisted arrest. Although a crowd of black people clearly were attacking Reynolds by hand and with frying pans, it is not at all clear that Hawkins himself represented any great danger to the sergeant. A black newspaper reported that Hawkins had been a "law abiding, peaceful man" of "Christian character" and declared that he had been "shot down for no other cause than that a negro has no rights which a police officer is bound to respect." Clearly members of the African American community viewed armed white policemen as a serious potential threat to the black people of the city.[52]

50. When Duffy died in May, 1899, the police surgeon attributed his death to the effects of the wound received in 1885 (*Annual Report of Board of Police Commissioners and Superintendent of Police*, 1900, p. 14).

51. *Daily Picayune*, April 4, 1889.

52. *Daily Picayune*, January 31, 1875, September 11, 1881, November 8, 1884, October 7, 1886; quotation in Eric Arnesen, *Waterfront Workers of New Orleans: Race, Class, and Politics, 1863–1923* (New York, 1991), 70.

The volatile mixture of policemen and guns constituted a formidable problem, one intricately interwoven with the social fabric. New Orleanians were a heavily armed people. In the late nineteenth century, 76 percent of homicides in New Orleans were committed with firearms, compared with 21 percent in Philadelphia; the overall homicide rate was six times as high in New Orleans as in Philadelphia, but the rate of homicides committed with firearms was twenty-three times greater in the Crescent City. A grand jury report of 1878 asserted that enforcement of the law against carrying concealed weapons was largely a dead letter. Complete repeal or stringent enforcement, the report suggested, were the only realistic alternatives, for slack enforcement of the existing law merely operated to the disadvantage of law-abiding citizens. The following year, the New Orleans *Times* observed that most crimes of violence in the South derived from passion rather than premeditation. Possible remedies were to be found, said the *Times*, in Tennessee, where a bill to tax firearms dealers and concealable weapons was before the legislature, or in Georgia, where one legislator advocated a ban on all handguns, "like exterminating vipers." In 1881 the *Daily Picayune* advanced the idea that a system of granting permits should be enacted because the current statute put people who obeyed it at the mercy of criminals. In that way, argued the *Picayune*, people with demonstrably high-risk occupations could have a legal chance at an equalizing means of self-defense because the undersized police force could hardly be relied on to stand between the individual citizen and the menace of crime.[53]

The city's elite did little to offer a good example of nonviolent self-restraint. Respectable gentlemen were often among the legions of illegal bearers of concealed weapons. The state attorney general commented in 1878 that among the people prosecuted for carrying concealed weapons "were many of high standing in the community, who, upon satisfying the sentence of the court by paying a small fine, left the court-house barely, if at all, conscious of having committed an offense." Their persistent disrespect for due process of law was painfully evident in the worst lynching episode of the nineteenth century. In 1891 a mob over ten thousand strong,

---

53. The homicide rate in New Orleans was considerably lower in the last decade of the century than it had been in the antebellum period. The rate for 1892–1900 was 13.7 per 100,000, down from about 35 per 100,000 during the years 1857–60. See *Annual Report of Board of Police Commissioners and Superintendent of Police*, 1892, p. 4, 1893, p. 17, 1894, p. 19, 1895, p. 23, 1896, p. 32, 1897, p. 23, 1898, p. 44, 1899, p. 36, 1900, p. 53; Lane, *Violent Death in the City*, 60, 62; *Times*, April 15, 1879; *Daily Picayune*, July 31, 1878, November 12, 1881.

headed by many of the leading citizens of New Orleans, broke into the parish prison and murdered eleven Italian-Americans who had been accused of complicity in the murder of Superintendent of Police David Hennessy the year before (three of the mob's victims had been acquitted the day before the lynching). This incident, which provoked a protest from the Italian government, was later condoned by another group of leading citizens, the grand jury.[54]

The problem of police misuse of deadly force was not resolved by the legislature, city council, state supreme court, district attorney, grand jury, police commanders, or anyone else in this period and showed only a tentative sign of amelioration near the end of the century. The state legislature authorized the carrying of concealed sidearms by police officers in 1898, thereby reconciling the letter of the law with long-standing police practice. This statutory change not only encouraged more respect for formal law by abating some measure of hypocrisy, but it also allowed the Board of Police Commissioners to standardize the police sidearm (a .32 Colt revolver) and the superintendent of police to recommend training in safety and marksmanship. Yet despite this change, the problem of an armed police in an armed society would persist, posing a continuing challenge to posterity.[55]

During the 1880s the New Orleans police in most ways set an example for other cities not to follow. Reform-minded New Orleanians viewed few of the changes in their police force in those years as improvements, with the exception of two developments modeled after reforms elsewhere in the country: the adoption of civil service reform and the inauguration of a rapid-response patrol wagon system.

In 1886 the municipal government had a system of telegraph boxes, developed by a Chicago firm, installed to facilitate quick reinforcement of patrolmen on the beat and removal of prisoners to jail. Although the system had only one hundred boxes at the outset, policemen could call in to one of three headquarters, from which a horse-drawn patrol wagon would be dispatched to the site of the call. The signal system's first trial run in December, 1886, yielded a response time of one and a half minutes. The

54. *Annual Report of the Attorney General*, 1877, pp. 38–39; Richard Gambino, *Vendetta: A True Story of the Worst Lynching in America, the Mass Murder of Italian-Americans in New Orleans in 1891, the Vicious Motivations Behind It, and the Tragic Repercussions That Linger to This Day* (Garden City, N.Y., 1977), 77–88, 155–81.

55. *Acts of Louisiana*, 1898, pp. 158–59.

system went into regular service in March, 1887, and although vandals smashed some of the glass roofs of the call boxes, the patrol and signal system proved highly successful. Indeed, Mayor Joseph Shakspeare recommended to the Common Council in 1889 that the addition of one or two patrol wagons would offer the cheapest means of compensating for the numerical weakness of the police force. Because the Common Council had steadfastly opposed higher police expenditures, this innovation was probably the most effective improvement in policing that was possible under the financial circumstances—and it had the additional advantage of being politically uncontroversial.[56]

In contrast to the patrol wagon and signal system, civil service reform proved to be highly controversial and much more difficult to achieve. Under the patronage system that prevailed until 1889, merit was neither necessary nor sufficient to gain appointment to the police. Only on rare occasion could men without strong political connections rise to high rank. The most conspicuous example of such a promotion was the appointment of Captain R. B. Rowley as chief of police in 1882. Mayor William Behan ignored his closest advisers, who argued in behalf of their favorites, Michael J. Sheehan or Zach Bachemin, and chose Rowley to fill the post over captains with more seniority. Behan, whose parents had emigrated from Ireland, had served in the Confederate army and the White League and had been a general in the state militia. Mayor Behan proved to have too much initiative to satisfy the regular or "Ring" Democrats who had supported him, and he lost a second bid for the mayor's office in 1884 in an election tainted by fraud. Chief Rowley was obliged to step down after Behan's loss, and the new mayor, Joseph Guillote, replaced him with Zach Bachemin.[57]

Behan's decision to choose a capable and apolitical man as chief of police

56. Ordinances and Resolutions of the Common Council (Council Series), No. 1674, March 2, 1886; *Daily Picayune*, January 20, March 16, June 2, December 29, 1886, March 2, 23, 1887, January 10, 1889.

57. When Rowley was still a sergeant, the *Picayune* observed that he has "doubtless made some enemies, as he shields neither friend nor foe when they have committed themselves. He is somewhat of a stickler at minor points, and will not overlook even a trifling deflection from the line of duty on the part of his subordinates." Bachemin almost immediately ran into trouble after succeeding Rowley, for the mayor suspended him and labeled him incompetent and unfit. The Police Examining Committee of the Common Council punished him with a suspension of fifteen days for incompetence, but the committee dropped a charge that he had mishandled money (*Daily Picayune*, December 1, 1881, November 18, 21, 24, 25, December 1, 6, 1882, May 21, 1884, February 11, August 5, 1885, December 14, 15, 1886).

did not constitute a reform movement, and the Ring politicians continued to dominate the city government until 1888. By the middle of the decade, however, organizations urging municipal reform began to appear and make themselves heard. In 1885 the Committee of One Hundred made an unsuccessful attempt to ensure the honesty of elections and then dissolved. The following year a similar group, the Law and Order League, failed to produce any significant reform. But another and more successful group, the Young Men's Democratic Association (YMDA), emerged in 1887 and offered a platform on which a broad coalition of reform could stand together. Calling former mayor Joseph Shakspeare out of retirement in 1888, the YMDA succeeded in electing an entire reform slate to serve in city government. Determined to prevent the Ring from stealing the election, the YMDA sent armed men to patrol the polls and maintain the honesty of the canvass.[58]

It was the YMDA that provided the impetus for civil service reform of the police department. The ideal of nonpartisan government service had attracted a national following strong enough by the early 1880s to take advantage of public alienation from the patronage system caused by President James Garfield's assassination at the hands of a disappointed office-seeker in 1881. Despite President Chester Arthur's initial ambivalence and considerable opposition from members of Congress, reform advocates secured a federal civil service law, the Pendleton Act, in 1883. Though this act covered only about 10 percent of federal jobs at the outset, it gradually expanded to encompass a larger and larger share of federal appointive offices. The movement also soon had an effect at the state and local levels when the Massachusetts, New York, New Jersey, and Ohio legislatures, for example, initiated civil service programs for the city police in Boston, Brooklyn, New York, New Brunswick, and Cincinnati in the mid-1880s; civil service did not come to Chicago until 1895 and not to St. Louis until 1905.[59]

The leaders of civil service reform around the country tended to be native-born Protestant Republicans, primarily in the professions and secondarily in business—men who regarded themselves as natural and proper

58. Jackson, *New Orleans in the Gilded Age*, 93–95.

59. *Daily Picayune*, November 19, 1885; Ari Hoogenboom, *Outlawing the Spoils: A History of the Civil Service Reform Movement, 1865–1883* (Urbana, 1961), 198–252, 279; Lane, *Policing the City*, 202; Walker, *Critical History of Police Reform*, 10, 39, 41, 74; Richardson, *New York Police*, 178.

community leaders and who distrusted the urban political machines that were heavily influenced by Catholic immigrants. In New Orleans civil service advocates included some Republicans, but most were Democrats, and they were less likely than reformers in the North to be motivated by anti-Catholic or nativist sentiment. Although the foreign share of white population in New Orleans in 1860 (45 percent) had been roughly comparable to that of major northern cities (48 percent in New York, 36 percent in Boston, 31 percent in Philadelphia, 50 percent in Chicago), thereafter the foreign-born proportion had fallen dramatically in New Orleans (to 19 percent in 1890) while declining only slightly in the urban North (in 1890 43 percent in New York, 36 percent in Boston, 27 percent in Philadelphia, 42 percent in Chicago). The political influence of immigrants had not remained as strong in the Crescent City as in the major northern cities.[60]

Through the influence of the YMDA, the Louisiana legislature enacted a civil service law for the New Orleans police in 1888. Ironically, Mayor Shakspeare, who had shown a genuine interest in honest government, opposed the bill on the grounds that it was an unconstitutional usurpation of municipal powers, and he apparently considered himself a better judge of honesty and efficiency than any as-yet-unnamed Board of Police Commissioners. Although the city won a favorable decision against the bill in the district court, the state supreme court reversed the lower court and upheld the reform act. In February, 1889, Shakspeare recommended to the Common Council that the civil service law be enforced, and the council then elected the Board of Police Commissioners.[61]

Under the new law, the board reviewed the qualifications of incumbent policemen, rejecting those who did not meet the new physical, educational, and moral standards. A few men with bad records or who were substandard in height were not reappointed, but most of the men were retained. Mayor Shakspeare's choice for chief of police in 1888, former detective David Hennessy, continued as superintendent of the reorganized force.[62]

Candidates for the civil service police had to be at least 5 feet 6 inches

60. *Compendium of the Eleventh Census: 1890. Part I—Population* (Washington, D.C., 1892), 544, 550, 551, 564, 572; Edward F. Haas, *Political Leadership in a Southern City: New Orleans in the Progressive Era, 1896–1902* (Ruston, La., 1988), 112–13.

61. *Daily Picayune*, July 25, 1888, February 13, 14, 1889; Jackson, *New Orleans in the Gilded Age*, 97–99.

62. *Daily Picayune*, April 22, May 2, 1888, February 20, March 10, 14, 17, 21, 28–31, April 2, 4, 18, July 4, 27, 1889.

tall, have no criminal convictions, and have five years' residence in the state and two years' in the city; long-standing—though vague—requirements of good character and physical fitness were continued as part of the civil service standards. A committee of the Board of Police Commissioners examined each candidate on his knowledge of the law, city ordinances, and departmental regulations, and the board ranked all candidates on the basis of their examination scores. The board was bound by law to make appointments to the force in order of rank on this eligibility list. Promotions were governed by similar procedures. Only policemen of the rank immediately below the vacancy were eligible for promotion, and they had to undergo a formal competitive examination. To guide policemen in their work, the board published a manual and issued copies in 1890.[63]

During the 1890s the police made increasing use of both traditional and modern means to enhance their effectiveness. For the first time since Reconstruction, a mounted contingent patrolled the less densely populated portions of the city. A bicycle corps chased fleet-footed offenders and policed bicycle traffic. The patrol wagon system expanded, answering an average of seven thousand calls per year, with additional wagons, horses, and telegraphic and telephonic call boxes to give the system greater reach. In December, 1896, the police began using the Bertillion system (an elaborate system of photographs, fingerprints, and body measurements) to record identifying information about offenders.[64]

In the 1890s the police force experienced relatively few changes in personnel. Average annual turnover for the years 1891–1900 was 10.2 percent, ranging from a low of 4.5 percent to a high of 16.3 percent. Low turnover led to an aging force; the mean age of policemen in 1900 was 43.1 years and the median 42.5 (this was roughly a decade older than in 1850, 1860, 1870, and 1880). Absenteeism hovered around a mere 2.0 percent per annum. Complaints against policemen were also relatively few; the number of police board trials for misconduct each year averaged less than one-half per man, somewhat below the rate for the Metropolitan years and far below the rate in the mid-1850s.[65]

63. *Acts of Louisiana*, 1888, pp. 64–70; *Daily Picayune*, November 28, 1889, February 6, 1890; *Manual of the City Police*.

64. *Annual Report of Board of Police Commissioners and Superintendent of Police*, 1891, pp. 14, 17, 1892, pp. 10–11, 1893, pp. 29–32, 1894, pp. 34–37, 1895, pp. 37–39, 1896, pp. 47–53, 1897, pp. 42–44, 1898, pp. 58–65, 1899, pp. 58–60, 1900, pp. 9, 78–80.

65. *Ibid.*, 1891, pp. 14–16, 1892, pp. 15–18, 1893, pp. 10–16, 1894, pp. 11–15, 21, 1895,

The police force of the 1890s differed from its forerunners in other ways, too. The department played a narrower institutional role, as the new police deemphasized social service. For decades the police had provided lodging in the stationhouse for homeless transients and vagrants. During the years of the Metropolitan Police, some fifteen thousand people annually availed themselves of this service, and even the Crescent City Police had accommodated a large number of lodgers, with nine thousand taking refuge in the stationhouses in 1884. From 1891 through 1900, however, fewer than fourteen hundred lodgers per year found refuge in the stationhouses, and even in the severe depression years of 1893–1895 the annual average rose only to slightly less than seventeen hundred. Another social service provided by the police, returning lost children to their families, declined by 55 percent from the *per capita* rate of 1868–1874 to that of 1891–1900.[66]

As the new police offered fewer social services they became more vigorous in exercising the power of arrest. The average number of arrests per policeman was much higher in the 1890s. In the mid-1850s the average number of arrests per policeman each year had been 47, and during the Metropolitan years it had ranged between 38 and 62 per annum. But the average rose to 86 in the years 1891–1900, ranging from a low of 67 to a high of 105. For three years in a row, 1893–1895, the average number of arrests made by each policeman was over 100. An increase in serious crime was not the source of the increase in number of arrests; some two-thirds of all arrests were for intoxication, disturbing the peace, and violations of minor city ordinances.[67]

The evidence of declining social service and increasing resort to arrests for petty offenses suggests a harsher, more punitive institutional role for

---

pp. 8–14, 1896, pp. 17–22, 1897, pp. 13–18, 1898, pp. 21–28, 30, 1899, pp. 16–23, 25, 27, 1900, pp. 19–32, 37–38.

66. *Ibid.*, 1891, p. 7, 1892, p. 7, 1893, p. 23, 1894, p. 24, 1895, p. 25, 1896, p. 34, 1897, p. 25, 1898, p. 46, 1899, p. 43, 1900, p. 60; *Daily Picayune*, January 16, 1885. No other institution played a major role in lodging the homeless. The city's almshouse was poorly funded and accommodated only about one hundred people at a time (Jackson, *New Orleans in the Gilded Age*, 192–93). For a thoughtful interpretation of lodgers and lost children, see Monkkonen, *Police in Urban America*, 86–147.

67. *Annual Report of Board of Police Commissioners and Superintendent of Police*, 1891, pp. 4–9, 1892, pp. 4–9, 1893, pp. 22–25, 1894, pp. 22–27, 1895, pp. 22–28, 1896, pp. 31–37, 1897, pp. 23–28, 1898, pp. 43–49, 1899, pp. 38–48, 1900, pp. 54–65.

the police near the end of the century. That development seems to have been roughly paralleled by the trend in race relations. White racism and the economic depression that began in 1893 made conditions worse for African Americans in New Orleans. In 1894–1895, white screwmen and longshoremen ended their interracial alliance with black workers and sought to exclude blacks from dockwork altogether, using considerable violence and getting some help from the police. Black Louisianans also lost virtually all of the modest political influence they had retained after Redemption. In 1896 the state legislature imposed a complicated voter registration system that purged most blacks from the voter rolls, and in 1898 a state constitutional convention effectively completed the process of disfranchisement by mandating literacy and property requirements for voting. Two years later New Orleans experienced the worst racial violence since Reconstruction when Robert Charles, a proud African American from Mississippi, refused to submit to police harassment. Charles shot and killed seven white people (including four white policemen) and wounded twenty others before being killed himself. These shootings triggered assaults by whites on innocent black New Orleanians, and at least six blacks were killed and seventy wounded before the rioting ended. In 1902 the state legislature forced the streetcar companies of New Orleans to institute racial segregation in the last public service to remain integrated from the Reconstruction period. It is not surprising, then, that in a city whose population was 27.1 percent black in 1900, African Americans remained very underrepresented on the police force (holding just 5.1 percent of police jobs) and were overrepresented among the people arrested by the police (constituting 38.1 percent of arrestees).[68]

Increasingly virulent racism was not the only expression of growing intolerance late in the century. Xenophobia resurged to a level unseen in New Orleans since the 1850s, this time targeting Italian immigrants. The city's Italian population was the only one of the seven largest foreign-born groups that grew in number during the period 1870–1890. Although Ital-

68. Arnesen, *Waterfront Workers of New Orleans*, 121–49; William Ivy Hair, *Bourbonism and Agrarian Protest: Louisiana Politics, 1877–1900* (Baton Rouge, 1969), 276–77; Hair, *Carnival of Fury: Robert Charles and the New Orleans Race Riot of 1900* (Baton Rouge, 1976), 139–40, 153, 155, 171, 185–86; Census of 1900, RG 29, NA; *Annual Report of Board of Police Commissioners and Superintendent of Police*, 1898, p. 42, 1899, p. 38, 1900, p. 54; Dale A. Somers, "Black and White in New Orleans: A Study in Urban Race Relations, 1865–1900," *Journal of Southern History*, XL (1974), 19–42, esp. 35–42.

ians accounted for only 3.2 percent of the foreign population of New Orleans in 1870, by 1890 that proportion had grown to 10.5 percent, and most of that growth occurred in the 1880s. In 1890 the Italians were the fourth largest immigrant group, outnumbered only by the Germans, Irish, and French. They were also highly concentrated in residence (most lived in the old French Quarter) and occupation (most were employed in the fruit, oyster, and fish businesses) and consequently highly visible.[69]

A common feature of the pattern of prejudice toward Italian immigrants was the assumption that they had a distinctive tendency toward criminal behavior. When Superintendent of Police David Hennessy was murdered in October, 1890, official suspicion focused on members of the Italian-American community. Hennessy had been investigating the shooting of several Italian immigrants (probably by other Italians), and a friend who was nearby on the night the chief was shot claimed that the fatally wounded Hennessy had whispered that "Dagoes" had assassinated him. Spurred by the Italophobic mayor Shakspeare, the police rounded up scores of Italians as suspects, and nineteen of them were indicted. When several of the trials ended in acquittal for some and hung juries for others, a number of the most influential and respectable men in the city organized a mob of ten thousand or more and stormed the parish prison, murdering eleven of the Italians held there, including three men who had been acquitted. The police made no effort to stop the lynching, and after it was over, the mayor and the grand jury condoned the murders.[70]

The new era marked by the inception of civil service reform for the New Orleans police thus showed signs of regression in the form of increasing ethnic and racial discrimination and decreasing commitment to social service. The inauguration of civil service did little to enlarge the police force, for the addition of men to the force over the next decade barely kept pace with the growth of the city's population. Municipal parsimony also held police salaries to the same low level that had made a police

---

69. Although the absolute number of Italian immigrants in New Orleans (3,662) was far below the number in New York (39,951), their share of the white population was roughly comparable: 2.7 percent in New York and 2.0 percent in New Orleans (*Ninth Census—Volume I*, 386–91; *Statistics of the Population of the United States at the Tenth Census*, 538–41; *Compendium of the Eleventh Census: 1890, Part II* [Washington, D.C., 1894], 636–37, 654, 656; Gambino, *Vendetta*, 18).

70. Gambino, *Vendetta, passim*; Humbert S. Nelli, *The Business of Crime: Italians and Syndicate Crime in the United States* (New York, 1976), 24–66.

career so unenticing to good men in the 1880s. Even in pursuit of the express goals of reformers, the civil service system was a partial success at best because it failed to produce a politically neutral police force. Police interference in elections remained a staple complaint of New Orleanians for decades, and political influence on police appointments and promotions persisted despite the formal mandate for merit-based personnel decisions. What civil service did accomplish was a sharp reduction in personnel turnover by making political dismissal of members of the force much more difficult. This led to an older, longer-tenured, and more experienced force—arguably a favorable development—yet it also made termination of mediocre personnel harder and perhaps allowed greater opportunity for covert graft by policemen especially skilled at malfeasance. Civil service thus proved to be not a panacea for all of the ills of the police but only a very limited reform.[71]

71. George M. Reynolds, *Machine Politics in New Orleans, 1897–1926* (1936; rpr. New York, 1968), 87, 131–32; Haas, *Political Leadership in a Southern City*, 82, 88.

# CONCLUSION

New Orleans stands out among American cities like a scarlet macaw in a flock of starlings. A city so colorfully eccentric and idiosyncratic might seem an odd choice to serve as the subject for a case study in the history of southern policing, though perhaps a good candidate for study as a unique case unto itself. The police force in nineteenth-century New Orleans emerges from this analysis as neither completely *sui generis* nor wholly typical of the police in the Deep South's larger cities. New Orleans apparently stood alone in its deliberate and definitive abandonment of the military style of policing in 1836, but until then it had shared that paramilitary approach with other southern cities. The Crescent City had the singular distinction of having a partitioned government between 1836 and 1852, when each of its three autonomous police forces had a territorial monopoly on municipal law enforcement within its jurisdiction, but otherwise the New Orleans police in those years closely resembled the forces that developed in New York, Philadelphia, and Boston in the 1840s and 1850s.

In some respects the circumstances that influenced policing in New Orleans were unusual in degree rather than unique in kind. A decline in the proportion of slaves in the city's population was a trend common throughout the urban South before the Civil War, but it was most pronounced in New Orleans. Many southern cities, especially the larger ones, had sizable concentrations of foreigners, but New Orleans consistently had the largest percentage of foreign-born in the Deep South—and in the antebellum period the largest concentrations of French, Spanish, and Italian immigrants—and stood second only to St. Louis in the entire slaveholding region. As a consequence, in 1860 immigrants accounted for 64 percent of the police in Charleston, 63 percent in New Orleans, and 58 percent in Savannah, and in 1870 the white police contingents in Charleston, Savannah, Mobile, Memphis, Vicksburg, and San Antonio all had more than 60 percent foreign-born personnel, and New Orleans had the largest proportion of all (68 percent).[1] Virtually every southern city and town was marked by at least some violence between the Know-Nothings and Democrats in the 1850s, and the level of this violence in New Orleans surely exceeded that in every other city in the South except Baltimore and Louisville. Of all the larger Deep South cities captured during the Civil War, occupation by Union forces was longest in New Orleans. After the war New Orleans became the first city in the South to integrate its police force, and in no other city did black policemen have a stronger, more full-fledged role in policing. Among the South's larger cities, only Charleston's tenure under military Reconstruction matched the length of that experience in New Orleans, and probably no other southern city witnessed such a stormy and bloody struggle between Republicans and Democrats in that period. After Reconstruction ended, New Orleans assumed yet another extreme position by hiring so few policemen and paying them so poorly— only one other sizable southern city, Mobile, paid its policemen a lower salary.

Although the New Orleans police were unique in a few ways and un-usual in several others, they shared many experiences with the police forces of most other major U.S. cities, especially in the second half of the nineteenth century. Partisan engagement of the police in municipal politics, which had clearly developed in New Orleans by midcentury, was the national norm in that period; several state governments intervened for partisan reasons in municipal policing, as Louisiana did during Reconstruction; and the adoption in the late nineteenth century of a nominally nonpartisan merit system of hiring and promotion took place in the Crescent City, neither very early nor very late, as part of a national movement. When the deployment of policemen to territorial patrol beats became virtually universal practice among the American urban police, the obstacles to effective supervision posed by this tactic plagued police supervisors in New Orleans just as they did throughout the rest of the country. With the advent of novel applications of technology to police work, such as the use of daguerreotypes and the telegraph in the 1850s, telephones in the 1880s, and the Bertillion system in the 1890s, New Orleans was neither first nor last among the major cities to adopt these innovations.

New Orleanians also closely resembled urban dwellers in the rest of the

1. The percentages of foreign-born policemen are derived from the census records cited in the source notes to Tables 12 and 16.

United States in their chronic dissatisfaction with police performance and their inclination to experiment with police reforms—especially cheap reforms. The early reform that installed the paramilitary Gendarmerie certainly failed in part because of the expensive mounted patrols. The city government retained the military style of policing in establishing the city guard but scrapped the horses and substantially reduced the cost of policing. Similarly, the demilitarization of 1836 allowed for a major institutional change without requiring an increased allocation to the police department. In the mid-1850s the American party initiated a reform that produced a big turnover of personnel, accompanied by a net reduction in the total number of policemen and concomitant savings to the city treasury. Only the Republican reforms of the Reconstruction period involved significant increases in spending, which exacerbated the hostility and opposition rooted in white Democrats' racism and partisan sentiment, and even the Republicans were compelled by shrinking revenues to resort to retrenchment. The Democratic reform that followed the end of Reconstruction not only reduced the share of jobs held by blacks and white Republicans but also cut expenditures for policing even more. The patrol wagon and telegraph system installed in the 1880s required some additional money from the city government, but it also permitted political leaders to rationalize the inadequate number of policemen by taking comfort in the thought that the new system enhanced police effectiveness without necessitating the employment of more men. The last reform of the period 1805–1889, civil service, cost the city almost nothing.

None of the changes in police organization and operation during the nineteenth century produced anything resembling satisfaction among New Orleanians. Perhaps public expectations of the police in America's heterogeneous society can never be fully met, but many of the reforms in New Orleans were guaranteed to alienate at least large minorities—or even a majority—of the city's population because they were motivated at times by racism, ethnic prejudice, invidious party spirit, or flinthearted parsimony. Political leaders rarely showed any desire or capacity to serve a larger, common public interest, acting instead to advance the agendas of narrowly self-interested constituencies and at times brazenly flouting the laws they had pledged to enforce. Many New Orleanians may have deserved no better, but surely some did.

# BIBLIOGRAPHY

## UNPUBLISHED GOVERNMENT DOCUMENTS

### CITY ARCHIVES, NEW ORLEANS PUBLIC LIBRARY

#### City Council

Alphabetical and Chronological Digest of the Acts and Deliberations of the Cabildo, 1769–1803. Typescript.

Documents and Letters of Laussat, Colonial Prefect and Commissioner of the French Government, and of the Commissioners of His Catholic Majesty. Typescript.

Journal of the Proceedings of the Board of Aldermen.

Journal of the Proceedings of the Board of Assistant Aldermen.

Ordinances and Resolutions of the City Council of New Orleans. Typescript.

Ordinances and Resolutions of the Common Council. Old Series; New Series; Administrative Series; Council Series.

Ordinances and Resolutions of the First Municipality Council.

Ordinances and Resolutions of the Second Municipality Council.

Ordinances and Resolutions of the Third Municipality Council.

Proceedings of Council Meetings. Typescript.

Reports of City Departments to the Board of Aldermen, 1866–69. Chief Thos. E. Adams to Mayor George Clark, April 12, 1866.

#### Mayor's Office

Biographies of the Mayors of New Orleans. Typescript.

Complaint Book, 1856–59.

Messages of the Mayors to the City Council. Typescript.

Messages of the Mayors to the First Municipality Council.

Messages of the Mayors to the General Council. Typescript.

Messages of the Mayors to the Second Municipality Council.

Messages of the Mayors to the Third Municipality Council.

#### Police Department

Arrest Books, 1881–90. Microfilm.

Personnel Records of the Police Department, 1856–68.
Reports of the Day and Night Police of the First Municipality.
Reports of the Day and Night Police of the Second Municipality.
Reports of the Day and Night Police of the Third Municipality.
Reports of the Third District Police.

*Other*

Charity Hospital Admission Books. Microfilm.
New Orleans Death Certificates. Microfilm.
Obituary Index. Card file.
Police Board Records, 1854–56. Scrapbook.
Tax Books of the Second Municipality.
Tax Registers and Ledgers, City of New Orleans.

### National Archives, Washington, D.C.

Records of the Adjutant General's Office. Record Group 94. No. 737, Final Report
of the Smith-Brady Commission.
Records of the Adjutant General's Office, 1780s–1917. Record Group 94. Index to
Compiled Service Records of Volunteer Union Soldiers Who Served in Or-
ganizations from the State of Louisiana. Microfilm.
Records of the Bureau of the Census. Record Group 29. Censuses of 1820, 1850,
1860, 1870, 1880, 1900. Microfilm.
Records of U.S. Army Continental Commands, 1821–1920. Record Group 393.
Part I, No. 1852, Applications for Positions as Police Officers, 1862–65, and
No. 1884, Letters Received by the Provost Marshal; Part IV, No. 1667, Letters
Received by the Chief of Police, and No. 1669, Orders and Circulars Issued by
the Chief of Police at New Orleans.
Records of the Veterans Bureau. Record Group 15.

### OTHER UNPUBLISHED DOCUMENTS

Criminal District Court, Parish of Orleans, Docket Books, 1879–90. New Orleans
Public Library.
First District Court, Parish of Orleans, Docket Books, 1856–66. New Orleans
Public Library.
First District Court, Parish of Orleans, Minute Books, 1855–74. New Orleans
Public Library.
*Helen M. Barnes* v. *City of New Orleans and Board of Metropolitan Police*, Superior
District Court, Parish of Orleans, Case 9240, 1873. New Orleans Public
Library.
Henry Clay Warmoth Papers in the Southern Historical Collection of the Uni-

versity of North Carolina Library. Microfilm. Howard-Tilton Memorial Library, Tulane University, New Orleans.

Pay List of the Day Police, Night Watchmen, and Lamplighters of the 3rd Municipality for the Month of May, 1841. Hill Memorial Library, Louisiana State University, Baton Rouge.

Payrolls of the City Guard. January, March, April, June, July, August, 1814, July, 1828. Historic New Orleans Collection.

Payrolls of the City Guard. May, 1814, December, 1820. Howard-Tilton Memorial Library, Tulane University, New Orleans.

Record of Inquests and Views, Coroner's Office, 1844–90. Microfilm. New Orleans Public Library.

Register of Convicts Received, February 13, 1866, to December 29, 1889. Louisiana State Penitentiary, Angola.

Superior Criminal Court, Parish of Orleans, Minute Books, 1874–76. New Orleans Public Library.

## PUBLISHED DIGESTS OF ORDINANCES AND LAWS

*The Charters and Ordinances of the City of Richmond, with the Declaration of Rights, and Constitution of Virginia.* Richmond, 1859.

*The Code of Ordinances of the City of Mobile, with the Charter, and an Appendix.* Compiled by Alexander McKinstry. Mobile, 1859.

*The Code of Virginia; with the Declaration of Independence and Constitution of the United States; and the Declaration of Rights and Constitution of Virginia.* Richmond, 1849.

*The Consolidation and Revision of the Statutes of the State, of a General Nature.* Compiled by Levi Peirce, Miles Taylor, and William W. King. New Orleans, 1852.

*Constitutions of 1812, '45, & '52. Also the Constitution of the United States, with Amendments. Articles of Confederation and the Declaration of Independence.* New Orleans, 1861.

*A Digest of All the Ordinances of the City of Savannah, and Various Laws of the State of Georgia, Relative to Said City, Which Were of Force on the 1st January, 1858, Together with an Appendix and Index.* Compiled by Edward G. Wilson. Savannah, 1858.

*A Digest of Ordinances, Resolutions, By-Laws and Regulations of the Corporation of New-Orleans, and a Collection of the Laws of the Legislature Relative to the Said City.* New Orleans, 1836.

*A Digest of the Acts of Assembly Relating to the City of Philadelphia and the (Late) Incorporated Districts of the County of Philadelphia, and of the Ordinances of the Said City and Districts, in Force on the First Day of January, A.D. 1856.* Compiled by William Duane, William B. Hood, and Leonard Myers. Philadelphia, 1856.

*Digest of the Acts of the Legislature, and Decisions of the Supreme Court of Louisiana, Relative to the General Council of the City of New Orleans, Together with the Ordi-*

*nances and Resolutions of the Former City Council, and the General Council of the City of New Orleans, in Force on the First of August, 1848.* Compiled by Perry S. Warfield. New Orleans, 1848.

*A Digest of the Ordinances and Resolutions of the General Council of the City of New-Orleans.* Compiled by T. Thiard and J. Reynes. New Orleans, 1845.

*Digest of the Ordinances and Resolutions of the Second Municipality; and of the General Council of the City of New-Orleans, Applicable Thereto.* Compiled by F. R. Southmayd. New Orleans, 1848.

*Digest of the Ordinances and Resolutions of the Second Municipality of New-Orleans, in Force May 1, 1840.* Compiled by John Calhoun. New Orleans, 1840.

*A Digest of the Ordinances of the City Council of Charleston, from the Year 1783 to Oct. 1844. To Which Are Annexed the Acts of the Legislature Which Relate Exclusively to the City of Charleston.* Compiled by George B. Eckhard. Charleston, 1844.

*A General Digest of the Ordinances and Resolutions of the Corporation of New-Orleans.* Compiled by D. Augustin. New Orleans, 1831.

*The Laws and General Ordinances of the City of New-Orleans, Together with the Acts of the Legislature, Decisions of the Supreme Court, and Constitutional Provisions, Relating to the City Government.* Compiled by Henry J. Leovy. New Orleans, 1857, 1866.

*The Laws and General Ordinances of the City of New Orleans, Together with the Acts of the Legislature, Decisions of the Supreme Court, and Constitutional Provisions Relating to the City Government.* Compiled by Henry J. Leovy and C. H. Luzenburg. New ed. New Orleans, 1870.

*The Ordinances and Resolutions of the City of Lafayette; Also the Act of Incorporation and Amendatory Acts.* New Orleans, 1845, 1848.

*The Ordinances and Resolutions of the City of Lafayette, Now in Force: Also the Act of Re-Incorporation, and Amendatory Acts.* Lafayette, 1851.

*Ordinances Issued by the City Council of New-Orleans, from the Promulgation of the Police Code Until the First of January 1812, with Two Acts of the Territorial Legislature Relative to Said City, to Serve as a Supplement to the Police Code.* New Orleans, 1812.

*Ordinances of the City of Charleston from the 14th September, 1854, to the 1st December, 1859; and the Acts of the General Assembly.* Compiled by John R. Horsey. Charleston, 1859.

*Ordinances of the Corporation of the City of Richmond, and the Acts of Assembly Relating Thereto.* Richmond, 1859.

*Ordinances Ordained and Established by the Mayor & City Council of the City of New-Orleans.* New Orleans, 1817. Bound with *Ordinances Ordained and Established by the Mayor and City Council of New-Orleans.* New Orleans, 1821. Bound with *An Act to Incorporate the City of New-Orleans, with Several Acts Relative to Said City.* New Orleans, 1818.

*Police Code, or Collection of the Ordinances of Police Made by the City Council of New Orleans. To Which Is Prefixed the Act for Incorporating Said City with the Acts Supplementary Thereto.* New Orleans, 1808.

*The Revised Statute Laws of the State of Louisiana from the Organization of the Territory to the Year 1869, Inclusive, with the Amendments Thereto. Enacted at the Sessions of the Legislature up to and Including the Session of 1876, and References to the Civil Code, the Code of Practice, and the Decisions of the Supreme Court of the State of Louisiana.* Edited by Albert Voorhies. New Orleans, 1876.

## OTHER PUBLISHED LEGAL MATERIAL

*Acts of Louisiana,* 1812–1900.

*Acts of the Orleans Territory,* 1806–11.

*Carmouche* v. *Bouis,* 6 Louisiana Reports 95 (1851).

*Duperrier* v. *Dautrive,* 12 Louisiana Annual Reports 664 (1856).

*Findlay* v. *Pruitt,* 9 Porter 195 (Alabama, 1839).

Foster, Sir Michael. *A Report of Some Proceedings on the Commission of Oyer and Terminer and Goal [sic] Delivery for the Trial of the Rebels in the Year 1746 in the County of Surry, and of Other Crown Cases. To Which Are Added Discourses Upon a Few Branches of the Crown Law.* Dublin, 1767.

Hale, Sir Matthew. *The History of the Pleas of the Crown.* 2 vols. London, 1736.

*Murdock* v. *Ripley,* 35 Maine Reports 472 (1853).

*Report of the Attorney General,* 1856–1900.

*State* v. *Brett,* 6 Louisiana Annual Reports 652 (1851).

*State* v. *J. T. Smith,* 11 Louisiana Annual Reports 633 (1856).

*State* v. *Lucy Bias,* 37 Louisiana Annual Reports 259 (1885).

Wharton, Francis. *The Law of Homicide in the United States.* Philadelphia, 1855.

———. *On the Criminal Law of the United States.* 3rd ed. Philadelphia, 1855.

## CENSUS MATERIAL (PUBLISHED)

*Aggregate Amount of Each Description of Persons Within the United States of America, and Territories Thereof, Agreeably to Actual Enumeration Made According to Law, in the Year 1810.* Washington, D.C., 1811.

*Census for 1820.* Washington, D.C., 1821.

*Compendium of the Eleventh Census: 1890. Part I—Population.* Washington, D.C., 1892.

Dawson, J. L., and H. W. DeSaussure. *Census of the City of Charleston, South Carolina, for the Year 1848.* Charleston, 1848.

*Fifth Census, or Enumeration of the Inhabitants of the United States. 1830. To Which Is Prefixed a Schedule of the Whole Number of Persons Within the Several Districts of the United States, Taken According to the Acts of 1790, 1800, 1812, 1820.* Washington, D.C., 1832.

Jackson, Ronald Vern, Gary Ronald Teeples, and David Schaefermeyer, eds. *Louisiana 1820 Census Index.* Bountiful, Utah, 1976.

———. *Louisiana 1830 Census Index.* Bountiful, Utah, 1976.

*New Orleans in 1805: A Directory and a Census.* New Orleans, 1936.

*Ninth Census—Volume I. The Statistics of the Population of the United States.* Washington, D.C., 1872.

*Population of the United States in 1860.* Washington, D.C., 1864.

*Report on Population of the United States at the Eleventh Census: 1890.* Part I. Washington, D.C., 1895.

*Return of the Whole Number of Persons Within the Several Districts of the United States: According to "An Act Providing for the Second Census or Enumeration of the Inhabitants of the United States." Passed February the 28th, One Thousand Eight Hundred.* Washington, D.C., 1802.

*The Seventh Census of the United States: 1850.* Washington, D.C., 1853.

*Sixth Census or Enumeration of the Inhabitants of the United States as Corrected at the Department of State in 1840.* Washington, D.C., 1841.

*Statistical View of the United States . . . Being a Compendium of the Seventh Census.* Washington, D.C., 1854.

*Statistics of the Population of the United States at the Tenth Census (June 1, 1880).* Washington, D.C., 1883.

Waring, George E., Jr. *Report of the Social Statistics of the Cities.* 2 vols. Washington, D.C., 1887.

## OTHER PUBLISHED DOCUMENTS

*Annual Report of Board of Police Commissioners and Superintendent of Police,* 1889– 1900.

*Annual Report of the Board of Metropolitan Police to the Governor of Louisiana,* 1868/ 69–1874/75.

*Annual Message of the Mayor, Together with the Budget of the City of New Orleans for 1871, and the Report of the Administrator of Public Accounts Thereon.* [New Orleans, 1871?].

*Annual Message of the Mayor to the Common Council of New Orleans. Submitted May 5, 1868.* [New Orleans, 1868].

*Biennial Report of the Board of Control of the Louisiana State Penitentiary for the Years 1890 and 1891, to His Excellency, the Governor of Louisiana, Baton Rouge, La., April 14, 1892.* Baton Rouge, 1892.

*Biennial Report of the Board of Control of the Louisiana State Penitentiary for the Years 1894 and 1895 to His Excellency Murphy J. Foster, Governor of Louisiana.* Baton Rouge, 1896.

*Communication of Charles M. Waterman, Mayor of the City of New Orleans, to the Board of Assistant Aldermen, and Their Action Thereon (June 18, 1858).* New Orleans, 1858.

*Congressional Globe.* 32nd Cong., 1st sess., 1851, 25, Appendix. Washington, D.C., 1852.

*General Message of Chas. M. Waterman, Mayor of the City of New Orleans, to the Common Council. October 1st, 1857.* [New Orleans, 1857?].

*House Reports.* 39th Cong., 2nd sess., 1867, No. 16.

*Journal of the Special Committee Appointed by the House of Representatives of Louisiana, to Investigate the Frauds Perpetrated in the State, During the Late Presidential Election.* New Orleans, 1845.

*Manual of the City Police, Adopted by the Board of Police Commissioners, January 1st, 1890.* New Orleans, 1889.

*Message of Gerard Smith, Mayor of the City of New Orleans, to the Common Council.* New Orleans, 1858.

*New Orleans Police Department 1973 Annual Report.* Metairie, La., [1974?].

*Proceedings and Debates of the Convention of Louisiana Which Assembled at the City of New Orleans January 14, 1844.* New Orleans, 1845.

"Proceedings of the Second Confederate Congress." *Southern Historical Society Papers,* Vol. LI [First Session]. Richmond, Va., 1958.

*Rules and Regulations for the General Government of the Police Department of the City of New Orleans.* New Orleans, 1852.

U.S. Bureau of Statistics (Treasury Department). *Immigration into the United States, Showing Number, Nationality, Sex, Age, Occupation, Destination, Etc., from 1820 to 1903.* Washington, D.C., 1903.

*The War of the Rebellion: A Compilation of the Official Records of the Union and Confederate Armies.* 130 vols. Washington, D.C., 1880–1901.

## CITY DIRECTORIES

*Cohen's New Orleans and Lafayette Directory.* New Orleans, 1849–51.

*Edwards' Annual Directory.* New Orleans, 1871–73.

*Gardner's New Orleans Directory.* New Orleans, 1860, 1866, 1868, 1869.

*Gibson's Guide and Directory of the State of Louisiana, and the Cities of New Orleans & Lafayette.* New Orleans, 1838.

*Graham's Crescent City Directory.* New Orleans, 1867, 1870.

*Michel & Co. New-Orleans Annual and Commercial Directory, for 1843.* New Orleans, 1842.

*Michel & Co. New Orleans Annual and Commercial Register for 1846.* New Orleans, 1845.

Montague, William L. *Montague's Richmond Directory and Business Advisor, for 1850–1851.* Richmond, [1850?].

*New-Orleans Directory, for 1841; Made by the United States Deputy Marshals, (While Taking the Late Census)*. New Orleans, 1840.

*Norman's New Orleans and Environs*. New Orleans, 1845.

Paxton, John Adams. *The New-Orleans Directory and Register*. New Orleans, 1822, 1823, 1830.

————. *Supplement to the New Orleans Directory of the Last Year*. New Orleans, 1824.

*Soards' Directory*. New Orleans, 1874–77.

*Whitney's New-Orleans Directory and Louisiana & Mississippi Almanac for the Year 1811*. New Orleans, 1810.

## TRAVEL ACCOUNTS, MEMOIRS, AND PUBLISHED LETTERS

*Annual Report of the American Historical Association for the Year 1902*. Vol. II. *Sixth Report of Historical Manuscripts Commission: With Diary and Correspondence of Salmon P. Chase*. Washington, D.C., 1903.

Benwell, J. *An Englishman's Travels in America: His Observations of Life and Manners in the Free and Slave States*. London, 1853.

Bernhard, Duke of Saxe-Weimar Eisenach. *Travels Through North America, During the Years 1825 and 1826*. 2 vols. Philadelphia, 1828.

Bingley, Rev. William. *Travels in North America, from Modern Writers*. London, 1821.

Cable, George W., ed. *Famous Adventures and Prison Escapes of the Civil War*. New York, 1893.

Chambers, William. *Things as They Are in America*. London, 1854.

Clapp, Theodore. *Autobiographical Sketches and Recollections, During a Thirty-Five Years' Residence in New Orleans*. Boston, 1857.

Corsan, W. C. *Two Months in the Confederate States, Including a Visit to New Orleans Under the Domination of General Butler*. London, 1863.

Darby, William. *A Geographical Description of the State of Louisiana*. Philadelphia, 1816.

Fearon, Henry Bradshaw. *Sketches of America*. 2nd ed. 1818. Reprint. New York, 1969.

Flint, Timothy. *Recollection of the Last Ten Years, Passed in Occasional Residences and Journeyings in the Valley of the Mississippi, from Pittsburgh and the Missouri to the Gulf of Mexico, and from Florida to the Spanish Frontier; in a Series of Letters to the Rev. James Flint, of Salem, Massachusetts*. Boston, 1826.

Hall, Captain Basil. *Travels in North America in the Years 1827 and 1828*. 3 vols. Edinburgh, 1829.

Hall, Margaret Hunter. *The Aristocratic Journey: Being the Outspoken Letters of Mrs. Basil Hall Written During a Fourteen Months' Sojourn in America, 1827–1828*. Edited by Una Pope-Hennessy. New York, 1931.

Hamilton, Captain Thomas. *Men and Manners in America*. 2 vols. Edinburgh, 1833.

Harden, William. *Recollections of a Long and Satisfactory Life.* New York, 1934.

Ingraham, Joseph Holt. *The South-West: By a Yankee.* 2 vols. New York, 1835.

King, Edward. *The Great South: A Record of Journeys in Louisiana, Texas, the Indian Territory, Missouri, Arkansas, Mississippi, Alabama, Georgia, Florida, South Carolina, North Carolina, Kentucky, Tennessee, Virginia, West Virginia, and Maryland.* Hartford, 1875.

Kingsford, William. *Impressions of the West and South During a Six Weeks' Holiday.* Toronto, 1858.

Latrobe, Benjamin Henry. *The Journal of Latrobe, Being the Notes and Sketches of an Architect, Naturalist and Traveler in the United States from 1796 to 1820.* New York, 1905.

Mackay, Alex. *The Western World; or, Travels in the United States in 1846–47.* 2 vols. From the second London edition. Philadelphia, 1849.

Mackay, Charles. *Life and Liberty in America; or, Sketches of a Tour in the United States and Canada, in 1857–8.* 2 vols. London, 1859.

Morgan, James Morris. *Recollections of a Rebel Reefer.* London, 1917.

Nichols, Dr. Thomas L. *Forty Years of American Life.* 2 vols. London, 1864.

Olmsted, Frederick Law. *A Journey in the Seaboard Slave States in the Years 1853–1854.* 2 vols. New York, 1904.

Parker, A. A. *Trip to the West and Texas. Comprising a Journey of Eight Thousand Miles, Through New-York, Michigan, Illinois, Missouri, Louisiana and Texas, in the Autumn and Winter of 1834–5. Interspersed with Anecdotes, Incidents, Observations. With a Brief Sketch of the Texian War.* 2nd ed. Boston, 1836.

Reed, Emily Hazen. *Life of A. P. Dostie; or, The Conflict in New Orleans.* New York, 1868.

Rowland, Dunbar, ed. *Official Letter Books of W. C. C. Claiborne, 1801–1816.* 6 vols. Madison, Wisc., 1917.

Rowland, Kate Mason, and Mrs. Morris L. Croxall, eds. *The Journal of Julia LeGrand, New Orleans, 1862–1863.* Richmond, 1911.

Russell, William Howard. *My Diary North and South.* Boston, 1863.

Sala, George Augustus. *America Revisited: From the Bay of New York to the Gulf of Mexico, and from Lake Michigan to the Pacific.* 5th ed. London, 1885.

Schultz, Christian. *Travels on an Inland Voyage Through the States of New-York, Pennsylvania, Virginia, Ohio, Kentucky and Tennessee, and Through the Territories of Indiana, Louisiana, Mississippi, and New-Orleans; Performed in the Years 1807 and 1808; Including a Trip of Nearly Six Thousand Miles.* 2 vols. New York, 1810.

Sealsfield, C. *The Americans as They Are; Described in a Tour Through the Valley of the Mississippi.* London, 1828.

Southwood, Marion. *"Beauty and Booty," the Watchword of New Orleans.* New York, 1867.

Stirling, James. *Letters from the Slave States.* London, 1857.

Stuart, James. *Three Years in North America*. 2 vols. Edinburgh, 1833.

Sullivan, Edward. *Rambles and Scrambles in North and South America*. London, 1852.

Tasistro, Louis Fitzgerald. *Random Shots and Southern Breezes, Containing Critical Remarks on the Southern States and Southern Institutions, with Semi-Serious Observations on Men and Manners*. 2 vols. New York, 1842.

Vandenhoff, George. *Leaves from an Actor's Note-Book; with Reminiscences and Chit-Chat of the Green-Room and the Stage, in England and America*. New York, 1860.

Warmoth, Henry Clay. *War, Politics and Reconstruction: Stormy Days in Louisiana*. New York, 1930.

Whipple, Henry Benjamin. *Bishop Whipple's Southern Diary, 1843–1844*. Edited by Lester B. Shippee. Minneapolis, 1937.

## NEW ORLEANS NEWSPAPERS

*Argus*, 1828.

*Bee*, 1831–61.

*Commercial Bulletin*, 1847–56.

*Daily Crescent*, 1851–66.

*Daily Delta*, 1847–63.

*Daily Orleanian*, 1851–54.

*Daily Picayune*, 1849–90.

*Daily States*, 1885.

*Daily Tropic*, 1843–45.

*Daily True Delta*, 1850–62.

*Deutsche Zeitung*, 1858.

*Louisiana Advertiser*, 1830–34.

*Louisiana Courier*, 1810–59.

*Louisiana Gazette*, 1808–25.

*Mercantile Advertiser*, 1831–34.

*Republican*, 1869–77.

*Times*, 1865–81.

*Times-Democrat*, 1884.

*Tribune*, 1867.

*True American*, 1836.

## SECONDARY BOOKS

Adams, William Forbes. *Ireland and Irish Emigration, from 1815 to the Famine*. 1932; rpr. New York, 1960.

Alfers, Kenneth G. *Law and Order in the Capital City: A History of the Washington Police, 1800–1886*. Washington, D.C., 1976.

Allen, Michael. *Western Rivermen, 1763–1861: Ohio and Mississippi Boatmen and the Myth of the Alligator Horse.* Baton Rouge, 1990.

Arnesen, Eric. *Waterfront Workers of New Orleans: Race, Class, and Politics, 1863–1923.* New York, 1991.

Arnold, Eric A. *Fouche, Napoleon, and the General Police.* Washington, D.C., 1979.

Asbury, Herbert. *The French Quarter: An Informal History of the New Orleans Underworld.* New York, 1968.

Ayers, Edward L. *Vengeance and Justice: Crime and Punishment in the 19th-Century American South.* New York, 1984.

Baker, Jean H. *Ambivalent Americans: The Know Nothing Party in Maryland.* Baltimore, 1977.

Beatty, Richmond Croom, Thomas Daniel Young, and Floyd C. Watkins, eds. *The Literature of the South.* Glenview, Ill., 1968.

Berlin, Ira. *Slaves Without Masters: The Free Negro in the Antebellum South.* New York, 1974.

Blassingame, John W. *Black New Orleans, 1860–1880.* Chicago, 1973.

Booth, Andrew B., comp. *Records of Louisiana Confederate Soldiers and Louisiana Confederate Commands.* New Orleans, 1920.

Brasseaux, Carl A. *Denis-Nicolas Foucault and the New Orleans Rebellion of 1768.* Ruston, La., 1987.

Bridenbaugh, Carl. *Cities in Revolt: Urban Life in America, 1743–1776.* New York, 1955.

———. *Cities in the Wilderness: The First Century of Urban Life in America, 1625–1742.* New York, 1955.

Bromwell, William J. *History of Immigration to the United States.* New York, 1856.

Brown, Richard Maxwell. *Strain of Violence: Historical Studies of American Violence and Vigilantism.* Oxford, 1975.

Cantwell, Edward P. *A History of the Charleston Police Force from the Incorporation of the City, 1783 to 1908.* Charleston, 1908.

Capers, Gerald M., Jr. *Occupied City: New Orleans Under the Federals, 1862–1865.* Lexington, 1965.

Castellanos, Henry C. *New Orleans as It Was: Episodes of Louisiana Life.* New Orleans, 1895.

Critchley, T. A. *A History of Police in England and Wales, 900–1966.* London, 1967.

Cunliffe, Marcus. *Soldiers and Civilians: The Martial Spirit in America, 1775–1865.* Boston, 1968.

Desdunes, Rodolphe Lucien. *Our People and Our History.* Edited and translated by Sr. Dorothea Olga McCants. Baton Rouge, 1973.

Du Bois, W. E. B. *The Suppression of the African Slave-Trade to the United States of America, 1638–1870.* 1898; rpr. New York, 1965.

Feldberg, Michael. *The Philadelphia Riots of 1844: A Study of Ethnic Conflict.* Westport, Conn., 1975.

———. *The Turbulent Era: Riot and Disorder in Jacksonian America*. New York, 1980.

Fischer, Roger A. *The Segregation Struggle in Louisiana, 1862–1877.* Urbana, 1974.

Fossier, Albert A. *New Orleans: The Glamour Period, 1800–1840.* New Orleans, 1957.

Fogelson, Robert M. *Big-City Police.* London, 1977.

Franklin, John Hope. *The Militant South, 1800–1861.* Cambridge, Mass., 1956.

Fraser, Walter J., Jr. *Charleston! Charleston! The History of a Southern City.* Columbia, 1989.

Friedman, Lawrence M., and Robert V. Percival. *The Roots of Justice: Crime and Punishment in Alameda County, California, 1870–1910.* Chapel Hill, 1981.

Gambino, Richard. *Vendetta: A True Story of the Worst Lynching in America, the Mass Murder of Italian-Americans in New Orleans in 1891, the Vicious Motivations Behind It, and the Tragic Repercussions That Linger to This Day.* Garden City, N.Y., 1977.

Gamble, Thomas, Jr. *A History of the City Government of Savannah, Ga., from 1790 to 1901. Compiled from Official Records by Thomas Gamble, Jr., Secretary to the Mayor, Under Direction of the City Council, 1900.* Savannah, 1901.

Gluckman, Arcadi. *United States Martial Pistols and Revolvers.* Harrisburg, Pa., 1960.

Greeley, Andrew M. *That Most Distressful Nation: The Taming of the American Irish.* Chicago, 1972.

Greenberg, Douglas. *Crime and Law Enforcement in the Colony of New York, 1691–1776.* Ithaca, 1976.

Haas, Edward F. *Political Leadership in a Southern City: New Orleans in the Progressive Era, 1896–1902.* Ruston, La., 1988.

Hair, William Ivy. *Bourbonism and Agrarian Protest: Louisiana Politics, 1877–1900.* Baton Rouge, 1969.

———. *Carnival of Fury: Robert Charles and the New Orleans Race Riot of 1900.* Baton Rouge, 1976.

Hall, Gwendolyn Midlo. *Africans in Colonial Louisiana: The Development of Afro-Creole Culture in the Eighteenth Century.* Baton Rouge, 1992.

Handlin, Oscar. *Boston's Immigrants: A Study in Acculturation.* Rev. and enlarged ed. New York, 1976.

Harring, Sidney L. *Policing a Class Society: The Experience of American Cities, 1865–1915.* New Brunswick, 1983.

Haven, Charles T., and Frank A. Belden. *A History of the Colt Revolver and the Other Arms Made by Colt's Patent Fire Arms Manufacturing Company from 1836 to 1940.* New York, 1940.

Henderson, Dwight F. *Congress, Courts, and Criminals: The Development of Federal Criminal Law, 1801–1829.* Westport, Conn., 1985.

Hindus, Michael Stephen. *Prison and Plantation: Crime, Justice, and Authority in Massachusetts and South Carolina, 1767–1878.* Chapel Hill, 1980.

Hirsch, Arnold R., and Joseph Logsdon, eds. *Creole New Orleans: Race and Americanization.* Baton Rouge, 1992.

Hoogenboom, Ari. *Outlawing the Spoils: A History of the Civil Service Reform Movement, 1865–1883.* Urbana, 1961.

Howard, Warren S. *American Slavers and the Federal Law, 1837–1862.* Berkeley, 1963.

Howe, William W. *Municipal History of New Orleans.* Baltimore, 1889.

International Association of Chiefs of Police, Field Operations Division. *A Survey of the Police Department: New Orleans, Louisiana.* Gaithersburg, Md., 1971.

Jackson, Joy J. *New Orleans in the Gilded Age: Politics and Urban Progress, 1880–1896.* Baton Rouge, 1969.

Johnson, David R. *American Law Enforcement: A History.* St. Louis, 1981.

———. *Policing the Urban Underworld: The Impact of Crime on the Development of the American Police, 1800–1887.* Philadelphia, 1979.

Kendall, John Smith. *History of New Orleans.* 3 vols. New York, 1922.

Kennett, Lee, and James LaVerne Anderson. *The Gun in America: The Origins of a National Dilemma.* Westport, Conn., 1975.

Landry, Stuart Omer. *The Battle of Liberty Place: The Overthrow of Carpet-Bag Rule in New Orleans, September 14, 1874.* New Orleans, 1955.

Lane, Roger. *Policing the City: Boston, 1822–1885.* Cambridge, Mass., 1967.

———. *Roots of Violence in Black Philadelphia, 1860–1900.* London, 1986.

———. *Violent Death in the City: Suicide, Accident, and Murder in Nineteenth-Century Philadelphia.* London, 1979.

McConnell, Roland C. *Negro Troops of Antebellum Louisiana: A History of the Battalion of Free Men of Color.* Baton Rouge, 1968.

McCrary, Peyton. *Abraham Lincoln and Reconstruction: The Louisiana Experiment.* Princeton, 1978.

Marchiafava, Louis J. *The Houston Police, 1878–1948.* Houston, 1977.

Miller, Wilbur R. *Cops and Bobbies: Police Authority in New York and London, 1830–1870.* Chicago, 1977.

Monkkonen, Eric H. *The Dangerous Class: Crime and Poverty in Columbus, Ohio, 1860–1885.* London, 1975.

———. *Police in Urban America, 1860–1920.* Cambridge, Eng., 1981.

Moore, John Preston. *Revolt in Louisiana: The Spanish Occupation, 1766–1770.* Baton Rouge, 1976.

Nau, John Frederick. *The German People of New Orleans, 1850–1900.* Leiden, Netherlands, 1958.

Neely, Mark E., Jr., Harold Holzer, and Gabor S. Boritt. *The Confederate Image: Prints of the Lost Cause.* Chapel Hill, 1987.

Nelli, Humbert S. *The Business of Crime: Italians and Syndicate Crime in the United States.* New York, 1976.

*New Orleans Police Department, Benefit of the Police Mutual Benevolent Association of New Orleans, History.* [New Orleans?], 1900.

Niehaus, Earl F. *The Irish in New Orleans, 1800–1860.* Baton Rouge, 1965.

Osterweis, Rollin G. *Romanticism and Nationalism in the Old South.* New Haven, 1949.

Palmer, Stanley H. *Police and Protest in England and Ireland, 1780–1850.* Cambridge, Eng., 1988.

Pierson, Marion John Bennett, comp. *Louisiana Soldiers in the War of 1812.* [Baton Rouge], 1963.

*Police Mutual Benevolent Association, Police Record.* New Orleans, 1912.

Rabinowitz, Howard N. *Race Relations in the Urban South, 1865–1890.* New York, 1978.

Rable, George C. *But There Was No Peace: The Role of Violence in the Politics of Reconstruction.* Athens, Ga., 1984.

Radley, Kenneth. *Rebel Watchdog: The Confederate States Army Provost Guard.* Baton Rouge, 1989.

Radzinowicz, Leon. *A History of English Criminal Law and Its Administration from 1750.* 4 vols. New York, 1948–68.

Reed, Merl E. *New Orleans and the Railroads: The Struggle for Commercial Empire.* Baton Rouge, 1966.

Reinders, Robert C. *End of an Era: New Orleans, 1850–1860.* New Orleans, 1964.

Reynolds, George M. *Machine Politics in New Orleans, 1897–1926.* 1936; rpr. New York, 1968.

Richardson, James F. *The New York Police: Colonial Times to 1901.* New York, 1970.

———. *Urban Police in the United States.* London, 1974.

Rightor, Henry. *Standard History of New Orleans, Louisiana.* Chicago, 1900.

Robinson, William H. *Justice in Grey: A History of the Justice System of the Confederate States of America.* Cambridge, Mass., 1941.

Scharf, Peter, and Arnold Binder. *The Badge and the Bullet: Police Use of Deadly Force.* New York, 1983.

Schneider, John C. *Detroit and the Problem of Order, 1830–1880: A Geography of Crime, Riot, and Policing.* Lincoln, 1980.

Shannon, William V. *The American Irish.* New York, 1963.

Sinclair, Harold. *The Port of New Orleans.* Garden City, N.Y., 1942.

Smith, Bruce. *The New Orleans Police Survey.* New Orleans, 1946.

Soulé, Leon Cyprian. *The Know Nothing Party in New Orleans: A Reappraisal.* Baton Rouge, 1961.

*Souvenir Program of the Joint Festival Given for the Benefit of the Firemen's Mutual Benefit and Relief Fund and Police Mutual Benevolent Association, Fair Grounds, Sunday, Oct. 6th, 1895.* New Orleans, [1905].

Steinberg, Allen. *The Transformation of Criminal Justice: Philadelphia, 1800–1880.* Chapel Hill, 1989.

Taylor, Joe Gray. *Louisiana Reconstructed, 1863–1877.* Baton Rouge, 1974.

Vincent, Charles. *Black Legislators in Louisiana During Reconstruction.* Baton Rouge, 1976.

Wade, Richard C. *Slavery in the Cities: The South, 1820–1860.* New York, 1964.

———. *The Urban Frontier: Pioneer Life in Early Pittsburgh, Cincinnati, Louisville, and St. Louis.* Chicago, 1959.

Walker, Samuel. *A Critical History of Police Reform: The Emergence of Professionalism.* Toronto, 1977.

———. *Popular Justice: A History of American Criminal Justice.* New York, 1980.

Wilkinson, Frederick. *Antique Firearms.* Garden City, N.Y., 1969.

Williams, Jack Kenny. *Vogues in Villainy: Crime and Retribution in Ante-Bellum South Carolina.* Columbia, S.C., 1959.

Wilson, Adelaide. *Historic and Picturesque Savannah.* Boston, 1889.

Wyatt-Brown, Bertram. *Southern Honor: Ethics and Behavior in the Old South.* New York, 1982.

## ARTICLES AND ESSAYS

Adler, Jeffrey S. "Streetwalkers, Degraded Outcasts, and Good-for-Nothing Huzzies: Women and the Dangerous Class in Antebellum St. Louis." *Journal of Social History,* XXV (1992), 737–55.

———. "Vagging the Demons and Scoundrels: Vagrancy and the Growth of St. Louis, 1830–1861." *Journal of Urban History,* XIII (1986), 3–30.

Bonner, James C. "The Historical Basis of Southern Military Tradition." *Georgia Review,* IX (1955), 74–85.

Burnham, John C. "The Social Evil Ordinance—A Social Experiment in Nineteenth Century St. Louis." *Bulletin of the Missouri Historical Society,* XXVII (1971), 203–17.

Chenault, William W., and Robert C. Reinders. "The Northern-born Community of New Orleans in the 1850s." *Journal of American History,* LI (1964), 232–47.

Deusner, Charles E. "The Know Nothing Riots in Louisville." *Register of the Kentucky Historical Society,* LXI (1963), 122–47.

Dormon, James H. "The Persistent Specter: Slave Rebellion in Territorial Louisiana." *Louisiana History,* XVIII (1977), 389–404.

Emsley, Clive. "'The Thump of Wood on a Swede Turnip': Police Violence in Nineteenth-Century England." *Criminal Justice History,* VI (1985), 125–49.

Ernst, Daniel R. "Beyond Police History: A Systemic Perspective." *Maryland Historian,* XVI (1985), 27–42.

Ethington, Phillip J. "Vigilantes and the Police." *Journal of Social History,* XXI (1987), 197–227.

Everett, Donald E. "Emigrés and Militiamen: Free Persons of Color in New Orleans, 1803–1815." *Journal of Negro History,* XXXVIII (1953), 377–402.

———. "Free Persons of Color in Colonial Louisiana." *Louisiana History*, VII (1966), 21–50.

Ferdinand, Theodore N. "The Criminal Patterns of Boston Since 1849." *American Journal of Sociology*, LXXIII (1967), 84–99.

———. "Criminality, the Courts, and the Constabulary in Boston: 1702–1967." *Journal of Research in Crime and Delinquency*, XVII (1980), 190–208.

———. "Politics, the Police and Arresting Policies in Salem, Massachusetts, Since the Civil War." *Social Problems*, XIX (1972), 572–88.

Gorn, Elliot J. "'Good-Bye Boys, I Die a True American': Homicide, Nativism, and Working-Class Culture in Antebellum New York City." *Journal of American History*, LXXIV (1987), 388–410.

Graff, Harvey J. "Crime and Punishment in the Nineteenth Century: A New Look at the Criminal." *Journal of Interdisciplinary History*, VII (1977), 477–91.

———. "'Pauperism, Misery, and Vice': Illiteracy and Criminality in the Nineteenth Century." *Journal of Social History*, X (1977), 245–68.

Haag, Pamela. "The 'Ill-Use of a Wife': Patterns of Working-Class Violence in Domestic and Public New York City, 1860–1880." *Journal of Social History*, XXV (1992), 447–77.

Hall, Jerome. "Legal and Social Aspects of Arrest Without a Warrant." *Harvard Law Review*, XLIX (1936), 566–92.

Haller, Mark H. "Historical Roots of Police Behavior: Chicago, 1890–1925." *Law and Society Review*, X (1976), 303–23.

Haunton, Richard H. "Law and Order in Savannah, 1850–1860." *Georgia Historical Quarterly*, LVI (1972), 1–24.

Holmes, Jack D. L. "The Abortive Slave Revolt at Pointe Coupée, Louisiana, 1795." *Louisiana History*, XI (1970), 341–62.

———. "The Effects of the Memphis Race Riot of 1866." *West Tennessee Historical Society Papers*, XII (1958), 58–79.

———. "The Underlying Causes of the Memphis Race Riot of 1866." *Tennessee Historical Quarterly*, XVII (1958), 195–221.

Hutcheon, Wallace S., Jr. "The Louisville Riots of August, 1855." *Register of the Kentucky Historical Society*, LXIX (1971), 150–72.

Ingalls, Robert P. "Lynching and Establishment Violence in Tampa, 1858–1935." *Journal of Southern History*, LIII (1987), 613–44.

Ingersoll, Thomas N. "Free Blacks in a Slave Society: New Orleans, 1718–1812." *William and Mary Quarterly*, XLVIII (1991), 173–200.

Jackson, Joy J. "Keeping Law and Order in New Orleans Under General Butler, 1862." *Louisiana History*, XXXIV (1993), 51–67.

Johnson, Bruce C. "Taking Care of Labor: The Police in American Politics." *Theory and Society*, III (1976), 89–115.

Johnson, David R. "The Origins and Structure of Intercity Criminal Activity,

1840–1920: An Interpretation." *Journal of Social History*, XV (1982), 593–605.

Jordan, Laylon Wayne. "Police Power and Public Safety in Antebellum Charleston, 1800–1860." *South Atlantic Urban Studies*, III (1979), 122–40.

Kendall, John Smith. "Old-Time New Orleans Police Reporters and Reporting." *Louisiana Historical Quarterly*, XXIX (1946), 43–58.

Kotlikoff, Laurence J., and Anton J. Rupert. "The Manumission of Slaves in New Orleans, 1827–1846." *Southern Studies*, XIX (1980), 172–81.

Lane, Roger. "Crime and Criminal Statistics in Nineteenth-Century Massachusetts." *Journal of Social History*, II (1968), 156–63.

————. "Crime and the Industrial Revolution: British and American Views." *Journal of Social History*, VII (1974), 287–303.

————. "Urbanization and Criminal Violence in the Nineteenth Century: Massachusetts as a Test Case." In *Violence in America: Historical and Comparative Perspectives*, ed. Hugh D. Graham and Tedd R. Gurr, 359–70. New York, 1969.

————. "Urban Police and Crime in Nineteenth-Century America." *Crime and Justice*, II (1980), 1–43.

Liebman, Robert, and Michael Poler. "Perspectives on Policing in Nineteenth Century America." *Social Science History*, II (1978), 346–60.

May, Robert E. "Dixie's Martial Image: A Continuing Historiographical Enigma." *Historian*, XL (1978), 213–34.

Miles, Edwin A. "The Whig Party and the Menace of Caesar." *Tennessee Historical Quarterly*, XXVII (1968), 361–79.

Monkkonen, Eric H. "A Disorderly People? Urban Order in Nineteenth and Twentieth Century America." *Journal of American History*, LXVIII (1981), 539–59.

————. "From Cop History to Social History: The Significance of the Police in American History." *Journal of Social History*, XV (1982), 575–91.

————. "The Organized Response to Crime in Nineteenth- and Twentieth-Century America." *Journal of Interdisciplinary History*, XIV (1983), 113–28.

————. "Systematic Criminal Justice History: Some Suggestions." *Journal of Interdisciplinary History*, IX (1979), 451–64.

Morgan, David T. "Eugenia Levy Phillips: The Civil War Experiences of a Southern Jewish Woman." In *Jews of the South*, ed. Samuel Proctor and Louis Schmier with Malcolm Stern, 95–106. Macon, Ga., 1984.

Morris, Christopher. "An Event in Community Organization: The Mississippi Slave Insurrection Scare of 1835." *Journal of Social History*, XXII (1988), 93–111.

Rabinowitz, Howard N. "The Conflict Between Blacks and the Police in the Urban South, 1865–1900." *Historian*, XXXIX (1976), 62–76.

Rankin, David C. "The Origins of Black Leadership in New Orleans During Reconstruction." *Journal of Southern History*, XL (1974), 417–40.

————. "The Tannenbaum Thesis Reconsidered: Slavery and Race Relations in Antebellum Louisiana." *Southern Studies*, XVIII (1979), 5–31.

Reynolds, Donald E. "The New Orleans Riot of 1866, Reconsidered." *Louisiana History*, V (1964), 5–27.

Rodriguez, Junius P. "Always 'En Garde': The Effects of Slave Insurrection upon the Louisiana Mentality, 1811–1815." *Louisiana History*, XXXIII (1992), 399–416.

Rousey, Dennis C. "Yellow Fever and Black Policemen in Memphis: A Post-Reconstruction Anomaly." *Journal of Southern History*, LI (1985), 357–74.

Saunders, Robert M. "Crime and Punishment in Early National America: Richmond, Virginia, 1784–1820." *Virginia Magazine of History and Biography*, LXXXVI (1978), 33–44.

Schafer, Judith Kelleher. "The Immediate Impact of Nat Turner's Insurrection on New Orleans." *Louisiana History*, XXII (1980), 361–76.

Schweninger, Loren. "A Negro Sojourner in Antebellum New Orleans." *Louisiana History*, XX (1979), 305–14.

Somers, Dale A. "Black and White in New Orleans: A Study in Urban Race Relations, 1865–1900." *Journal of Southern History*, XL (1974), 19–42.

Tansey, Richard. "Out-of-State Free Blacks in Late Antebellum New Orleans." *Louisiana History*, XXII (1981), 369–86.

———. "Prostitution and Politics in Antebellum New Orleans." *Southern Studies*, XVII (1980), 449–79.

Thompson, Thomas Marshall. "National Newspaper and Legislative Reaction to Louisiana's Deslondes Slave Revolt." *Louisiana History*, XXXIII (1992), 5–29.

Tracy, Charles A., III. "Police Function in Portland, 1851–1874." *Oregon Historical Quarterly*, LXXX (1979), 5–30, 134–70, 287–322.

Tregle, Joseph G., Jr. "Political Reinforcement of Ethnic Dominance in Louisiana, 1812–1845." In *The Americanization of the Gulf Coast, 1803–1850*, ed. Lucius F. Ellsworth, 78–87. Pensacola, 1972.

———. "The Rise of Nativism in New Orleans." In *St. Patrick's of New Orleans, 1833–1958*, ed. Charles Dufour, 23–29. New Orleans, 1958.

Tunnell, Ted. "Free Negroes and the Freedmen: Black Politics in New Orleans During the Civil War." *Southern Studies*, XIX (1980), 172–81.

Urban, Chester Stanley. "New Orleans and the Cuban Question During the Lopez Expeditions of 1849–1851: A Local Study in 'Manifest Destiny.'" *Louisiana Historical Quarterly*, XXII (1939), 1095–1159.

Vandal, Gilles. "The Nineteenth-Century Municipal Responses to the Problem of Poverty: New Orleans' Free Lodgers, 1850–1880, as a Case Study." *Journal of Urban History*, XIX (1992), 30–59.

Von Hoffman, Alexander. "An Officer of the Neighborhood: A Boston Patrolman on the Beat in 1895." *Journal of Social History*, XXVI (1992), 309–30.

Walker, Samuel. "The Police and the Community: Scranton, Pennsylvania, 1866–1884, a Test Case." *American Studies*, XIX (1978), 79–90.

Watson, Richard L., Jr. "Congressional Attitudes Toward Military Preparedness, 1829–1835." *Journal of American History*, XXXIV (1948), 611–36.

Watts, Eugene J. "The Police of Atlanta, 1890–1905." *Journal of Southern History*, XXXIX (1973), 165–82.

Wilentz, Sean. "Crime and Poverty and the Streets of New York City: The Diary of William H. Bell, 1850–1851." *History Workshop*, VII (1979), 126–55.

Young, Tommy R. "The United States Army and the Institution of Slavery in Louisiana, 1803–1815." *Louisiana Studies*, XIII (1974), 201–22.

## DISSERTATIONS AND THESES

Alfers, Kenneth G. "The Washington Police: A History, 1800–1886." Ph.D. dissertation, George Washington University, 1975.

Bacon, Selden D. "The Early Development of American Municipal Police: A Study of the Evolution of Formal Controls in a Changing Society." Ph.D. dissertation, Yale University, 1939.

Cei, Louis Bernard. "Law Enforcement in Richmond: A History of Police-Community Relations, 1737–1974." Ph.D. dissertation, Florida State University, 1975.

Denham, James Michael. "'A Rogue's Paradise': Violent Crime in Antebellum Florida." Ph.D. dissertation, Florida State University, 1988.

Everett, Donald Edward. "Free Persons of Color in New Orleans, 1803–1865." Ph.D. dissertation, Tulane University, 1952.

———. "Legislation Concerning Free Persons of Color in Orleans Parish, 1840–1860." Master's thesis, Tulane University, 1950.

Hepler, Mark Kerby. "Color, Crime and the City." Ph.D. dissertation, Rice University, 1972.

———. "Negroes and Crime in New Orleans, 1850–1861." Master's thesis, Tulane University, 1960.

Ketcham, George Austin. "Municipal Police Reform: A Comparative Study of Law Enforcement in Cincinnati, Chicago, New Orleans, New York and St. Louis, 1844–1877." Ph.D. dissertation, University of Missouri, 1967.

Kolp, John Leslie. "Suburbanization in Uptown New Orleans: Lafayette City, 1833–1852." Master's thesis, University of New Orleans, 1972.

Levett, Alan Edward. "Centralization of City Police in the Nineteenth Century United States." Ph.D. dissertation, University of Michigan, 1975.

Maniha, John Kenneth. "The Mobility of Elites in a Bureaucratizing Organization: The St. Louis Police Department, 1861–1961." Ph.D. dissertation, University of Michigan, 1970.

Marchiafava, Louis J. "Institutional and Legal Aspects of the Growth of Professional Urban Police Service: The Houston Experience, 1878–1948." Ph.D. dissertation, Rice University, 1976.

————. "The New Orleans Police Department, 1852–1860: The Road to Reform." Master's thesis, University of New Orleans, 1972.

Mowrey, Robert Thompson. "The Evolution of the Nashville Police from Early Times to 1880." Senior thesis, Princeton University, 1974.

Reichard, Maximilian Ivan. "The Origins of Urban Police: Freedom and Order in Antebellum St. Louis." Ph.D. dissertation, Washington University, 1975.

Rider, Eugene Frank. "The Denver Police Department: An Administrative, Organizational, and Operational History, 1858–1905." Ph.D. dissertation, University of Denver, 1971.

Schafer, Judith Kelleher. "The Long Arm of the Law: Slavery and the Supreme Court in Antebellum Louisiana, 1809–1862." Ph.D. dissertation, Tulane University, 1985.

Spletstoser, Frederick Marcel. "Back Door to the Land of Plenty: New Orleans as an Immigrant Port." 2 vols. Ph.D. dissertation, Louisiana State University, 1978.

Tansey, Richard Randall. "Economic Expansion and Urban Disorder in Antebellum New Orleans." Ph.D. dissertation, University of Texas at Austin, 1981.

Taylor, Paul Wayne. "Mobile, 1818–1859, as Her Newspapers Pictured Her." Master's thesis, University of Alabama, 1951.

Tregle, Joseph G., Jr. "Louisiana in the Age of Jackson: A Study in Ego-Politics." Ph.D. dissertation, University of Pennsylvania, 1954.

Vandal, Gilles. "The New Orleans Riot of 1866: The Anatomy of a Tragedy." Ph.D. dissertation, College of William and Mary, 1978.

Winters, John David, Jr. "Confederate New Orleans." Master's thesis, Louisiana State University, 1947.

# INDEX

Abell, Edmund, 116, 119
Absenteeism, 54, 54n, 55, 96, 96n, 127–28, 192
Adams, Eugene, 87
Adams, Lionel, 175–77
Adams, Thomas E., 79, 100, 114–15, 118, 119, 122–23, 125
African Americans: as police, 7, 28–29, 29n, 102, 119, 123, 125, 126, 135–43, 138n, 160, 167, 186, 198; as citizens from 1865, pp. 8–9, 102–103, 114, 115–19, 121–23, 132, 134, 148, 148–49n, 160, 167, 184–85, 186, 194; number of, 11, 29, 39, 121, 197; as slaves, 18n, 20, 21n, 22–24, 30, 91, 92–93, 93n, 111–12, 119, 140n, 141, 174; as free persons before 1865, pp. 92–93, 93n, 112, 119–21
Age: of arrestees, 158; of police, 56, 57, 98n, 139, 192, 196
American party, 66, 68–80, 95n, 98, 101n, 198
Amite, 154
Anglo-Americans, 6, 12, 28, 28n, 40–41, 40n, 65
Arrests, 9n, 86n, 90–94, 93n, 132, 133–34, 138, 138n, 147–48, 148–49n, 193–94
Assault and battery, 86n, 93
Atlanta, 75, 137, 146, 163, 165
Attorney general, 47–48, 85, 187
Augusta, 75, 137, 146, 163

Bachemin, Zach, 175, 178, 189, 189n
Bacon, Selden, 1, 4
Badger, A. S., 131, 132, 133, 145, 153, 155–56

Badges, 100, 127
Baird, Absalom, 116, 118
Baltimore, 80, 81n, 120, 121, 125n, 137, 164, 165, 198
Banks, Nathaniel P., 110, 112
Benwell, J., 21
Bernhard, duke of Saxe-Weimar Eisenach, 20, 40
Bertillion system, 192, 198
Bicycle corps, 192
Blassingame, John, 148–49n
Board of Metropolitan Police, 124, 132, 136–38, 143, 148n, 150–51
Board of Police, 66–67, 68, 69–70, 70–71, 74–76, 77, 84, 94–95, 99, 121–22, 170, 186, 188, 191–92
Boasso, Theodore J., 171–72
Boatmen, 15, 89
Boats, 73, 108, 126, 130–31
Boré, Etienne, 16, 28
Boston, 3, 4, 12, 14, 24, 38, 38n, 58, 67, 85, 86n, 164, 190, 191, 197
Boylan, Thomas, 98n, 156, 157, 166, 171
Brooklyn, 190
Burke, John, 113
Butler, Benjamin F., 106–107, 110, 114

Cabildo, 15
Cabildo, Battle of, 153
Cain, George L., 125, 131, 133, 152
Cambre, Antoine, 87
Canary Islands, 27
Chambers, William 23
Charity Hospital, 56–57, 61
Charles, Robert, 194

Charleston, 1, 3, 4, 5–6, 13, 19–22, 20n, 21n, 24, 25, 36–37, 38, 39n, 67, 75, 137, 163, 165, 197, 198
Chattanooga, 125n, 165
Chicago, 67, 125n, 164, 190, 191
Cholera, 12
Cincinnati, 125n, 164, 190
City guard, 3–4, 17–21, 199
Civil service, 98–99, 161, 188, 189–92, 195–96, 199
Civil War, 102–13, 103n, 159, 161, 198
Clapp, Theodore, 26n
Clare, Louis, 172
Cleveland, 164
Colonial policing, 2–3, 14–15
Commissaries of police, 14
Committee of One Hundred, 190
Common Council, 67–68, 70–71, 71n, 74, 76, 78–79, 83, 96, 100, 121, 124, 157, 161–64, 166, 170, 172, 174, 189
Confederacy, 102–112, 115–16, 115n, 144
Constables, 2–3, 15, 17–18, 48
Conway, Hugh, 124
Crossman, Abdil, 68

Deadly force, 9–10, 32–34, 53, 65, 65n, 66, 69, 80–90, 117–19, 127, 151–56, 160–61, 165, 167, 168, 170–71, 172–88, 177n, 178n, 179n, 180–81n, 194, 195
Delinquency by police, 17, 38, 51–53, 56, 56n, 84–85, 87–89, 94–95, 94–95n, 112, 134, 143–44
Democrats, 6–7, 62, 66–67, 68–71, 76, 78, 95n, 101n, 116, 125n, 152, 154–58, 189, 190–91, 199
Detectives, 144, 169–72
Detroit, 164
Devereaux, Thomas, 170–71
Dintinger, Barbara, 52–53, 52n, 53n
District attorney, 47, 85
Dostie, Anthony P. 103–104, 116
Duffy, Thomas, 185–86, 186n

Economic status: of arrestees, 93–94n, 148,

148–49n; of police, 96–97, 97n, 140–41, 140–41n
Elliott, Benjamin, 62
Emsley, Clive, 8
European Brigade, 106, 108

Fees, 2, 3
Finland, 27
Fire companies, 98, 109, 117
First Municipality, 43, 44, 44n, 45, 46, 47, 48, 49, 55, 56, 56n, 60, 64, 82, 93, 93n
Fischer, Roger, 149n
Flanders, Benjamin F., 98, 104
Fogelson, Robert, 8
Forno, Henry, 52, 77, 79, 79n, 97
Forstal, Edouard, 17
Franco-Americans: as citizens, 6, 11–12, 40–41, 40n, 43, 65; as police, 26–28
Franklin, John Hope, 4
French: as police, 26–27, 59–60, 73, 74, 145, 168; as citizens, 59–60, 73–74, 145, 147–48, 195, 197
French, Jonas, 107, 112
Freret, William, 49–50

Gabriel [Prosser], 22
Galveston, 137, 146–47, 163
Gambling, 46–48, 166
Gendarmerie: in New Orleans, 16–17, 16–17n, 24–25, 130, 199; in France, 19
General Council, 45, 47, 48
Germans: as police, 26–27, 59–60, 73–74, 108, 135, 139, 147, 168; as citizens, 59–60, 63, 73–74, 77, 104, 109–110, 145, 148, 195
Graft, 91, 94, 99, 134, 166, 169–70, 196
Grand juries, 73, 99, 101n, 116, 166, 168, 187, 195
Griffin, John, 184–85
Gros, Jean, 87–88
Guerin, Arthur, 87
Guillote, Joseph, 175, 177–78, 189

Hall, Basil, 23
Hall, Margaret Hunter, 23

Harris, Robert, 170
Haunton, Richard, 1
Hawkins, James, 186
Heath, Edward, 122–23
Hennessy, David, 171, 186, 188, 191, 195
Hennessy, Mike, 171
Hire, William, 117
Hoffman, Henry, 26
Holland, 27
Homicide: rates of, 85, 85–86n, 187n; law on, 174, 176–77, 177n
Horses, 16–17, 17–18n, 126, 130, 161, 188–89, 192, 199
House of refuge, 46, 170–71

Immigrants: as police, 6–7, 24, 25–28, 26–27n, 36, 58–63, 72–75, 145, 147, 167–68; as citizens, 38, 41, 58–60, 63–65, 72–75, 93, 145–46, 148, 168, 190–91, 194–95, 195–98
Independent movement, 78
Ingraham, Joseph Holt, 13
Irish: as police, 6–7, 27–28, 41, 58–63, 62n, 68, 68n, 69, 72–73, 74–75, 77, 95, 95n, 135, 144–46, 167–68; as citizens, 58–63, 60n, 61n, 72, 74–75, 93, 104, 112, 143, 148, 195
Italians: as police, 59, 73–74, 145, 168; as citizens, 59, 73–74, 145, 148, 168, 171, 187–88, 194–95

Jacquess, Jonathan A., 79
Jails, 93–94n, 101n
James, William, 69, 69n, 71, 71n, 83, 97
Johnson, David, 5
Jordan, Laylon W., 5–6

Kansas City, 80
Kavanagh, M. D., 113
Kellogg, William P., 152, 154–55, 156, 157
Kennedy, Hugh, 113
Ketcham, George A., 1
Kingsford, William, 21

Lamplighters, 17, 26

Lane, Roger, 1, 8
Law and Order League, 190
Legislature: and partition of New Orleans, 6, 43; and deadly force, 82–83, 85, 173–74, 188; and police reform, 98–99, 102–103, 124–26, 150–51, 191
LeGrand, Julia, 112
Lewis, John, 71, 76, 78, 83, 98
Lexington (Ky.), 75, 146, 163
Liberty Place, battle of, 145, 154–56
Literacy: of arrestees, 93n, of police, 98n
Loan, William F., 147n, 170
Lodging, 92, 132–33, 193, 193n
Longstreet, James, 155
López, Narciso, 64
Louisville, 75, 81n, 137, 146, 163, 164, 198

Magistrates, 2, 34, 68, 85, 88, 103, 116, 174, 176, 185–86
Marital status: of police, 56–57; of arrestees, 134
Mather, James, 33
McCann, Nathaniel, 88
McClelland, John, 103, 112
McEnery, John D., 152–53, 155
McLaughlin, Michael, 173
Mealey, Patrick, 172
Mechanics' Institute riot, 102, 115–19, 115n, 117n, 118n
Memphis, 7n, 75, 114, 125n, 137, 146, 163, 165, 197
Metropolitan Police: of London, 19; of New Orleans, 126–58
Military-style police: in Charleston, 3–6, 13–14, 19–21, 21n, 24, 38–39, 39n; in Mobile, 3–6, 13–14, 22, 24, 38–39, 39n; in New Orleans, 3–6, 13–14, 16–19, 17n, 18–19n, 24–25, 29–34, 36–39, 39n, 197, 199; in Richmond, 13–14, 22–23, 24, 38–39, 39n; in Savannah, 3–6, 13–14, 21–22, 24, 38–39, 39n
Militia, 3–4, 15–16, 18, 18–19n, 21n, 31n, 70, 129, 152–56, 174
Miller, Wilbur, 8
Milwaukee, 89, 164

Mobile, 3–6, 13–14, 22, 24, 38–39, 39n, 75, 137, 146, 147, 163, 165, 197, 198
Mondelli, J. E., 111
Monkkonen, Eric, 5, 193n
Monroe, John, 105–106, 114–16, 118–19, 122
Montgomery, 75, 137, 146, 163, 165
Morgan, Philip H., 103
Moynan, Alexander F., 71, 73, 77, 77n
Mumford, William, 106

Nashville, 75, 125n, 137, 146, 163
New Brunswick, 190
New Orleans: population of, 11, 13, 74, 132; economy of, 12–13, 17, 42–44, 64, 71, 96–97, 108, 159; public institutions of, 12, 122–23, 132–33, 159, 166, 194
New York, 1, 3, 4, 12, 14, 24, 38, 38n, 67, 79–80, 89, 100, 125n, 164, 190, 191, 195n, 197
Nicholls, Francis T., 157
Night watch, 2, 14–15, 17, 26, 35, 49–51, 53–56
Noble, Jordan B., 142
Norfolk, 114, 136, 137, 163, 165

O'Leary, Stephen, 68–70, 68n, 95, 100
Olmsted, Frederick Law, 21, 23, 58

Packard, Stephen B., 157
Panic of 1819, p. 12
Partition, 6, 37, 40–48, 40n, 197
Patrol work, 2–3, 14, 34–35, 48–49, 50–51, 128–29, 130–31, 161, 188–89, 192, 199
Pensions, 96, 126, 128, 164
Petersburg (Va.), 75, 136, 137, 146, 163
Petrie, Charles, 52–53, 52n, 53n
Philadelphia, 3, 4, 12, 14, 24, 38, 38n, 58, 67, 85, 100, 164, 187, 191, 197
Phillips, Eugenia Levy, 106–107
Photographs, 67, 100, 134n, 192, 198
Politics, 30–39, 31–32n, 59–60, 62–65, 66–80, 97–99, 98n, 101, 103–11, 113–17, 119, 121–25, 136, 145–47, 149–50, 156–

58, 160, 167–69, 172, 189–91, 196, 198–99
Poole, John, 88
Portsmouth (Va.), 137, 163
Prieur, Denis, 26, 36–37, 45–46
Private police, 165, 171
Public Guard, 22–24
Public order, 90–91, 132, 165, 193–94. See also Riots

Rabinowitz, Howard, 7
Ramos, Clement, 71
Rankin, David C., 120n
Rattle (for signaling), 35
Reconstruction, 102–103, 114–58
Reform (of police), 4, 6, 7–8, 13–39, 41–42, 50, 64–65, 67, 76, 79–80, 98–101, 102–103, 107, 114–15, 119, 121–23, 124–38, 157–58, 161, 166, 168–69, 175, 177–78, 187–99
Republicans, 7, 102–103, 114–16, 118, 122–25, 125n, 126–34, 145–47, 149–58, 161, 190–91, 198–99
Residence (of police), 56–57
Retrenchment, 7, 43–44, 71–72, 131, 150–51, 161–66, 199
Rey, Octave, 138, 142–43
Reynolds, Thomas, 173, 178, 186
Richardson, James, 4–5, 8
Richmond, 13–14, 22–23, 24, 38–39, 39n, 67, 75, 137, 146, 163
Riots, 63–64, 70–71, 91, 114, 115–19, 124–25, 127, 151–57, 165
Rivery, Pierre Achille, 15
Robinson, Boyd, 107, 113, 145
Rowley, R.B., 189, 189n
Russell, William Howard, 66, 101n, 103

Sailors, 32–33, 89
St. Louis, 67, 75, 89, 125n, 134, 137, 146, 164–65, 190, 197
St. Martinville (La.), 154
Sala, George A. H., 160
Salaries, 2, 3, 4, 14, 16, 36, 43–44, 95–97,

121, 150–51, 160, 162–65, 173, 195–96, 198
San Antonio, 75, 137, 146, 163, 197
San Francisco, 164
Savannah, 3–6, 13–14, 21–22, 24, 38–39, 39n, 75, 136, 137, 146, 163, 165
Schneider, John, 8
Second Municipality, 43, 44, 44–45n, 45, 47, 49, 52, 54, 55, 56, 56n, 60, 63, 64–65, 68, 82, 93n
Seuzeneau, Peter, 71–72
Shakspeare, Joseph, 166, 170, 171, 178n, 189, 191
Shepley, George, 121
Sheridan, Philip, 122
Sheriffs, 3, 48, 48n, 66, 168
Sherman, Henry T., 70–71
Size of police force: in New Orleans, 7, 24, 26–27n, 30n, 35, 44, 71, 73–74, 113, 126, 130–31, 135, 145, 151, 157, 160, 162, 163, 164, 165, 198–99; in other cities, 24, 163, 164
Slaughterhouse Cases, 130n
Slavery, 3–6, 11, 13–16, 18n, 19–24, 29–30, 36, 39, 39n, 91, 92–93, 111–12, 119–120, 140n, 141, 174
Slidell, John, 62
Social service, 7, 90, 92, 126, 129–30, 132–34, 166, 193, 193n
Soulé, Pierre, 106
Spanish: as police, 26, 59, 60, 74, 145, 147, 168; as citizens, 63–64, 139, 140, 147, 148, 197
Spanish army, 15, 19
Special officers, 117, 172
Special police, 70, 78–79, 83, 165
Stith, Gerard, 78, 79, 97–98
Strikes, 91, 165
Stuart, James, 20
Sullivan, Edward, 80–81
Summers, H. M., 69–70, 98
Supernumeraries, 54, 95–96, 96n, 122n
Surgeons, 127–28
Sweden, 27
Syndics, 14, 18

Tasistro, Louis, 20, 20n
Taylor, Willie, 184–85
Telegraph, 67, 100–101, 161, 188–89, 192
Telephones, 159, 192
Third Municipality 28, 43, 44, 44–45n, 45, 46, 47–48, 49, 51, 54, 55, 56, 56n, 60, 63, 68n, 82, 93n
Timrod, Henry, 102
Training (of police), 84n, 95–96, 126, 131
Turner, Nat, 30, 30n
Turnover, 38n, 54–55, 54–55n, 96, 96n, 112, 192
Twain, Mark, 159

Uniforms, 2–3, 3–4, 5, 6, 13, 14, 17, 19, 19n, 21, 22, 23, 29, 34, 38n, 50, 67, 100, 121, 122n, 138
United States Army, 15, 16, 18

Vandal, Gilles, 115n, 117n
Vicksburg, 137, 146, 147, 163, 197
Vigilance committees, 34, 78–79, 166
Voorhies, Albert, 116, 118–19

Wade, Richard, 4
Walker, Mary E., 133
Walker, Samuel, 5, 8
War of 1812, pp. 12, 18–19n
Washington, D.C., 121, 137, 164–65
Waterman, Charles, 76–78, 98
Watts, Eugene, 1
Weapons: swords, 3, 4, 13, 15, 19, 22, 32, 33, 173–74; muskets, 4, 17, 19, 21, 22, 32, 33, 36, 174; revolvers, 14, 38n, 67, 80–90, 117, 139, 153, 174–75, 177–83, 180–81n, 184–86, 185n; pistols, 17, 21, 22, 32, 33, 65, 80, 87, 175, 179; bayonets, 22, 23, 32, 33; spontoons, 35, 82, 173–74; knives, 65n, 77, 80–81, 83–84, 86–87, 88, 107, 167; laws regarding, 67, 85, 90, 160–61, 173–79, 183–84, 187–88; shotguns, 70; slung-shots, 80, 83–84; rifles, 130, 139, 152, 153; cannon, 130, 153, 155; Gatling guns, 130, 155

Whigs, 62, 63, 66, 68, 68n
White, Henry, 109
White League, 154, 189
Williamson, J. J., 123–24, 125, 135
Winter, J. L., 82

Women, 52–53, 52n, 53n, 87–88, 89–90n,
   91–92n, 93, 133–35

Youenes, John, 47, 68, 68n, 97
Young Men's Democratic Association, 190